PHRYNE OF THESPIAE

WOMEN IN ANTIQUITY

Series Editors: Ronnie Ancona and Sarah B. Pomeroy

This book series provides compact and accessible introductions to the life and historical times of women from the ancient world. Approaching ancient history and culture broadly, the series selects figures from the earliest of times to late antiquity.

Cleopatra
A Biography
Duane W. Roller

Clodia Metelli
The Tribune's Sister
Marilyn B. Skinner

Galla Placidia
The Last Roman Empress
Hagith Sivan

Arsinoë of Egypt and Macedon
A Royal Life
Elizabeth Donnelly Carney

Berenice II and the Golden Age of Ptolemaic Egypt
Dee L. Clayman

Faustina I and II
Imperial Women of the Golden Age
Barbara M. Levick

Turia
A Roman Woman's Civil War
Josiah Osgood

Monica
An Ordinary Saint
Gillian Clark

Theodora
Actress, Empress, Saint
David Potter

Hypatia
The Life and Legend of an Ancient Philosopher
Edward Watts

Boudica
Warrior Woman of Roman Britain
Caitlin C. Gillespie

Sabina Augusta
An Imperial Journey
T. Corey Brennan

Cleopatra's Daughter
And Other Royal Woman of the Augustan Era
Duane W. Roller

Perpetua
Athlete of God
Barbara K. Gold

Zenobia
Shooting Star of Palmyra
Nathanael Andrade

Eurydice and the Birth of Macedonian Power
Elizabeth Donnelly Carney

Melania the Younger
From Rome to Jerusalem
Elizabeth A. Clark

Sosipatra of Pergamum:
Philosopher and Oracle
Heidi Marx

Helena Augusta:
Mother of the Empire
Julia Hillner

Radegund:
The Trials and Triumphs of a Merovingian Queen
E.T. Dailey

Phryne of Thespiae:
Courtesan, Muse, and Myth
Laura McClure

PHRYNE OF THESPIAE

COURTESAN, MUSE, AND MYTH

Laura McClure

OXFORD
UNIVERSITY PRESS

Oxford University Press is a department of the University of Oxford.
It furthers the University's objective of excellence in research, scholarship,
and education by publishing worldwide. Oxford is a registered trade mark of
Oxford University Press in the UK and in certain other countries.

Published in the United States of America by Oxford University Press
198 Madison Avenue, New York, NY 10016, United States of America.

© Oxford University Press 2024

All rights reserved. No part of this publication may be reproduced, stored in
a retrieval system, or transmitted, in any form or by any means, without the
prior permission in writing of Oxford University Press, or as expressly permitted
by law, by license or under terms agreed with the appropriate reprographics
rights organization. Inquiries concerning reproduction outside the scope of the
above should be sent to the Rights Department, Oxford University Press, at the
address above.

You must not circulate this work in any other form
and you must impose this same condition on any acquirer

Library of Congress Cataloging-in-Publication Data
Names: McClure, Laura, 1959– author.
Title: Phryne of Thespiae: Courtesan, Muse, and Myth / Laura McClure.
Description: New York, NY : Oxford University Press, [2024] |
Series: Women in antiquity | Includes bibliographical references and index.
Identifiers: LCCN 2024013791 (print) | LCCN 2024013792 (ebook) |
ISBN 9780197580844 (hb) | ISBN 9780197580851 (pb) | ISBN 9780197580868 |
ISBN 9780197580882 | ISBN 9780197580875 (eb)
Subjects: LCSH: Phrynē. | Women—Greece—Athens—Biography. |
Courtesans—Greece—Athens—Biography. |
Sex role—Greece—History—To 1500. Classification:
LCC DF233.8.P65 M44 2024 (print) | LCC DF233.8.P65 (ebook) |
DDC 938/.5092 [B]—dc23/eng/20240403
LC record available at https://lccn.loc.gov/2024013791
LC ebook record available at https://lccn.loc.gov/2024013792

DOI: 10.1093/9780197580882.001.0001

Contents

Acknowledgments   xi

Introduction: Toward a Biography of Phryne   1
1. Her Story, in Quotations   18
2. Precarious Lives, Unstable Identities   28
3. Sex and the Ancient City   65
4. Phryne's Receptions in Greek Art   92
5. The Prosecution of Phryne   123
Epilogue   153

Notes   157
Works Cited   185
Index   195

Detailed Contents

Acknowledgments   xi

Introduction: Toward a Biography of Phryne   1
   Conclusion   17

1. Her Story, in Quotations   18
   Sources and Challenges   20
   Myth or Reality?   25

2. Precarious Lives, Unstable Identities   28
   Brothel Slaves and Flute Girls   30
   Hetaeras and Concubines   31
   The Case against Neaera: Hetaera or Lawful Wife?   35
   Women at the Symposium in Attic Vase Painting   41
   Hetaera Names?   54
   Wayward Lives   60
   Conclusion   62

3. Sex and the Ancient City   65
   Sex and Athenian Democracy   66
   Under the Sign of Aphrodite   67
   The Topography of Sex   72
   Drinking with Men, "As a Hetaera Would"   75
   The Business of Sex   78
   Woman-Owned   81
   Fourth-Century Hetaeras   84
   Toward a Biography of Phryne   90

4. Phryne's Receptions in Greek Art   92
   Female Portrait Statues and Dedications   94
   Praxiteles' Portraits   97
   The Thespian Triad   99

The Happy Hetaera   103
Phryne's Portrait Statue at Delphi   104
Phryne and the Invention of the Female Nude   108
Phryne and the *Cnidian Aphrodite*   115
Conclusion   121

5. The Prosecution of Phryne   123
Women and the Athenian Legal System   124
The *Graphe Asebeias*   130
A Climate of Suspicion   132
Women and Impiety   134
Hyperides' In Defense of Phryne   140
The Disrobing   143
Conclusion   151

Epilogue   153

Notes   157
Works Cited   185
Index   195

Acknowledgments

Like every book, this one is the product of many individuals. It would not have come into being without the efforts of the editors, Ronnie Ancona and Sarah Pomeroy, who first invited me to contribute a volume on Phryne to Oxford University Press's Women in Antiquity series. I am also deeply grateful to Stefan Vranka, executive editor at Oxford University Press, for his patience and encouragement, especially during pandemic-related disruptions. His careful reading of the final manuscript was extremely helpful and attests to the care he takes as an editor. Thanks are also owed to Chelsea Hogue and the production staff at OUP for their superb work in shepherding the manuscript through the production process.

Many thanks to the anonymous referees who read the original proposal and the completed manuscript. Their insights and suggestions have been invaluable to the formulation and organization of this book. Special thanks to Allison Glazebrook for so many conversations over the years about prostitution in classical Athens, for specific feedback at various stages, and for her many scholarly contributions to the field.

Of supreme importance to all my research endeavors over the past several years has been my term as senior fellow at the Institute for Research in the Humanities at the University of Wisconsin–Madison, which gave me much-needed time off from teaching every spring to write. I am grateful to IRH director, Steve Nadler, for his collegiality, support, and friendship over the years. I have also been fortunate in the IRH friends and colleagues who have sustained me intellectually and socially during this strange time. Special thanks go to all my online writing partners, Cherene Sherrard, Justine Walden, Simon Newman, Andrea Harris, Jennifer Ratner-Rosenhagen, and Maryellen MacDonald. IRH staff members, Ann Harris, Katie Apsey, and Lizzie Neary, also deserve praise for creating such a hospitable, supportive, and productive environment for fellows.

I would also like to acknowledger UW colleagues Anna Andrzejewski (art history) for encouraging me to include Phryne's receptions in the introduction to this volume and to Claire Taylor (history) for historical advice on ancient Thespiae, numerous conversations on women in classical Athens over the years, and, most of all, her excellent essay on hetaera names.

The Kellett Mid-Career Research Award from the Graduate School at the University of Wisconsin and a recent appointment to the Halls-Bascom Professorship by the College of Letters and Science have generously funded various research-related expenses, including books, computers, and production-related costs, incurred during the writing of this book.

Lastly, I would like to recognize my colleagues in Classical and Ancient Near Eastern Studies for their forbearance in allowing me to pursue these research opportunities and for so graciously shouldering a heavier teaching and service burden in my absence. I have also been especially fortunate in being able to teach an exceptional group of graduate students during the writing of this book. Their enthusiasm, insights, and research related to the study of women, gender, and sexuality in the ancient world have been infectious and sustaining. Particular thanks to classics graduate student Marina Grochocki for her careful proofreading of the original manuscript at the initial submission stage.

Lastly, much love and appreciation go to my family, and especially to my husband, Richard Heinemann, who is, as always, the *sine qua non*.

Laura McClure
Madison, Wisconsin
January, 2024

Cover
Franz von Stuck, *Phryne*, Portland Art Museum, Gift of Dr. Anna Berliner, 62.9

xii   Acknowledgments

Introduction

Toward a Biography of Phryne

> All archives are incomplete—such historical accounts written primarily by the most powerful have overwhelmingly informed our understanding of the past. (Connolly and Fuentes 2016: 105)

Phryne of Thespiae was purportedly the most famous hetaera in fourth-century Athens, and she became even more famous in her post-classical receptions, from the Hellenistic period to the modern age.[1] The term hetaera, discussed more fully in Chapter 2, simply means "female companion" but, in the absence of a modern equivalent, is often translated "courtesan."[2] Indeed, it is hard to imagine Phryne apart from her numerous images that proliferated during the nineteenth century, best known from Jean-Léon Gérôme's work, *Phryne before the Aeropagus* (Figure I.1), exhibited at the Salon, Paris' premier art exhibition, in 1861. Known for his lucrative history paintings of classical subjects that undercut the genre as high art, Gérôme depicts the most notorious incident in the life of the hetaera, the baring of her breasts at her trial for impiety. At left, her defender, the orator Hyperides (c. 390–330 BCE), pulls off her pale blue robe to expose her stark white body as if removing a drop cloth from a statue. At right a semi-circle of male jurors in red confront her nakedness with a mixture of shock and pleasure as Phryne turns away and covers her face in shame. Instead of representing a heroic moment from antiquity, Gérôme serves up a sexual fantasy to an elderly group of voyeurs and, of course, lets his (presumably) male

Phryne of Thespiae. Laura McClure, Oxford University Press. © Oxford University Press 2024.
DOI: 10.1093/9780197580882.003.0001

FIGURE I.1 Jean-Léon Gérôme, *Phryne before the Aereopagus*, 1861. Hamburg, Kunsthalle, HK-1910.

viewers in on the secret, much to the dismay of his critics.³ And yet despite the numerous retellings of this episode from antiquity onward, this event almost certainly never happened, at least not in the way later writers and artists portrayed it. Gérôme's painting thus must be viewed not as an unmediated representation of the hetaera based on reliable sources from antiquity, but rather as the result of a complex process of transmission, interpretation, and adaptation of a mythology generated entirely from the perspective of men that had become entrenched by the first century CE and subsequently rediscovered and reimagined by male painters, sculptors, and popular culture in the years leading up to his composition and beyond.⁴ This book seeks to disentangle the legacy of Phryne from the historical reality of the women who lived and worked as hetaeras in ancient Greece, beginning with her rise as an international symbol of the glorified *courtisane* in fine art and popular media of the nineteenth century. Even as post-classical artists mined the ancient sources for their own creative works, they nevertheless refashioned her into an icon for their own age, as a harbinger of alternative sexualities, new representational modes, and diverse Hellenisms. By examining the uses of Phryne in the modern era, this chapter illustrates the challenges implicit in separating fantasy from fact in all of the accounts of the hetaera from antiquity onward. Indeed, one might say that Phryne's signature characteristic is her ability to elude definition, to be continually re-imagined and transformed in ways that reflect shifting historical realities and values.

The modern Phryne is very much a French construction, the product of a literary and artistic tradition that celebrated notable Greek hetaeras such as Lais, Phryne, and Pancaste/Campaspe, the mistress of Alexander the Great, as well as more recent historical French courtesans.[5] They featured in accounts such as Catherine Bédacier's *Les belles grecques: ou, L'Histoire des plus fameuses courtisanes de la Grece* (1712); Pierre Dufour's eight-volume *Histoire de la prostitution chez tous les peuples du monde depuis l'antiquité la plus reculée jusqa' nos jours* (1861); Henry de Kock, *Histoire des courtisanes célèbres* (1869), which includes a chapter on Phryne; and moral and cultural compendia like Jakob von Falke's *Hellas und Rom: Eine Culturgeschichte des Classischen Alterthums* (1882). In her first appearances in painting, however, Phryne's status as a prostitute is muted and her presence subordinated to larger themes, such as the triumph of reason over passion or the artist at work. For instance, the Italian painter Salvator Rosa (1615–1673) depicts the hetaera's encounter with the philosopher, Xenocrates, a disciple of Plato, in *Phryne and Xenocrates* (1662; private collection, Rome). As recorded by Diogenes Laertius and repeated by Valerius Maximus, Xenocrates allowed Phryne to take refuge under his roof and even to share his narrow bed in order to protect her from alleged assailants.[6] When her repeated attempts to seduce him were rebuffed, she quipped that he was "not a man but a statue," playing on the pun between the words *andros* and *andriantos* in ancient Greek.[7] This story stresses foremost the self-restraint of the philosopher, evoking Socrates' legendary disdain for physical pleasure, as exemplified by his refusal to yield to Alcibiades' advances at the end of Plato's *Symposium*.[8] But it also reminds us of two important aspects of Phryne's characterization in antiquity, her witticisms and verbal dexterity at the symposium and her widespread association with artists and artworks, most notably as the model for Praxiteles' *Cnidian Aphrodite* and Apelles' lost painting, *Aphrodite Rising from the Sea*, also known as the Anadyomene, and to a lesser extent for dedications of her portrait statues in Greek sanctuaries, a subject discussed more fully in Chapter 4. Thanks to Rosa's painting, Phryne became widely known throughout Europe because of an engraving by printmaker Simon Francis Ravenet the Elder produced in 1770 and distributed by the British publisher John Boydell.[9] The painting features the pair in half figure against a plain, dark background. Wearing a white gown, Phryne dominates the scene as she leans back against a cushion at right and converses with the less visually prominent Xenocrates at left. A large, ornate bed post projects above the rumpled sheets behind her back. Although Phryne is fully clothed, her reclining posture, open legs, and the disheveled bed gesture to her eroticism. While the hetaera may be a visual focal point, the choice of theme and its chaste rendering underscore the moral fortitude of the philosopher rather than amorous aspect of their meeting.

A century later, Phryne attracted the interest of the celebrated Swiss history painter Angelica Kauffmann (1741–1807), whose home on the via Sistina in Rome, which she shared with her husband, Antonio Zucchi, from 1782 onward, became a popular stop for fashionable visitors on the Grand Tour.[10] Like many other seventeenth-century painters, Kauffmann regularly turned to classical themes, particularly the subject of the artist at work and artist and model based on ancient narratives; indeed, two bookcases from an inventory of her salon attest to her interest in antiquity and the Renaissance.[11] An early painting, *Zeuxis Choosing His Models for the Painting of Helen of Troy* (1778; Providence, RI, Brown University, Annmary Brown Memorial Museum), brings to life a popular story in which Zeuxis, a painter known for his verisimilitude, seeks to combine the best features of several young women to capture the unparalleled beauty of Helen. A subsequent painting, *Alexander Leaves Campaspe to Apelles* (1782–1783; Landeshaupt, Bregenz), deals with another artist/model narrative from antiquity. In this story, the painter Apelles fell in love with his model, Campaspe, when commissioned to paint a nude portrait of her, whereupon Alexander, her lover, bequeathed her to him as an expression of his magnanimity and self-control.[12] The interchangeability of these women is illustrated by Jean-Michel Moreau's engraving for the history of ancient painters published in Robillard-Péronville's *Le Musée francais* (1803) in which he swaps out Campaspe for Phryne in this scene.[13]

Given Phryne's exceptional association with artists and artworks in antiquity, it is not surprising that she figures prominently in a group of classically inspired paintings that Kauffmann completed between 1788 and 1795 for her London patron, George Bowles: *Phryne Seducing Xenocrates* (1794, private collection) and *Praxiteles Showing Phryne the Statue of Cupid* (1794) (Figure I.2), together with a pair based on popular Roman themes, *The Nymph Egeria in Her Religious Colloquy with Numa Pompilius* and *Roman Charity*.[14] The first painting clearly draws

FIGURE I.2 Angelica Kauffmann, *Praxiteles Giving His Eros to Phryne*, Providence, RI, Rhode Island School of Design, Museum of Art, 59.008.

on Rosa's earlier version of the anecdote, whether Kauffmann had direct experience of the painting or knew it only through Ravenet's widely circulated engraving.[15] In her rendering, Kauffmann presents the two half figures in an intimate scene. Clad in a soft white gown that modestly exposes only her shoulder, Phryne approaches the philosopher at right, seeming to interrupt his thoughts as she grasps his forearm. Produced in the same year, *Praxiteles Showing Phryne the Statue of Cupid* imagines a less commonly depicted motif, the hetaera's preference for Praxiteles' statue of Eros over his Satyr, which she later dedicated it to her native city of Thespiae.[16] The Eros was a well-known and extremely popular statue in classical antiquity, as we will see in Chapter 4, that generated numerous Hellenistic epigrams in which it symbolizes the love of the philosopher for the hetaera, such as this one:

> Praxiteles accurately rendered the Love that he suffered,
> taking the model from his own heart, giving me to Phryne in

Introduction 5

payment for myself. But I give birth to passion no longer by shooting arrows, but by darting glances.[17]

Rather than showing the artist at work, as in other such scenes, Kauffmann instead follows epigrammatic convention by depicting the painter as the lover of his beautiful mistress.[18] Phryne, seated in profile at right, turns toward Praxiteles, who stands at left. He holds and points to a small statue of Cupid as the embodiment of his passion, a winged male infant with a bow and arrow held loosely at his side, as the two lovers intently gaze into one other's eyes. Thanks to these and other receptions, Phryne's appeal in the late eighteenth century reached far beyond fine art. Her familiarity among popular audiences is illustrated by a drawing of the London cartoonist James Gillray (1756–1815). It depicts the Earl of Derby, the short, stout figure at right, with his tall, slim mistress, Elizabeth Farren, a well-known comic actress, inspecting various art works (Figure I.3). She is made to admire "Zenocrates (*sic*) & Phryne," while he considers a hunting scene entitled "the Death." Part of the joke, of course, is that she herself is a mistress gazing upon her ancient antecedent.

Whereas Kauffmann introduced a romantic element into Phryne's narrative, de-emphasizing the sensual aspects of her stories by depicting a fully clothed hetaera deep in conversation with her male interlocutors, eighteenth- and nineteenth-century French painters took her image in a new direction, stressing her sexual status as a *courtisane* and focusing almost exclusively on the display of her naked body, drawing on ancient accounts of her public nudity at her impiety trial or at various religious festivals. A mid-eighteenth-century rendering in washed pen by Jean-Baptiste-Henri Deshays (1729–1765) features a voluminously draped hetaera standing with downcast gaze before the judges who sit on a podium above, while the orator clutches her veil from behind.[19] A miniature gouache by Pierre-Antoine Baudouin (1723–1769), *Phryne Before the Athenian Judges*, exhibited at the 1763 Salon, uses a similar compositional structure, but allows the viewer a glimpse of Phryne's naked breasts as she looks modestly downward while her defender removes her veil with his right hand.[20] Subsequent renditions, such as the drawing of Jacques-Louis David (1748–1825), produced around 1818 (Figure I.4), increasingly emphasize her frontal nudity. Drawn in black charcoal on medium wove paper, David's image depicts three male judges at left, two of whom gaze directly at the hetaera, while the third

FIGURE I.3 James Gillray, "A Peep at Christies; – or – Tally-ho & his Nimeny-Pimeney Taking the Morning Lounge" (1796). New York, Metropolitan Museum, 1975.558.1.

FIGURE I.4 Jacques-Louis David, *Phryne before her Judges* (c. 1816–1820). Cleveland, OH, Cleveland Museum of Art, 2013.249.

looks away. Exoticized by cropped, tight curls, beaded necklace, and naked breasts, Phryne appears to glance defiantly beyond the frame. The narrative of the disrobing appears to have been a favorite among David's circle, which introduced a new aspect of her iconography instrumental to Gérôme's painting. In one example, the hetaera stands almost completely naked before the fully clothed male jurors, her transparent garment falling around hips and thighs, creating a dramatic contrast with the darkness surrounding her, while the orator hales her by the sheer veil around her head. [21]

From this point onward, variations on the theme of Phryne's judicial nudity rapidly begin to multiply among French painters and sculptors, becoming a regular part of the annual Salon exhibitions from the 1840s through the 1850s.[22] As time goes on, however, these depictions become increasingly detached from their original narrative context, deemphasizing the jurors while focusing on the naked body of the hetaera. At one extreme is the *Phryne* (1850) (Figure I.5) of Gustave Boulanger (1824–1888), a close friend of Gérôme, which abandons any mythic pretext, producing instead an almost entirely pornographic image of the hetaera seemingly figured as a brothel worker. Clearly influenced by his visit to Algiers in 1845, Boulanger represents Phryne déshabillé as she reclines on a low bed piled high with textiles in a darkened room. Her dark brows and eyes, pronounced nose, heavy earrings, serpentine bracelet, and ankle beads, along with the letters ΦΡΥΘΝΗ (Phryne) embroidered in red on the blanket, suggest her exotic origins. This Phryne is not on trial but rather has become "metonymic for courtesans in general": a racialized other, sexually predatory, and intrinsically dangerous.[23] The trend toward eroticizing and Orientalizing Phryne belongs to a larger set of discourses set in motion around the mid-nineteenth century that rejected the sanitized Hellenism of Johann Joachim Winckelmann (1717–1768), the "noble simplicity and quiet grandeur" of Greece in favor of a "decadent" or "dissident" Hellenism that sanctioned the dark and irrational forces underlying human experience, including illicit sex.

Gérôme's *Phryne before the Areopagus* fits squarely within this idiom in its embrace of a completely eroticized, naked Phryne as the object of the collective male gaze within both the fictional courtroom and the external milieu of the Salon's exhibition hall. His mentor, the Swiss

FIGURE I.5 Gustave Boulanger, *Phryne* (1850). Amsterdam, Van Gogh Museum, inv./cat.nr s 456 S/1996.

Introduction   9

painter Charles Gleyre (1806–1874), whose atelier Gérôme briefly joined in 1844, seems to have also dabbled in the subject of Phryne during the 1850s, producing a sketch of her trial, as well as other compositional studies on the same theme.[24] Importantly, the former depicts the hetaera facing forward, unclad except for the loose drapery that she clutches over her lower body, as the male jurors leer behind her. Another immediate precedent was a version of the trial by Victor Mottez (1809–1897) in which the jurors are moved to a semi-circle in the foreground and almost completely submerged in darkness as they gaze at the naked body of Phryne dramatically illuminated in white on the podium above them while her defender unspools her drapery from above.[25] Working in close proximity to these works, Gérôme began preparation for his version of Phryne with an oil sketch produced in 1857, which situates Hyperides behind the hetaera as well as moves the trial indoors for the first time.[26] He also turned to the new art of photography for his rendering of the hetaera, anxiously awaiting some photographs of the nude studio model, Christine Roux (1820–1863), from the photographer Nadar, pseudonym for Gaspard-Félix Tournachon (1820–1920), in the months before the 1861 exhibition.[27] Like Phryne, Roux was a widely sought-after artists' model whose pose, captured in a photograph by Nadar (Figure I.6), served as a basis for Gérôme's Phryne. Photography was a new medium that offered for the first time an easily mass-produced format for the circulation of "artistic nudes" of anonymous working-class women to a broad sector of society through the Victorian black market, at a much cheaper price than Gérôme's lucrative paintings.

Phryne before the Areopagus, however, shifts the focus away from previous representations of the scene in a number of important ways. Like Mottez, he increases the number of jurors, but by moving them out of the darkness and into a lighted interior so that they occupy most of the frame, he is able to articulate with great specificity their individualized reactions to Phryne's disrobing. In so doing, he stresses the perspective of the male jurors and the vulnerability of the hetaera to their collective gaze. He further follows Mottez in highlighting the hetaera's unclothed body, but the de-emphasis on brushwork and absence of body hair and other coloration invites the viewer to see her as an art work rather than as a living woman, a "statue vivante," as Théophile Gautier (1811–1872) remarked in a review of the piece, evoking not only the myth of Pygmalion, but also the Greek statuary displayed in private collections and public museums throughout Europe from the seventeenth century

10   Phryne of Thespiae

FIGURE I.6 Nadar (Gaspard-Félix Tournachon), Standing Female Nude (1860–1861). New York, Metropolitan Museum, 1991.1174.

onward.[28] Indeed, the orator theatrically removes Phryne's blue robe with both hands as if to reveal at last his ideal creation, reinforced by the inscription on her sash, ΚΑΛΗ ("lovely"), resting on the ground beside her feet. The golden statuette of Athena in full military regalia placed on a statue base inscribed with her name, ΑΘΗΝΗ, along with an olive branch and Attic vase, further underscores the sculptural theme, contrasting virgin and hetaera by positioning it directly to the right of Phryne's lower torso. Finally, Gérôme very subtly Orientalizes Phryne not only by means of her gold necklace and bracelet, but also by the display of her full-body nudity before a crowd of men, a motif later repeated in his six slave-market scenes. For instance, *The Slave Market,* painted soon after the 1861 exhibit, translates Phryne to a Middle Eastern or North African context, in which a prospective male buyer inspects the teeth of a female slave, who stands before him completely naked but for her heavy metal collar as a signifier of her bondage.[29] Another painting produced several years later, *The Roman Slave Market* (1884), reverses the original Phryne image, showing the naked female slave from behind, her raised arms covering her face in shame, as she faces the crowd of male bidders standing before her.[30] The painting thus invites the male viewer to be the judge of Phryne's innocence, to gaze lustfully at her nakedness, and to purchase her services in the form of the painting. Not surprisingly, Gérôme's history paintings met with huge success in the private art market, landing him a lucrative exclusive contract with the leading art dealership Groupil & Cie.[31]

Gérôme's version of Phryne's trial was wildly popular with nineteenth-century viewers, immediately sparking a number of reproductions, adaptations, and appropriations across a wide spectrum of media, including engravings, photographs, sculpture, painting, cartoons, tableaux vivants, operettas, and even modern dance. Indeed, "it was the most frequently reproduced, imitated, and caricatured interpretation of the Phryne motif in the nineteenth century."[32] Since these receptions alone could form the subject of an entire book, this discussion will be confined to a few major trends and important examples. The familiarity of popular audiences with Gérôme's Phryne and both sides of the Atlantic is illustrated by a cartoon Bernhard Gillam (1856–1896) produced for the American humor magazine *Puck*, entitled *Phryne before the Chicago Tribunal* (1884) (Figure I.7). It depicts journalist Whitelaw Reid pulling off the cloak of Republican presidential candidate James G. Blaine to reveal him wearing shorts and a bib labeled "Magnetic Pad,"

FIGURE I.7 Bernhard Gillam, *Phryne before the Chicago Tribunal* (June 4, 1884). Library of Congress Prints and Photographs.

and covered with tattoos that reference his various corrupt dealings as he stands before the Republican delegates dressed as Greek jurors. The accompanying caption reads, "Ardent Advocate: 'Now, Gentlemen, don't make any mistake in your decision! Here's purity and magnetism for you—can't be beat!'" By translating Gérôme's iconography to a contemporary political context, Gillam not only exposes Blaine as a prostitute willing to sell himself to the highest bidder, but also pokes fun at the hypocrisy of the Republican party.

In the world of fine art, Gérôme's Phryne had an immediate and long-lasting impact. Just after the 1861 exhibition, Alexandre Falguière (1831–1900) created two small-scale bronze sculptures in the same pose (1868), with arm covering her eyes, which led to several three-dimensional versions of the hetaera. Most alter the pose to indicate the disrobing by including the garment behind or alongside the naked woman, as rendered by Louis Tuaillon (1884): Reinhold Begas (1886), Aristide Maillol (c. 1900), and Ferdinand Lepcke (1908).[33] Fin-de-siècle painters also turned with enthusiasm to the subject, producing increasingly abstract representations of Phryne as archetypal nude and model. In a painting by Polish artist Artur Grottger (1837–1867), produced in 1867, Phryne faces front, her red robe falling to her feet, leaving her completely exposed to the viewer as she covers her eyes with

Introduction   13

her left hand (Figure I.8). Although most of the references to the original mythic context have been stripped away—her defender, the jurors, and the courtroom—the painting elliptically alludes to the trial with her discarded garment.

By far the most famous of the nineteenth-century representations of the hetaera after Gérôme is *Phryne at the Posidonia in Eleusis* (1899) by Russian-born painter Henryk Siemiradzki (1843–1902), a massive historical work that reimagines another myth, the hetaera's disrobing at a religious festival in preparation for immersion in the sea.[34] Positioned at the center of the frame, Phryne enters the procession stripped by her servants, her body fully exposed except for a knotted garment slung over her lower body, as she loosens her hair and descends to the sea before an enthusiastic crowd of mostly men. This theme is subsequently taken up by British painters Frederic Leighton (1830–1896), with his *Phryne at Eleusis* (c. 1882), and Edward Burne-Jones (1833–1898), *Bath of Venus* (1888). A few years later, José Frappa (1854–1904) returns to the subject of her trial in his painting, *Phryne* (1904), but portrays the hetaera as a willing participant in her own disrobing, showing her from the back as she removes her red robe and confidently displays her breasts to the jurors before her. Symbolist painter Franz von Stuck (1863–1928) in his *Phryne* (1917), the cover image for this book, returns the hetaera to her front-facing pose while eliminating the original narrative context: Standing in an interior, possibly a bedroom, with a bright red wall, Phryne spreads her wing-like purple garment edged with golden tassels behind her to display her slim, stylized figure. The American painter William MacGregor Paxton (1869–1989) offers a similar statue-like pose in his *Phryne* (1923), who holds aloft her red drapery from behind to illuminate her full-frontal nudity.[35]

Gérôme's *Phryne before the Areopagus* became an instant sensation among popular audiences, beginning with the tableau vivant of French singer, model, and *courtisane* Blanche d'Antigny (1840–1874), staged in 1869, which served as a prelude to almost a dozen operettas about the hetaera, including one by Jacques Offenbach (1819–1880) and another by Camille Saint-Saëns (1835–1921). With a libretto by Lucien Augé de Lassus, Saint-Saëns' operetta premiered at the Opéra-Comique on May 23, 1893, and featured the American singer, Sybil Sanderson (1864–1903), in the title role.[36] The performance culminated with a memorable scene in which an evanescent Sanderson emerged as Aphrodite from the sea before an astonished audience. Even early modern dance embraced the

14   Phryne of Thespiae

FIGURE I.8 Artur Grottger, *Phryne* (1867), Cracow, Poland, Czartoryski Museum, The Picture Art Collection / Alamy Stock Photo.

subject of Phryne, most notably in the work of Adorée Villany, the pseudonym for a dancer and choreographer of unknown origins and uncertain date who appears to have performed sort of refined striptease in her "Dance of Phryne" circa 1900 (Figure I.9). Such venues allowed female performers, many of whom had sat as models or engaged in sexual labor or longer-term liaisons for financial support, an opportunity to reinterpret Phryne from their own perspectives. In her book, *Tanz-Reform und Pseudo-Moral: Kritisch-satyrische Gedanken aus meinem Bühnen und Privatleben*, a response to her arrest for public indecency in 1911, Villany argued that "to overcome the pervasive fear of the female

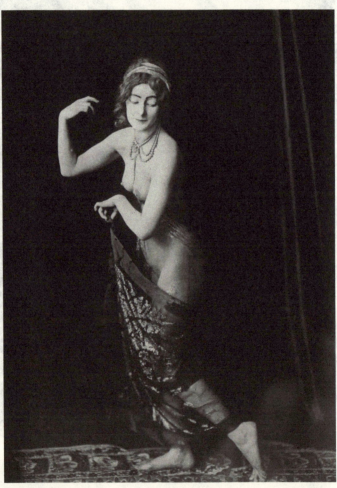

FIGURE I.9 Adorée Villany performing "Dance of Phryne," circa 1900. Library of Congress.

body one had to gaze at it with the same seriousness that one applied to the contemplation of artworks."[37] For her, inhabiting Phryne through nude dance expressed a form of female autonomy and sexual empowerment that challenged her objectification and commodification by male practitioners of nineteenth-century high art.

Conclusion

Phryne's modern receptions reflect the varied and often complex forms that Hellenism assumed from the seventeenth century onward, sparked by a new enthusiasm for ancient Greek art, literature, and culture, that became fused in France with a specific cultural interest in the figure of the *courtisane*. By the late nineteenth century, Phryne had become an international cultural icon thanks to Gérôme's rendering of her impiety trial and the numerous reproductions, variations, and adaptations it engendered. For many of these artists, Phryne's legacy in art as a model for the *Cnidian Aphrodite* along with the sensationalized stories of her public nudity legitimated representations that bordered on the pornographic and rendered her a lucrative commodity in the private art market. At the same time, her pervasive presence during this period points to a new and experimental sense of sexual and social freedom justified by pre-Christian conceptions of sexuality, homo-eroticism, and sexual labor and embodied by the fin-de-siècle women who performed Phryne. Finally, tracing Phryne's modern receptions affords insight into how this process might have played out in the ancient world as specific historical incidents became embellished and reinterpreted according to later tastes, ideologies, and experiences. At the same time, this brief survey reminds us of the need to remain vigilant about how male concerns and perspectives have shaped narratives of the hetaera from antiquity to the present, as the epigraph from Connolly and Fuentes cautions above, and to consider the liberatory possibilities for how we might construct a new feminist biography of Phryne.

Introduction 17

1

Her Story, in Quotations

What we "know" of Phryne consists of a random collection of anecdotes, much of which resists efforts to construct a coherent biography.[1] Most of our information comes from late second-century CE Greek writers living in the Roman Empire writing hundreds of years after her floruit, most notably the rhetorician and grammarian Athenaeus (late second/ early third cent. CE). His lengthy treatise, *Dining Sophists*, itself lacks an overt narrative structure, consisting rather of thousands of quotations from earlier texts, many now lost. From these fragments, we learn that Phryne, a word meaning "Toad," was her professional name, so-called because of her sallow complexion, but that her original name was Mnesarete, a common name for women in Athens and Attica.[2] She was originally from Thespiae in Boeotia, a city about 80 kilometers from Athens, the daughter of a man named Epicles.[3] Athenaeus distinguishes two Phrynes, one with the epithet Klausigelôs ("Laughing through Tears") and the other, Saperdion ("Little Fish"), although he does not specify which one haled from Thespiae.[4] She is further differentiated from the Phryne known as Sestos ("Swindler"), because she "fleeced" her clients.[5] Her childhood was spent in poverty, but eventually she amassed enormous wealth by charging a high price for her body.[6] Phryne's legendary riches facilitated several public benefactions. She offered to fund the rebuilding of the Theban walls after they had been destroyed by Alexander the Great, but only on the condition that the citizens inscribe the words "Alexander tore them down, but Phryne built them up them again."[7] Phryne made dedications to her native city, including its major tourist attraction, a statue of Eros by the sculptor Praxiteles (c. 390–322), with whom she was erotically linked.[8] In return, the Thespians dedicated a gilded statue of the hetaera at Delphi, also

Phryne of Thespiae. Laura McClure, Oxford University Press. © Oxford University Press 2024.
DOI: 10.1093/9780197580882.003.0002

wrought by Praxiteles, and installed it between images of the king of Sparta and Philip II (Alexander's father), with the words "Phryne, the daughter of Epicles of Thespiae" inscribed on its base.[9] Its placement and costliness led the Cynic philosopher Crates (365–285) to denounce it as a monument to Greek depravity.[10] She rejected those lovers who displeased her, even when they had paid lavishly for her services, and indulged the impecunious.[11] Phryne was a contemporary of several other famous hetaeras mentioned in comedy, including Lais, Plangon, Gnathaena, Myrrhine, and Nannion.[12] She was further known for her caustic and coarse rejoinders made at the drinking parties of men.[13]

Much of the discourse about Phryne, however, revolves around her exceptional beauty and public nudity, particularly in religious and legal contexts.[14] She concealed her body when in public by wearing a close-fitted tunic and avoiding the baths, yet revealed it before all of the Greeks at two religious festivals called the Eleusinia and Posidonia.[15] The sight of her naked body after she stripped and entered the sea inspired Apelles' painting, *Aphrodite Rising from the Sea*, a prototype for Botticelli's *Birth of Venus*. The pervasive association of the hetaera with the goddess informs the story that Praxiteles used Phryne as the model for his *Cnidian Aphrodite*, the first life-size female nude in the Western artistic tradition.[16] But the most shocking display of her body occurs in narratives surrounding her impiety trial, an event that made her famous from the fourth century onward according to a contemporary source, Posidippus' (c. 315–260 BCE) comic play, *Ephesia* ("Woman from Ephesis"): "Before our time, Phryne was far and away the best known courtesan there was; because even if you're younger than that, you've heard about her trial."[17] Indicted by Euthias (dates known), she was successfully defended by the orator Hyperides (390/1–322 BCE).[18] The only thing that saved her from conviction was a clever stratagem. When the orator's arguments appeared unpersuasive, he dramatically ripped off her upper garments, exposing her naked breasts to the jurors, a sight that induced not lust but piety: "the jurors fearful of this priestess and temple-attendant of Aphrodite, and to incline toward pity rather than the death penalty."[19] According to another source, she won acquittal for herself, "just barely—with her tears," by "taking the jurors' hands, one by one."[20] This is all that we "know" of Phryne, and yet it is the product of a literary tradition largely constructed hundreds of years after her death.

Her Story, in Quotations   19

Sources and Challenges

Reconstructing the lives of historical women in ancient Greece and Rome poses many challenges, as previous scholars in the Women in Antiquity series have observed.[21] Athenian citizen women are frustratingly inaccessible foremost because of the exiguous and fragmentary literary and archaeological remains—what constitutes the archive for classicists—and the fact that many of the sources were written centuries after the events they record. These narratives were constructed almost entirely by men, reflecting male priorities and biases that often objectify women and moralize about their actions. The problem is even more acute in the case of marginalized, non-elite women, such as prostitutes, who inhabited the fringes of their communities and whose social identities, because not securely linked to the polis ("city-state") through marriage to citizen men and the birth of legitimate children, were elusive. The widespread practice of not naming elite women in public has further contributed to their obscurity, while the multiplicity of names publicly attributed to hetaeras can paradoxically occlude rather than identify them in the archive. For instance, more than one hetaera seems to have gone by the name of Phryne and the one that this book concerns originally bore the name of Mnesarete. Moreover, each of these hetaeras was differentiated by nicknames. Indeed, one of the speakers in Plutarch's *Oracles at Delphi* points out the confusion perpetuated by nicknames during a discussion of Phryne/Mnesarete, "In many instances, apparently, nicknames cause the real names to be obscured. For example, Polyxena, the mother of Alexander, they say was later called Myrtale and Olympias and Stratonice."[22] Importantly, this passage suggests that not only hetaeras but other important female figures, including elite women, such as Olympias, the mother of Alexander the Great, could have multiple names, a topic to which we shall return in the next chapter.

Greek hetaeras have left virtually no record in their own voices, even though some writings are attributed to them, including sex manuals and sympotic verse. The best-known such treatise, composed by Philaenis (c. 300 BCE), survives in the form of a few tattered scraps:

> Philaenis the Samian, daughter of Ocymenes, wrote this
> work for those who want to know the true things in life and
> not just in passing . . . having worked at it myself . . . About
> seductions: it is necessary that the seducer be unbeautified and

20   Phryne of Thespiae

uncombed so that the woman has no realization of what he is doing . . . in thoughts . . . by saying that a woman . . . is like a goddess, that an ugly woman is full of charm, and that an old woman is like a young maid. How to kiss.[23]

The only such papyrus to come down to us, the work appears to be composed of various sections containing advice about seduction, kissing, and probably sexual positions.[24] Even if written by a man adopting a feminine persona, as some scholars believe, it nonetheless supports the view that the attribution of this type of work to a hetaera was culturally plausible. But such sources are tantalizingly beyond our reach.

Marginalized non-citizen women in classical Athens were often identified as prostitutes, whether they actually engaged in commercial sex or not, because their behavior did not conform to prevailing social norms for citizen women.[25] And yet the figure of the hetaera, a woman who consorted with famous men and inhabited the public, male-only spaces of the city, such as the theater, the law court, and the private drinking parties of elite men, was symbolically central. The words and deeds of the most illustrious such women began to populate the literary discourses of the fourth century BCE, when historical hetaeras proliferated in Athens as resident aliens or metics. They are particularly prominent in new and middle comedy (most of which exists only in fragmentary form), Attic oratory, and the Socratic dialogues of Xenophon (c. 430–355/4 BCE) and Plato (c. 427/8–348 BCE). Although many of the women encountered in these texts were arguably historical figures, the literature that began to coalesce around them became increasingly fictionalized as the tradition evolved and as the process of textual transmission moved away from classical Athens. This study therefore embraces a paradox: the actual prostitutes that populated ancient Athens, whether brothel slaves or semi-independent, wealthy hetaeras, most of whom were metics, left virtually no trace of their actual lives, while at the same time, some of them, like Phryne, engendered multiple literary and artistic receptions, constructed wholly by men.

Accounts of Phryne span a period of over a thousand years, starting in the fourth century BCE and continuing well into the sixth century CE as part of a larger burgeoning discourse on Athenian prostitution. The principal fourth-century sources include the fragments of Greek middle comedy, the least well-attested phase of Attic comedy, the plays and fragments of Menander (342/1–c. 290), also known as

Greek new comedy, and the forensic speeches of Attic oratory, particularly Aeschines 1, pseudo-Demosthenes 59, Lysias 3 and 4, and Isaeus 6. Material culture, in the form of vases, inscriptions, and architecture, also attest to their historical presence. The two genres that most often reference prostitutes and women of ambiguous social and sexual status, comedy and oratory, are highly unreliable because in aiming to entertain and persuade, respectively, they tend to distort and exaggerate rather than convey historically accurate information about Athenian society. Indeed, forensic speeches do not attempt to give an objective statement of the facts but rather to win an argument, often deploying a negative discourse of prostitution against various women, whether they engaged in prostitution or not, highlighting their former enslaved status and their sexual availability.[26] Nonetheless these sources can offer valuable insights into Athenian social practices, attitudes, and assumptions about gender, sexuality, non-marital liaisons, marriage, and legitimacy. For example, marriage alliances in Menander's *Dyskolos* closely adhere to contemporary marital and inheritance practices, while the structure of dowries across his works is consistent with situations epigraphically and historically attested.[27] Similarly, the portrayal of the hetaera Chrysis in his fragmentary play, *Samia*, illustrates how free Athenian women could preserve their independence through commercial sex.[28] Although forensic speeches are prone to serious misrepresentation, particularly in the portrayal of a speaker's opponents, they require plausibility for success and thus reliably represent Attic law and the assumptions underlying litigants' claims.[29] For example, when the citizen Simon in Lysias' *Against Simon* states that he entered into a formal contract for sex with a boy named Theodotus, it may be impossible to verify his claim, but it can be inferred that such an arrangement in classical Athens was not only commonplace but an alternative morally superior to forcible abduction.[30] Similarly, when forensic speeches allege that a number of Athenian political leaders prostituted themselves in their youth, it seems reasonable to assume that an Athenian jury would not have found such allegations inconceivable.[31]

The most extensive fourth-century account of Phryne was Hyperides' speech, *In Defense of Phryne*, an enormously popular text in antiquity and beyond, which generated a major strand of her biography, although only a few fragments remain (frr. 171–80 Kenyon). Her prosecution was not unique among late fifth- and fourth-century BCE forensic cases, as a number of hetaeras were brought to trial during this

22   Phryne of Thespiae

period on various charges, beginning with Aspasia, as we shall see in Chapter 5. A prosecution speech, variously attributed to Aristogeiton (second half of the fourth cent. BCE), Euthias (mid-fourth cent. BCE), and Anaximenes (second half of the fourth cent. BCE), is also attested.[32] Even as oratory borrowed comic tropes and plots revolving around hetaeras, so, too, comedy subsequently made use of famous forensic figures, either as targets of abuse or as protagonists, as, for example, the *Neara* plays of Philemon (c. 300 BCE) and Timocles (late fourth cent. BCE), and Epicrates' *Antilais* (c. 380–350 BCE) and the *Nannion* play of Eubulus (c. 400–330 BCE), no doubt produced after the prosecutions of these women.[33] Indeed, the shift away from mythic titles and plots in Attic comedy after 350 BCE toward plays named after contemporaries indicates that at least some of the characters were drawn from real life, including hetaeras.[34] For instance, the prosecution of Phryne is recounted in Posidippus' *Ephesia*, as quoted previously in this chapter, a play that was produced sometime after 290 BCE, when the poet was active, suggesting that almost a half century later, the trial had taken root in the Athenian imagination.[35] Phryne is also named in several other fourth-century middle comedies, including the *Neottis* of Anaxilas (date uncertain), Timocles' *Neaera* and *Orestautocleides*, and *The Female Barber* of Amphis (mid-fourth cent. BCE).[36]

Subsequent references to Phryne are scattered throughout a wide variety of texts, including Hellenistic prosopographies and treatises, ancient biography, Greek epigram, geography, historiography, and pagan and Christian moral discourses, most of which are preserved in Second Sophistic literature.[37] Indeed, the Greek hetaera was a popular literary figure during this period, when Greek writers living in the Roman Empire sought to reify the Attic past by a mix of selective and inventive source manipulation.[38] Works such as *Dialogues of the Courtesans* by Lucian (c. 125–80 CE), which does not explicitly mention Phryne, and the *Letters of the Courtesans* by Alciphron (late second to early third cent. CE), which does, borrow characters and vignettes from fourth-century comic discourse, especially those involving hetaeras, as filtered and refracted through intermediary Hellenistic materials, none of which have survived. Athenaeus' *Dining Sophists* is by far our most important source for the Greek hetaera from this period, and Phryne looms large in his narrative.[39] The work recounts a fictional banquet held at the house of a Roman friend of the author's, Larensis, and includes a guest list of famous

Her Story, in Quotations   23

intellectuals such as Plutarch, Galen, and Ulpian. The conversation revolves around every aspect of sympotic dining, from furniture, cooks, exotic foods, wine, women, and song illustrated by hundreds of excerpts from earlier texts. Book 13, *Peri Gynaikon* ("Concerning Women"), is devoted to the subject of women as objects of erotic pleasure. It mentions, at least in passing and sometimes at great length, almost all the major accounts of hetaeras from earlier periods of the Greek literary tradition. Among these, Athenaeus cites almost twenty previous sources on Phryne, now lost, including quotations from her fourth-century contemporaries, the orators Hyperides and Aristogeiton, and the comic poets Timocles, Amphis, and Posidippus.[40] Most of the quotations, however, are drawn from later Hellenistic biography, geography, historiography, hetaera treatises, and comic prosopographies, some of which are intentionally esoteric. For instance, Book 13 contains the only extant reference to Alcetas (date uncertain), an author probably obscure even to Athenaeus, and his treatise, *On the Dedications at Delphi*, which describes Phryne's statue and inscription in the sanctuary.[41] One of the primary speakers, Theodorus, known by the nickname Cynulcus, lists several authors who produced treatises on prostitutes that circulated in antiquity, none of which exist today.[42] Although not mentioned in Book 13, Philaenis' "scandalous work about sex" is alluded to several times throughout the larger work.[43] These literary excerpts were probably culled from commonplace books, compilations of pre-selected quotations and anecdotes, representing a critical intermediate stage in the development of the romanticized Athenian hetaera.[44] A handful of these anecdotes are repeated by other first- to third-century CE authors, such as Plutarch (c. 25–120 CE), Pausanias (fl. 150 CE), and Diogenes Laertius (c. 250 CE), suggesting that Phryne's biographical tradition by this time was already well developed and widely circulated. By the late second century CE, Phryne's name, often paired with that of another celebrated hetaera in her circle, Lais, had become synonymous with prostitution and debauchery.[45] Her continued importance to the tradition of oratory is attested as late as the rhetorical declamations of Choricius (491–518 CE). These authors used their sources freely, often paraphrasing them under the guise of citations, without regard for context, and gradually the original meaning of these texts became lost.[46]

24   Phryne of Thespiae

Myth or Reality?

In contrast to Aspasia and Neara, Phryne has only begun to receive comprehensive scholarly treatment, despite the explosion of research on prostitutes and hetaeras in ancient Greece produced over the past three decades.[47] Most recent studies of the subject, such as James Davidson (1997), McClure (2003a), Leslie Kurke (1999), and Kate Gilhuly (2009), approach the hetaera, and sexual labor in Greece more generally, as a discursive construct or literary invention of the Second Sophistic period. Kurke argues that the study of ancient Greek prostitution requires recognition of its discursive or representational function because the extant texts tell us very little about "real" women.[48] She views the hetaera as the invention of the archaic, aristocratic symposium, the private drinking party hosted by elite men, as a deliberate political strategy by which elite symposiasts could distinguish themselves from the rise of commerce and commercial wealth, although Phryne is not part of this discussion. For Gilhuly, Phryne exemplifies the discursive strategy of the "feminine matrix" that structures the feminine through the interplay of public roles, "the prostitute is defined against the wife, but aligned with the ritual agent."[49]

Within this scholarship, Phryne is treated largely as a literary character not only because of the lack of hard evidence for her historical reality but also because of the large number of romantic and sensational stories that became attached to her, and which had particular appeal for nineteenth-century painters, as discussed in the introduction. Craig Cooper, for instance, believes that Phryne's disrobing at her trial is a creation of later antiquity based on a misreading of the original defense speech.[50] Christine Havelock in her exploration of Phryne's artistic receptions in antiquity similarly views her as "largely a fictitious character, and her liaison with Praxiteles is probably a fantasy."[51] Interpreters of Phryne as a discursive construct, including this writer, have accordingly emphasized her pervasive association with art objects, rhetorical display, and stories of voyeurism.[52] Phryne is unique among the rich and famous hetaeras in her shrewd manipulation of Athens' visual economy. Her high price guaranteed that she remained beyond the reach, and out of sight, of most men, "the high fee, like the gift, maintains the hetaera's exciting oscillation on the threshold of availability."[53] Helen Morales goes so far to suggest that Phryne was largely a fictional character and "much of her story, if not herself, was invented." [54] In her view, the stories about Phryne's exposed body and viewers' reactions to it function as allegorical narratives about the creation and reception of art.

The outsized importance of Athenaeus' Book 13 to these discussions would, of course, lead to the conclusion that the Greek hetaera is an almost entirely fictitious character, "or at least a heavily-enhanced reality."[55] As I have written elsewhere, the Athenian hetaera by the Second Sophist period operated as a literary and cultural construction that carried symbolic value, an idealized but distant and alien figure, a relic from the remote past absent from the Roman table.[56] Konstantinos Kapparis attributes this fictionalized hetaera to "revisionist interference": the literature of the Second Sophistic interjected prostitutes into Athenian history through the reinterpretation of famous works of art, monuments, and dedications by linking them to hetaeras in order to sensationalize their stories or dilute homoerotic content.[57]

Several scholars, however, do in fact believe that Phryne was a real woman who was involved in actual historical events, although her story became much embellished by later authors. Kapparis, for instance, considers her prosecution for impiety and the trial "historical facts."[58] He believes she intentionally manufactured her own personal mythology for future generations.[59] Esther Eidinow also considers Phryne a historical figure, as one of three named, real women put on trial for illicit supernatural activities, or "witchcraft," in the fourth century BCE, a topic to which we shall return at more length in Chapter 5.[60] And although Catherine Keesling does not deal directly with the question of Phryne's historicity, she treats her monument at Delphi as authentic, examining it in the context of honorific portrait statues of individuals that became increasingly popular in late classical period and onward.[61] In another discussion of the statue, Antonio Corso reads Phryne's biographical tradition quite literally, viewing her as a historical figure who fled war-torn Thespiae, moved to Athens, became the girlfriend of Praxiteles, and inspired his art as one of two models for his *Cnidian Aphrodite*.[62]

In constructing a biography of Phryne, therefore, one must navigate between these two conflicting but intersecting strands of scholarship on Athenian prostitution. As Davidson observes, "It is a travesty to treat the Greek courtesan as a literary figment and equally mistaken to see her as pure unadulterated fact. She operates at the intersection."[63] On the one hand, we cannot fully access the historical core beneath the stories layered over Phryne in her literary afterlife. On the other, we might construct a life for Phryne based on what we can piece together not only

26   Phryne of Thespiae

from literary quotations, but also from our knowledge of the historical realities of hetaeras and other sexual laborers in fourth-century Athens, and what we know of women in ancient Greece more generally. But this methodology poses an important question for the feminist scholar: how do we recuperate a life entangled with, and impossible to differentiate from, a tradition that fantasized and fetishized Phryne without becoming complicit in this narrative? Saidiya Hartman's concept of "critical fabulation," first set forth in her essay "Venus in Two Acts," offers one possible path for a feminist biography of Phryne. The limitations of the historical record for recovering the lives of marginalized and oppressed women can be mitigated by combining a critical reading of the evidence with the creation of new narratives and "exploiting the capacities of the subjunctive."[64]

To re-imagine Phryne in this way, it is necessary first to acknowledge the limitations of the source evidence, as we have in the preceding discussion, and then to foreground possible aspects of her agency by considering her self-fashioning, or the ways she could have helped to shape her own reception, as "a remarkable woman who played an active and knowing role in creating her own mythology."[65] In the next chapter, we will consider issues of identity, legitimacy, and belonging in the classical Athenian polis that conspired to erase the historical realities of Phryne and other women like her and begin to rewrite her story in new ways.

2

Precarious Lives, Unstable Identities

Despite the widespread fascination with Athenian hetaeras in the ancient literary tradition and the attested presence of such women in the social landscape of fourth-century Athens, modern scholars have struggled to arrive at a consistent set of criteria by which to identify them in the historical record. Attempts to distinguish with certainty hetaeras from other types of prostitutes, and even from citizen women, whether by terminology, dress, cosmetics, special shoes, activities, ethnicity, or naming practices, have largely failed.[1] Even male citizens could not be securely distinguished from slaves and foreigners by their dress and physical appearance alone.[2] Attic oratory routinely plays on the pervasive ambiguity of social status: for instance, during a raid on a citizen's farm, men seeking to enforce a financial judgment seized the debtor's son, mistaking him for a slave, and then brutally beat an elderly free woman, also mistaking her for a slave.[3] In another case, a young man intentionally trespassed on a neighbor's property hoping that the owner would think him a slave, strike him, and be forced to pay damages for the assault of a free person.[4] Then there is the fuller Pancleon, who manifested to some of his acquaintances as a citizen and to others as a foreigner, while to still others as a slave.[5]

The mobility of female social identity at Athens makes it even more difficult to determine who was and was not a free citizen woman because girls did not undergo the same level of social and political scrutiny as their brothers and became displaced into other households when they married. A speech about an inheritance dispute by the

Phryne of Thespiae. Laura McClure, Oxford University Press. © Oxford University Press 2024.
DOI: 10.1093/9780197580882.003.0003

orator Isaeus (first half of the fourth cent. BCE) revolving around the estate of an Athenian man named Euctemon is instructive as to how the Athenians constructed and verified social and political identities for men and women. Euctemon's wife, three sons, and two daughters were all known to his relations, to his kin association (known as a phratry), and to members of his local political district (called demesmen).[6] In other words, their identities as citizens were well attested at all levels of Athenian society.[7] The sons had participated in important civic rituals and were accepted by immediate family, the phratry, and deme, which provided evidence of the family's free standing as Athenian citizens.[8] Although Euctemon's daughters did not undergo the same processes of incorporation and civic confirmation, their marriages to Athenian men and the birth of legitimate offspring attested to their status as lawful Athenian wives and mothers. As Rebecca Kennedy observes, "Without deme or phratry records, the legitimacy and citizen status of a woman was dependent on the ability to muster up ample relatives to act as witnesses to one's birth, marriage, dowry, childbearing and more."[9]

This chapter explores the difficulties inherent in recovering the historical presence of hetaeras like Phryne in fourth-century Athens from the literary, artistic, and historical remains, and of differentiating them from other types of prostitutes, and even from citizen wives. Their unstable identities and precarious lives are at the heart of three ongoing scholarly debates about Athenian prostitution arising, first, from the meanings of the terms used to refer to hetaeras, their ambiguous representation in Attic red-figure vase painting, and the diversity of personal names applied to them. As will be evident from this discussion, the signification of marginalized women was inextricably bound up with how Athenians defined and defended legitimate marriage and legal offspring from the earliest period of polis development, while the mobility of female social identity left many women, even legitimate female citizens, vulnerable to charges of prostitution and fraud. The final portion of the chapter considers, briefly, the social fluidity and upward and downward mobility of women on the margins of Athenian society that made their lives precarious and subject to uncontrollable external forces, such as pregnancy, poverty, abuse, and the capricious whims of their lovers and alleged husbands.

Brothel Slaves and Flute Girls

In other cities, sexual conventions are straightforward and well-defined, but at Athens they are complicated.[10]

Almost without exception, prostitutes in fourth-century Athens were either slaves or foreigners, often immigrants known as metics, like Phryne, a refugee from Thespiae.[11] Athenians permitted visitors to remain in the polis for a brief period while they conducted their business, but those who wished to stay longer as metics were required by law to register with the state, to secure an Athenian sponsor or *prostates*, and pay an annual tax, called the *metoikion*, in the amount of twelve drachmas for a man and six for a woman.[12] This process allowed metics to be recognized as free persons permanently living in Attica under the protection of the Athenian state and its judicial system. In the fourth century, there were proportionately more foreigners resident in Athens than in most Greek cities, and they played a vital role in the Athenian economy.[13] Many metics were well-known, wealthy professionals, such as the orators Lysias (?459–post-380 BCE), who came from a family of prosperous metics originally from Syracuse, and Deinarchus (c. 360–post-292/1 BCE), a metic from Corinth. Failure to comply with rules governing *metoikia* could result in prosecution for an immigration violation and was punishable by enslavement, a topic to which we shall return in Chapter 5. Female metics who resided with citizen men as concubines were exempt from this tax, but if they separated from their partners, they suddenly became vulnerable to prosecution for not meeting the legal requirement of a sponsor. Moreover, marriage between a metic and a citizen was illegal due to a law introduced by Pericles in 451 that limited the right of citizenship to children born exclusively of two Athenian parents.[14] Although this decree fell into disuse in the waning years of the Peloponnesian War, a stricter version was later passed, exact date unknown, that imposed penalties on any individual who married or pretended lawful marriage to a foreigner. Engaging in this form of fraud could invite prosecution on a charge of immigration fraud, as we will see in our discussion of Neaera later in this chapter.

Scholars have traditionally divided the purveyors of commercial sex into three basic categories: *porne* (*pornos* if male), *hetaera*, and *pallake* (note that there is no male equivalent for the latter two categories), in addition to numerous derogatory slang terms.[15] At the lower end of the

30   Phryne of Thespiae

social scale was the *porne*, a name derived from the Greek verb *pernemi* ("to sell"), referring to an anonymous enslaved woman or girl who could be purchased for a nominal fee at a brothel.[16] Female sex slaves offered immediate sexual gratification to "anyone who wishes," a formula that always implies degrading and compulsory prostitution. Occasionally a *porne* can be represented as a partner in a longer-term, more stable relationship, as in the case of Lysias 4, in which two wealthy men are said to own jointly a woman described as a *porne* and slave woman, two terms that are often paired, although her actual status is ambiguous and her identity unknown.[17] Indeed, the term is clearly pejorative and stresses that the woman is a sexual commodity, while the actual social standing of the woman is equivocal, contingent upon the rhetorical aims of the speaker.[18] The *auletris*, a female musician who played the aulos, an ancient Greek flute-like instrument, denotes a woman hired to perform at the symposium (about which more later in this chapter), and does not technically denote a woman who offers sex for pay, although vase depictions of this figure often have sexual connotations. The *aulteris* and other female performers such as the *orchestris* ("dancer") seem to have had more freedom, made more money, and operated under less coercion than the *porne*.[19] Indeed, some of the most illustrious of the fourth-century hetaeras were flute players, such as the hetaera Lamia.[20] Or she could become a *pallake*; Philoclean in Aristophanes' *Wasps*, for example, promises to make the *auletris* his partner after manumitting her.[21]

Hetaeras and Concubines

> Mistresses (*hetaerai*) we keep for the sake of pleasure,
> concubines (*pallakai*) for the daily care of our persons, but
> wives (*gynaikai*) to bear us legitimate children and to be
> faithful guardians of our households.[22]

Nearly every discussion of Greek terminology related to female prostitution begins with these words, from a prosecution speech delivered against the Corinthian hetaera Neaera, which we will be discussing in more detail later in this chapter. Taking a cue from this statement, the hetaera has accordingly been grouped with *pallake* as forming a category distinct from the brothel and hired-out prostitutes described previously, and yet one that potentially encroached on the rights and prerogatives of legally recognized Athenian wives and mothers.[23] A *pallake* could be either a free woman or slave, as evidenced by the archaic law that allowed the killing of a man caught sleeping with another man's wife and pertained to the *pallake* only if she was "kept on the terms that her children would be free."[24] The *pallake* participated in a quasi-marital arrangement with a single man, usually created with an explicit contract, giving her "some security and recourse but not legitimating her offspring."[25] In the fourth century, concubinage seems to have been a response to a law in effect in 349/8 prompted by the proliferation of alien hetaeras that prohibited an alien man, or woman, to live with (*sunoikein*) a citizen, that is, to pretend to be legitimately married to one.[26] Since the male partner was normally an unmarried citizen and the woman a metic, their union was ineligible for marriage and their children not recognized as citizens and legal heirs.[27] The most famous example is Aspasia, who came to Athens from Miletus and entered into a relationship with Pericles, discussed more fully in the next chapter.[28] Although a *pallake* was maintained by one man who may have originally purchased her, their ongoing relationship was not a commercial one and had no term limit, as in the case of hetaeras and other prostitutes.[29]

The meaning of the term hetaera, in contrast, has been widely debated. At one extreme, Leslie Kurke insists on the absolute binarism of *porne* and hetaera.[30] Along with James Davidson, she argues that although the hetaera offered sexual gratification for material rewards like the *porne*, she participated in an economy of gift exchange rather than coinage.[31] Kapparis has argued that there is no absolute distinction between the terms *porne* and hetaera and that they are often used interchangeably, with hetaera operating as a subcategory of *porne*.[32] At the other end of the spectrum, scholars such as Daniel Ogden and Simon Goldhill maintain that the hetaera is defined not by opposition to *porne* but rather to wife, standing outside of marriage as a legal institution more generally.[33] Ogden argues that it is impossible to make any kind of sustained or absolute categorial distinction between hetaera and *pallake* as both types of women entered into lasting, exclusive relationships with a single man; indeed, Menandrian comedy offers several examples of a hetaera becoming a *pallake*.[34] However, there does appear to be a spatial difference. A concubine resided in her lover's household, presumably in the absence of female kin, while a hetaera did not, and introducing her into one's home when womenfolk were present was considered an egregious violation of their modesty.[35] Rebecca Kennedy argues that the

32   Phryne of Thespiae

term hetaera applied to a wide range of women, many of whom did not sell their bodies, but were independent women, many of them metics, but sometimes citizens, whose relationships were not protected by law.[36]

Unlike a *porne*, a hetaera sought and could negotiate an exclusive, contractual arrangement with one man, principally someone with great wealth and power, as only such an individual could afford her costly companionship. She exerted considerably more control over not only her choice of partners but also certain aspects of their relationship, such as when and under what conditions she might gratify her lover and whether to end the affair if she was mistreated or lost interest. Remunerated for a period of time rather than for a discrete sexual act, a hetaera accompanied men to places where respectable women could not go, such as to symposia and the theater, and to mixed-gender religious festivals like the Panathenaea, the annual civic celebration of Athena at Athens, and the Eleusinian mysteries, the secret initiation rituals of Demeter. In addition, she could join in the nocturnal revels of the *komos*, a noisy procession through the streets of Athens that took place after the symposium, involving singing and dancing to the music of the flute. In this respect, a hetaera, like a *pallake*, functioned as a sort of second wife, or "Ersatzfrau," but one who was not confined to the house and could participate in the public sphere alongside her lover while at the same time fulfilling his sexual fantasies of exoticism, literary sophistication, and cosmopolitan élan.[37]

The concept of the hetaera does not seem to have entered the Athenian imagination until the late sixth and early fifth centuries BCE, when Athens first saw an influx of women from Asia Minor, facilitated by an increase in long-distance trade.[38] Herodotus is the first author to use the term hetaera to refer to a female prostitute, in reference to a woman named Rhodopis, who was originally a Thracian slave but later earned her freedom and reaped enormous wealth from her exceptional beauty.[39] We will return to this figure at the end of the next chapter. The word hetaera does not occur with any frequency in written sources until the fourth century BCE; indeed, Kapparis proposes that Herodotus appropriated the term to describe Rhodopis' profession and that it was subsequently adopted by later authors.[40] By the fourth century, however, the term hetaera appears to have applied to a range of women, mostly metics or resident aliens at Athens, but sometimes citizen women, who were unmarriageable, or lived outside of male guardianship, and/or may have temporarily turned to prostitution to support themselves.[41] Indeed, multiple fourth-century texts, especially Attic oratory, attest to the mutability of this new category of woman. A case in point is the uncertain social status of the unnamed woman in Lysias' 4: as we saw earlier, the speaker disparages her as a "prostitute slave nobody" and, as such, claims that she can be subjected to judicial torture for evidence.[42] His opponent, however, maintains that the woman is free and denies that she was ever held in common as property.[43] The fact that the woman had been living in a long-term relationship with the opponent as either a hetaera or *pallake* suggests that the deployment of demeaning terms for prostitution is part of a larger rhetorical strategy to vilify the woman, whose anonymity and ambiguous social status rendered her vulnerable to exploitation by the speaker for political aims.[44]

Isaeus 6, a dispute over property inheritance discussed at the beginning of this chapter, offers another example of how the unstable and ambiguous status of a woman could be manipulated for the sake of a legal argument. The case revolves around the status of the mother of two previously unknown sons and potential heirs to the estate of Euctemon. The mother of these boys, the speaker alleges, was an emancipated slave named Alce who worked for many years as a brothel slave and then in old age managed one of Euctemon's properties as a brothel, selling young women or *paidiskai*.[45] She appears to have been living with Euctemon in the guise of a citizen wife, persuading him to introduce the elder of her sons into his phratry as if he were his father.[46] The speaker repeatedly indicates Alce's low status by naming her, contemptuously referring to her as an *anthropos*, and emphasizing her lack of a male guardian or other close relatives.[47] Although a slave, Alce attempted to pass herself off as a wife not only by seeking her son's entry into Euctemon's phratry but also by participating in the annual rites of the Thesmophoria, an Athenian festival in honor of Demeter that promoted the agricultural fertility of the city reserved exclusively for citizen women.[48] Although never called a hetaera or *porne*, the woman's status as a former slave and her lack of local kin ties reinforces her low economic and likely non-Athenian status. In all these cases, there is no concrete evidence for the social standing of the woman in question, whether hetaera, *porne*, *pallake*, or even lawful wife. Rather these passages suggest that a multitude of terms relating to female sexual status could be applied to the same woman, reflecting the social mobility, upward and downward, of women who lived on the margins of Athenian society and the rhetorical objectives of the speaker.[49]

34   Phryne of Thespiae

Moving from oratory to comedy, the figure of Chrysis in Menander's *Samia* (c. 315–309 BCE) illustrates both the close alignment of hetaera with *pallake* and the difficulty and yet necessity of distinguishing their arrangements with citizen men from lawful marriage, namely, by delimiting the oikos ("household") as "the privileged and protected space of legitimate procreation."[50] Chrysis is an alien from the island of Samos in eastern Greece who worked as a hetaera until Demeas, an Athenian citizen, purchased her to live with him at his home in an exclusive relationship, explicitly as a *pallake*.[51] Demeas initially feels shame at keeping a hetaera and bringing her into his oikos, even in the absence of female kin, and hides this relationship from his son.[52] Like a citizen woman, Chrysis participates in female social networks, visits often with the neighbor woman next door, and celebrates religious festivals such as the Adonia, a private celebration of Aphrodite, with them, but she is not a lawful wife.[53] When Demeas mistakenly believes she has given birth to his child and begun to rear it, he exclaims, "My hetaera's now become my wife (*gameten hetairan*), it seems, without my knowledge!"[54] The phrase "hetaera wife," and his son's reaction, "A wife? How?! I don't understand!," point to the incompatibility of female sexual availability and licit motherhood, underscoring the idea that the hetaera and *pallake* had no legitimate reproductive function within the oikos.[55] As Daniel Ogden explains, "a hetaera is characterized as someone that does not or should not bear children, and it is shameful if she usurps a wife's role in doing so."[56] In Isaeus 3, a woman's childlessness is adduced as proof of her status as a hetaera who accepts "anyone who wishes," while in another legal speech a man named Olympiodorus, in taking up with a hetaera, is said to have rendered his household barren.[57]

The Case against Neaera: Hetaera or Lawful Wife?

The mutability and instability of the social and sexual categories that would have applied to Phryne and which undoubtedly led to her prosecution underpin the most extensive account of a hetaera to survive from fourth-century Athens, the forensic speech *Against Neaera* attributed to the orator Demosthenes (384–322 BCE) but likely the work of Apollodorus delivered between 343 and 340 BCE. It is our only extant text of a litigation involving a hetaera, a subject that will be taken up in more detail in Chapter 5, when we turn to Phryne's trial.[58] The speech not only affords significant insights into the ambiguous social status of women on the margins, not least, the difficulty of distinguishing them from wives, but also the use of prostitution as a rhetorical trope and legal strategy. Neaera was indicted on a charge of illegal marriage to a citizen man. Interestingly, the prosecutor at one point insinuates a far more serious crime, that of impiety, but then drops it, probably because it would be more difficult to prove.[59] (The tenuous nature of impiety charges will be explored more fully in Chapter 5 in connection with Phryne.) Apollodorus then goes on to allege that Stephanus, an Athenian citizen, unlawfully lives together with Neaera, a *xene* or alien woman, passing her off as a citizen and legitimate wife. He further accuses him of introducing her sons into his phratry and deme registers, and giving her daughter, Phano, formerly known as Strybele, in marriage to a citizen man as if they were his legitimate offspring:[60]

> I too have come before you to prove that Stephanus is living
> together with an alien woman (*xene gynaiki*) as if in marriage
> (*sunoikousa*) contrary to the law; that he has introduced
> children not his own to his phratry and demesmen; that he
> has given in marriage the daughters of hetaeras as though they
> were his own; that he is guilty of impiety toward the gods; and
> that he nullifies the right of y/˘our people to bestow its own
> favors, if it chooses to admit anyone to citizenship.[61]

The first part of the speech (1–49) constructs an image of Neaera as a brothel slave, who began her career in Corinth, a harbor town famous for its prostitution, as a *paidiske* or brothel slave, owned and raised under the tutelage of Nicarete, a freedwoman of Charisios of Elis and the wife of his cook, Hippias, and let out to customers far too young.[62] Apollodorus twice refers to her former enslaved status and her open traffic in sex to position her rhetorically as a *porne*, at least in her early years: she is the property of others, makes a living off her body, receives payment for her sexual services, and is available to anyone who wants her:[63]

> I wish for the moment to return to the defendant Neaera, and
> prove to you that she belonged to Nicarete, and that she lived
> as a sex worker letting out her person for hire to those who
> wished to enjoy her.[64]

36   Phryne of Thespiae

The word hetaera is first used of the prepubescent Neaera when she accompanies Simos of Aleuadae, one of the richest and most powerful men in Greece, to Athens for the festival of the Panathenaea and stays at the house of Ctesippus with Nicarete, drinking and dining in the presence of many men "in the manner of a hetaera."[65]

After years of deriving profits from her, Nicarete sold Neaera for thirty minas to two bachelors, Timanoridas of Corinth and Eukrates of Leukas, who kept her as their private mistress.[66] In this relationship, she is alternately characterized as their personal sex slave and as a hetaera, indicating that the two terms could plausibly be applied to the same woman, or perhaps suggesting a transition from brothel slave to a woman used exclusively by one or two wealthy owners.[67] About to enter into legitimate marriages with citizen women, they decided to get rid of Neaera, giving her the opportunity to buy her freedom at the cut rate of twenty minas on the condition that she no longer work in Corinth, threatening to sell her back to a *pornoboskos* or pimp if she ever did so.[68] Unable to raise the entire sum by herself from a combination of her own earnings and contributions of her former lovers, Neaera accepted the offer of a wealthy Athenian citizen by the name of Phrynion to make up the difference for her manumission.[69] She returned with him to Athens, where she accompanied him to dinner parties, joined him in the nocturnal revels of the *komos*, and even had sex with him in public "as though a hetaera."[70]

Phrynion's wanton and abusive behavior violated the rules of propriety even for a hetaera, compelling Neaera to flee to Megara "since she was mistreated outrageously by Phrynion, and was not loved as she expected to be, and since her wishes were not granted by him."[71] There she eked out a living by selling her body for another two years during wartime until another Athenian, Stephanus, came to her rescue, staying at her house and having sex with her. With Stephanus as her *prostates*, a requirement of all metics in Athens, as discussed previously, Neaera returned with him to the city after he promised to take her as wife and to introduce her sons into his phratry and make them citizens.[72] At Athens, Neaera continued to work as a non-exclusive hetaera, entertaining lovers in Stephanus' house, which allowed her to charge a higher fee for her services because of her status as the "wife" of an Athenian citizen.[73] This arrangement also facilitated a blackmail scheme that involved enticing rich, unwitting foreigners into having sex with Neaera, a putative wife, and then extorting a hefty sum by accusing them of

Precarious Lives, Unstable Identities

adultery.[74] Meanwhile, Phrynion found out that Neaera had returned to Athens and immediately claimed her as his runaway slave. Stephanus intervened, asserting her freedom according to the law, and after arbitration, which involved the testimony of Neaera herself, she was declared "a free woman and guardian (*kurian*) of her own person."[75] The speaker then brings this narrative to a close, arguing that he has proven that Neaera was originally a slave who was sold twice and worked with her body as a hetaera.[76]

The question of female legitimacy in the Athenian polis and the mutable identities of marginal women is also at the heart of the second part of the speech (50–93), which makes a factually weak and unconvincing case that Phano, Neaera's daughter, was also an alien, indeed a prostitute, posing as a citizen woman, like her mother. In contrast to Neaera, however, Apollodorus never directly calls Phano a hetaera or *porne*, but rather hints at her questionable status with the phrase "that sort of woman," probably because, in fact, she was neither.[77] Instead he creates, in the words of Cynthia Patterson, a "fictional two-headed monster" by conflating mother and daughter.[78] Matronymic references to her as "the daughter of Neaera" reinforce her questionable social standing by downplaying the legitimacy of Stephanus as her father and thereby calling into question her eligibility for citizenship as a hetaera's daughter.[79] The repeated naming of Phano and the reminder that she was originally called Strybele again associate her with her mother's profession.[80] Although given in marriage to an Athenian citizen named Phrastor, Phano's lack of modesty and obedience led to her being cast out while pregnant with his child. Phrastor later took her back, acknowledging the baby as his own, but his phratry and genos refused to recognize his son on the grounds that Phano was not the legitimate daughter of Stephanus but rather of Neaera.[81]

Apollodorus further presents Phano as Neaera's daughter by alleging that she participated in a variation of the extortion plot contrived earlier by Stephanus. When he caught Epaenetos, a former lover of Neaera's, consorting with Phano, he accused him of adultery and extorted from him a sum of thirty minas. Epanetos in turn indicted Stephanus, accusing Phano of prostitution by referring to her as an *anthropos* and using the same verb for intercourse previously used of Neaera.[82] He further argues that the law against adultery does not apply to "women who sit in a brothel or openly sell themselves."[83] In a final act of insolence, Stephanus married Phano a second time, to a man named Theogenes,

38   Phryne of Thespiae

the archon basileus, a type of Athenian magistrate, which gave her a prominent and controversial position in Athenian cult, requiring her to make secret offerings during the festival of the Anthesteria on behalf of the city as *Basilinna*, a public office restricted to citizen women.[84] The charges against Phano amplify the representation of Neaera as an alien hetaera whose offspring would be ineligible for citizenship status while at the same time underscoring her vulnerability to charges of commercial sex and civic disenfranchisement in light of any hard evidence to the contrary.

When Apollodorus returns to the subject of Neaera over fifty chapters later, his escalation of rhetoric against her again demonstrates the fungibility of the terminology for prostitution and its uses and abuses in forensic oratory:

> Will you leave a woman who has blatantly sold herself
> throughout the whole of Greece (*peporneumenen*) unpunished
> for insulting the city so shamefully . . . ? For where has this
> woman not made her living from her body? To what place has
> she not gone in quest of her daily wage? What do you suppose
> a woman does who is subject to men who are not her kinsfolk,
> and who follows in the train of him who pays her? Does she
> not serve all the lusts of those who deal with her?[85]

The participle *peporneumene*, and the allusions to spatial mobility, to working with her body and charging a fee, and to being sexually available to all without discrimination, clearly limn Neaera as a *porne*.[86] Although Apollodorus deploys various terms for prostitution and social marginality throughout the speech as a rhetorical tactic to denigrate the defendant, from *xene*, *doule*, and *porne* to hetaera and *pallake*, Neaera's actual status, and that of her daughter, in the end remain unclear.[87] By the time of the trial, Neaera would have been in her late fifties, having lived with Stephanus in relative obscurity for around two decades.[88] To the extent that she would have been familiar to the jurors, it would have been through her relationship to Stephanus rather than her previous history as a brothel slave or hetaera plying her trade in the sex market in Corinth and Megara, as Apollodorus claims. As he goes on to propose in anticipation of arguments for the defense, Neaera may well have been a freedwoman employed to manage Stephanus' household and even care for his children, that is, Phano and her two brothers, in the absence of a legitimate wife and mother.[89] She could have been his long-term sexual partner as a *pallake*, or a hetaera, as he alleges, but not the mother of Stephanus' children, or, indeed, his legal and legitimate wife. As Glazebrook observes, "The uncertainty surrounding her story and her relationship to Stephanus' household remains in place at the end of the piece."[90] Indeed, Apollodorus' rhetorical strategy, contingent as it is on a broad array of terms to convey the low social standing of female others in classical Athens, would not have worked if the jurors knew exactly who Neaera was.

Whatever the actual status of Neaera and Phano, the speech reflects contemporary male anxieties about foreign women operating outside of the institution of marriage, whether as brothel slaves, hired-out prostitutes, or the more lasting arrangements of *pallake* and hetaera, and their potential to encroach upon the categories of lawful Athenian womanhood. Clearly the main offense is that Neara, as well as her daughter, Phano, by masquerading as citizen wives threaten to subvert social hierarchy, thereby legitimating the practice of prostitution for impoverished citizen daughters and granting to hetaeras the prerogatives of free women, particularly the right to bear children and to share in the religious privileges of the city.[91] For this reason, Apollodorus famously attempts to articulate the distinction between the two types of women available to men in his final remarks quoted at the beginning of this section: hetaeras and *pallakes* for sex and the care of their bodies, and wives for the bearing of legitimate children and the management of their households. And yet, as *Against Neaera* demonstrates again and again, authenticating the actual social standing of these three categories of women was far from straightforward. Indeed, a hetaera had everything to gain if she could pass herself off as a legitimate wife, as did Neaera and Phano, and possibly Alce, Phile, and some of the other female denizens of Attic oratory, while actual citizen women had everything to lose if suspected of adultery, or worse, trafficking in sex. As we have seen, distinctions between hetaera and legitimate wife or daughter could easily be flouted. Posing as a wife not only enabled Neaera to command a higher fee for her services as a "respectable" married woman living with her husband, it also allowed her to carry out a lucrative blackmail operation by threatening to accuse her customers of adultery.[92] Nicarete, the woman who reared Neaera to prostitution, called her and the other girls "daughters" so that "by giving out that they were free women, she might exact the largest fees from those who wished

40   Phryne of Thespiae

to enjoy them."[93] Whether a former hetaera or not, Neaera apparently passed for decades as a citizen woman, living in relative obscurity with Stephanus until her late fifties at the time of the trial.[94] Moreover, Phano is able to infiltrate the highest ranks of Athenian citizens by marrying the archon basileus, even presiding with him over ancient rites.[95] A hetaera with the means to pass as a wife would have had every reason to do so, but conversely the same system rendered a legitimate wife vulnerable to charges of adultery and commercial sex. As Julia Assante astutely observes, the idea of lawful marriage as a reliable and fixed constant in classical Athens against which other relationships can be measured is a myth, since the boundary between the two was often porous and unstable, paving the way for allegations of illicit sexual and other suspicious activities.[96] Phryne, we might imagine, would have lived much like Neaera, as a foreigner in Athens, entering into long-term, illegitimate relationships and eliciting envy and mistrust for her violation of gender norms.

Women at the Symposium in Attic Vase Painting

A second important debate surrounding hetaeras that has proved inconclusive involves the iconography of female nudity in Attic red-figure vase painting and parallels in comic texts. This complex question has particular relevance for Phryne, whose stories situate her at the intersection of "respectable" female nudity and erotic provocation, to be considered more fully in Chapters 4 and 5. To date, scholars have yet to establish reliable criteria for identifying hetaeras on Attic vases and how to distinguish them from other types of prostitutes and even citizen women. As with terminology, many scholarly interpretations begin with the assumption that the category of hetaera is linguistically and visually distinct from wife. Accordingly, it has been argued that the primary attribute of the hetaera in Attic vase painting is nudity, a category perceived as incompatible with the construction of the citizen wife, as first set forth by Larissa Bonfante in her exploration of the meanings of nudity in ancient art. She argues that female figures stripped of their clothing on Athenian pots typically signify the sexual vulnerability and low social or alien status associated with female entertainers.[97] Carola Reinsberg in her study of the iconography of prostitution in Attic vase painting similarly identifies every nude female, even when alone in a private setting or in an exclusively female environment, and every female who engages in erotic behavior, even an embrace or affectionate gaze, as a hetaera.[98] In addition to nudity, elements of commercialism, such as a pouch or money bag, are also considered signs of prostitution. For instance, Jennifer Neils argues that hetaeras are "easily recognizable" on vases because of their nudity and/or the presence of a money bag in a male companion's hand.[99] Further, whether clothed or naked, women depicted on a specific type of drinking cup used in the symposium called a *kylix* that typically represents sympotic scenes and practices are likely candidates for prostitution, although not necessarily hetaeras.

Another attribute that supposedly confirms the presence of a hetaera are name inscriptions, especially those scholars have identified with prostitution. The Thalia cup, an Attic bilingual (red and black) figure kylix from around 510 BCE, depicts several naked women engaging in sexual activities with men, with several inscribed female names: Thalia ("Blooming"), Corone ("Crow"), and Smica ("Tiny").[100] Other name inscriptions that have been associated with hetaeras in vase iconography include Aphrodisia and Obole ("Obol"), the labels given to two women spinning wool on a late sixth-century cup by the Ambrosios painter belonging to a private collection, and Callisto, a delicate young woman portrayed together with a symposiast on the tondo of another red-figure kylix (c. 490 BCE), and Rhodopis, whose name appears on a black-figure hydria (c. 520 BCE).[101] Although some of these are found among fourth-century hetaeras over a hundred years later, many are indistinguishable from the names of citizen women. For instance, Rhodopis is the name attributed to the first attested hetaera in the literary record, but the female figure bearing this name on an Attic red-figure hydria is one of four modest maidens drawing water from a fountain![102]

Even textile production, the supreme symbol of female fidelity and domestic virtue in ancient Greece, has been used to identify hetaeras on Attic vases, beginning with the so-called spinning hetaeras debate. Almost a century ago, G. Rodenwalt argued that a young female spinning wool on an Attic red-figure alabastron by the Pan Painter (Figure 2.1), now lost, is a high-priced hetaera because of the apparent money bag held in the outstretched hand of the youth at right.[103] His novel interpretation, that textile activities conferred respectability on the female brothel worker, thereby increasing her value, recalls Nicarete's "daughters" and the advantages for hetaeras of passing as citizen women.

42   Phryne of Thespiae

FIGURE 2.1 A seated girl at left spins wool while a youth at right holds out a pouch. Attic red-figure alabastron by the Pan Painter, c. 470–460 BCE. Berlin, Antikensammlung F2254.

Since then, almost every image of a woman working wool, nude, in the presence of men, or on a sympotic vessel, has been identified as a hetaera. For instance, the sedate figure of a woman seated on a chair and holding a distaff and spindle on an Attic red-figure kylix (Figure 2.2) has been identified as a madame overseeing her customers, despite the fact that she is fully clothed and there are no clear attributes of commercial sex.[104] Because of the (questionable) link established between textile production and prostitution among scholars, the presence of a large number of loom weights in the deposits of Building Z located in the Kerameikos has been taken as evidence that the site served as an inn or brothel.[105] Certainly these indicate a female presence, but not necessarily sexual laborers moonlighting as weavers, which may be identified by other assemblages, as we will see in the next chapter. The legacy of the spinning hetaera has similarly influenced the view that the women designated as *talasiourgoi* ("wool-workers") in Athenian manumission records, known as the phialai inscriptions, were not domestic slaves but actually prostitutes attempting to mask their true professions.[106]

Scholars have more recently questioned these assumptions, moving away from trying to establish a set of reliable criteria by which to distinguish hetaeras from wives in the visual record to an increasing awareness of the challenges and ambiguities presented by vase iconography. Ulla Kreilinger has decisively demonstrated that female nudity can be

FIGURE 2.2 A seated woman spinning between two male and female pairs. Attic red-figure kylix, c. 450 BCE, attributed to the Euaion Painter. Berlin, Antikensammlung F31426.

deployed in a variety of contexts on Greek vases, many of which either have no erotic associations, as for instance, the famous image of Cassandra at the altar after the fall of Troy (Figure 2.3), whose nakedness emphasizes not sexual availability but rather vulnerability and fear.[107] It also conveys her abject status as a suppliant who takes refuge at the altar of Athena while reaching toward a warrior to beg for her life.[108] Indeed, the act of baring the breasts in the literary tradition is often a form of supplication rather than erotic, as in the case of Hecuba, who pleads with Hector not to return to battle, or Clytemnestra, who asks Orestes to take pity on her as the source of his life.[109] As part of the preparations for sex and its aftermath, female nudity in scenes of bathing can also have a wide variety of connotations, from prostitution to pre-nuptial rites. Indeed, nuptial scenes increasingly feature both male and female nudity in Attic pottery from the late fifth century onward, including the idealized image of the kneeling bather, as examined in Chapter 4.[110] Another exception is athletic nudity, as in the case of a red-figure

FIGURE 2.3 Cassandra at the altar. Attic red-figure hydria by the Cleophrades painter, 500–474 BCE. Naples, Museo Nazionale Archeologico 2422. INTERFOTO / Alamy Stock Photo.

Precarious Lives, Unstable Identities

amphora that depicts a group of naked women apparently at the beach, apart from men: one woman swims freestyle among the fishes at the lower register, while another at her right perches on the tips of her toes, arms forward, back curved, ready to dive into the water.[111] Chapter 4 will address in greater detail the influence of these earlier representations of female nudity on the development of the first female sculptural nude, the *Cnidian Aphrodite.*

In most cases, however, the social and sexual status of women in Attic vase painting is entirely ambiguous, as Sian Lewis and others have observed, "Just as in reality, there was no method of distinguishing a prostitute from any other woman simply by looking . . . Nothing on its own signifies that a woman sells sex for a living."[112] Items such as amulets, diaphanous garments, mirrors, and various types of hairstyles and foot-wear associated with hetaeras in the Greek literary tradition are com-monplace elements of the iconography of all types of women in Greek art, as Mireille Lee has demonstrated. For instance, the *sakkos*, a kind of hairnet or snood that held back the hair, is worn both by free adult women as well as hetaeras and slaves.[113] The respectability of the spinner on the alabastron discussed previously in this chapter (Figure 2.1) has been restored by Gloria Ferrari, who believes that the pouch is not a money bag, but rather a container for knucklebones, a favorite game of girls, proffered as an innocent gift.[114] Sheramy Bundrick similarly argues that many images of women on Attic vases are intended to have mul-tiple and even contradictory meanings, such that hetaera and house-wife are often interchangeable, in order to maximize the marketability of the vase. She takes as an example an Attic red-figure hydria by the Harrow Painter (Figure 2.4), which shows at left a woman seated under a portico, wrapped in a mantle, wearing a *sakkos*, and holding a mirror. A small boy faces her, wrapped in a himation, while a bearded, half-draped man leans on a staff outside, holding a pouch in his left hand. Scholars are divided over the identity of the seated woman, with the majority arguing that she is a hetaera and the building a brothel, while the minority view holds that she is a legitimate wife at home among her male kin.[115] In Bundrick's view, the Harrow hydria depicts a domestic scene in which the male *kyrios* or guardian brings home money to his wife in order to idealize and promote "the social roles of the members of the classical Athenian oikos."[116] Athenian vase painters thus kept the ico-nography of textile scenes deliberately open-ended in order to appeal to a broad range of clientele.[117] It is noteworthy that in the case of all three

46   Phryne of Thespiae

FIGURE 2.4 A seated young woman holding a mirror and wearing a *sakkos* with man at right holding pouch. Attic red-figure hydria, c. 470 BCE, attributed to the Harrow Painter. Tampa, Florida, Tampa Museum of Art, Joseph Veach Noble Collection, purchased in part with funds donated by Mr. and Mrs. James L. Ferman, 1986.070.

vases just discussed there is nothing about the female figure, in either her appearance or demeanor, that overtly signifies sexual availability or a non-domestic setting.

The most likely place to find hetaeras in Attic vase painting are the sympotic scenes that adorn the exteriors and interiors of drinking cups, or *kylikes*, used by the participants, based on their representations of female nudity and sexual activities. These are vases intended to be used

FIGURE 2.5 Woman sexually gratifying two men (detail of exterior). Attic red-figure kylix attributed to the Pedieus Painter, c. 510 BCE. Paris, Louvre G13.

and viewed exclusively by men, in contrast to the types of vessels associated with women, such as cosmetic jars, *epinetra* or thigh covers used for working wool, and vases used for ritual purposes like weddings and funerals.[118] To begin with one of the more graphic depictions of naked female bodies used for the sexual gratification of men, let us turn to the disturbing image of sexual assault found on an Attic red-figure kylix by the Pedieus Painter (Figure 2.5). Part of a group-sex scene featuring four women and eight men involved in threesomes and foursomes, the detail shows a nude woman balancing precariously on a stool, attempting to steady herself with her right hand while her left dangles at her side. To the left, a man forces her to perform oral sex on his oversized member, grasping her by her back, while to the right, another man enters her from the rear while restraining her with his left hand, a sandal at the ready in case she disobeys. The men in this scene and elsewhere on the vase direct and dominate the activities, a point visually reinforced by their placement in the upper register, while the women are portrayed as subordinate and passive as they squat or crouch on all fours below them.[119] Indeed, they are forced to submit to degrading sex acts such as anal sex and fellatio that are regularly associated with brothel slaves.[120] Despite the presence of these images on a cup used for the symposium, there are oddly few sympotic attributes, perhaps signifying a perversion of sympotic protocol or that events are taking place elsewhere. The brutal sexuality in this scene is reminiscent of the explicit abuse that Neaera rejects from Phrynion when he forced her "to have sex with him openly everywhere whenever he wished" and failed to protect her from being raped by multiple men at a party while she was drunk.[121] Even hetaeras were not expected to tolerate such mistreatment, and it was in fact an act of hybris for any man to attempt it, and in the case of sexual assault, legally actionable, as demonstrated by Lysias' forensic speech, *Against Philonides for Rape*, discussed in Chapter 4.

As if to counter the violent and almost bestial sexuality on the cup's exterior, the interior tondo (Figure 2.6) features a quiet scene between a fully clothed female lyre player and her male companion, who delicately embraces her with one arm while holding a cup in the other. For Kurke, this sudden visual transition embodies the discursive polarities occupied by the hetaera, from abased object of male desire, on the one hand, to "idealized mystification," on the other.[122] However, it is unlikely that the objectified female figures depicted on the exterior of Pedieus kylix and similar vases were originally intended to represent the celebrity hetaeras of fourth-century Athens, like Phryne, given that almost all of the erotic scenes on Attic red-figure vases precede 450 BCE, some by more than fifty years, well before the first attested use of the term hetaera.[123] Moreover, the cultural construct of the hetaera, which is largely based on exclusivity, limited availability, lack of public nudity, and long-term liaisons with a single man, undermines the argument that the women depicted in scenes of explicit and demeaning sex in a sympotic or komiastic context are hetaeras.[124] Rather it is more likely that we are meant to view the Pedieus cup as depicting brothel slaves, freelance prostitutes, or even domestic slaves on its exterior and a refined, fully clothed, and cherished musician-hetaera on its tondo.

One legible type of prostitute regularly referenced on sympotic vessels is the female flute player or *auletris*. A red-figure kylix from Corpus Christi College, Oxford (Figure 2.7), portrays a naked flute player surrounded by half-dressed men reclining on couches in various stages of inebriation; her total nudity, whether a fantasy or not, advertises her potential sexuality availability, as do the attempt of the symposiast at right to grope her body.[125] In contrast to the Pedieus vase, however, the attributes of a symposium are in clear evidence, including, in addition to her flute, drinking cups, a lyre hanging on the wall, full-length couches,

FIGURE 2.6 Female lyre player accompanying a male symposiast, tondo, Attic red-figure kylix attributed to the Pedieus Painter, c. 510 BCE. Paris, Louvre G13.

cushions, and pillows. The tondo of another red-figure kylix (Figure 2.8) portrays a similarly sedate and intimate scene between a fully clothed *auletris* and her male companion, who listens intently to her song. The female flute-player was not only a staple of the symposium, she was also a key participant in the afterparty or *komos*, in which the inebriated symposiasts and their hetaeras took their party to the streets led by the music of the flute.

The genres of old and middle comedy provide numerous parallels for the association of public nudity and graphic sexual activity with hetaeras and brothel slaves; indeed, they routinely feature in the concluding scenes of Aristophanic comedy. Scantily clad or fully naked female performers and mutes regularly appeared on Aristophanes'

FIGURE 2.7 A naked *auletris* at center playing the aulos surrounded by male symposiasts, Attic red-figure kylix by the Foundry Painter, c. 490–480 BCE, Athens. Cambridge, Fitzwilliam Museum Loan Ant. 103.18. (On loan from Corpus Christi College.)

FIGURE 2.8 An *auletris* entertaining a male symposiast, tondo, Attic red-figure cup, c. 480 BCE, Vulci. Paris, Louvre Museum, G135.

Precarious Lives, Unstable Identities   51

comic stage, in the form of the two "little treasures" who accompany Dicaeopolis at the end *Acharnians*; the "little golden beetle" or *auletris*, a figure that often provides the pretext for a joke about fellatio, who accompanies Philocleon in *Wasps*; Procne, the "delicate little bird," also depicted as a flute player, in the *Birds*; and the dancer summoned by Euripides to entice the Scythian Archer in *Thesmophoriazusae*.[126] Explicit sexual allusions to the anatomies of these figures, such as to the breasts of the girls in Acharnians, to the buttocks of Opora, and to Diallage's genitals, anus, breasts, and legs, as well as incitements to grasp or fellate the penis, or references to their spatial mobility, indicate that they are meant to be understood as lower-order prostitutes; indeed, they are never referred to as hetaeras.[127] Whether actual women played these roles, or whether they were performed by men in costume, these bodies were visually and verbally exposed before assembled male spectators in Attic old comedy, just as they were in the symposium and in Attic vase painting.[128]

The frequent and detailed descriptions of prostitutes in the fragments of middle comedy preserved by Athenaeus suggest that encounters with such women were a regular occurrence on Athenian streets. A common theme is the low cost, variety, and availability of brothel prostitution as a safe alternative to adultery:

> There are very attractive girls in the brothels, girls you can see basking in the sun with their breasts bare, lined up one after another in a column, half-naked. A man can pick whichever one he likes—thin, fat, round, tall, withered up, young, old, middle-aged, ancient . . . And you can (have sex with) any of them without fear, and cheaply, during the day, in the evening, however you want. Whereas the women you can't see, and can't see clearly when you do see them, [make you] fearful, having your life in your hand . . . .[129]

The passage draws a clear contrast between the bodies of prostitutes which can be viewed by all, outside in broad daylight, and those of citizen wives, which exist in the shadowy realm of the house, unseen, or barely visible, even in a furtive sexual encounter.[130] These comic fragments combined with the visual evidence indicate that the nudity of common prostitutes was highly visible to men in the democratic polis and intersected in important ways with democratic laws and institutions, whether in the theater, the symposium, or the city streets, a topic to which we shall return in the next chapter.

As this brief discussion has shown, the images of women in Attic red-figure vase painting pose substantial interpretative challenges for the modern viewer. Women of all types—foreigners, slaves, hetaeras, and wives—can share similar iconographic attributes, such as the *sakkos*, diaphanous garments, as well as wool-working implements, and are thus indistinguishable by physical appearance and activities alone. Although women engaged in innocuous domestic activities, such as spinning, are portrayed on vessels intended to be looked at and used by men at the symposium, they cannot be securely identified as hetaeras. A pouch (Figures 2.1 and 2.3), or even a gift associated with women, such as a jewelry box or alabastron (Figure 2.2), given by a man to a girl or woman does not necessarily allude to commercial sex. Female nudity, previously considered an undisputed marker of sexual availability, can occur in a variety of contexts, in connection with both citizen women and mythic figures, especially in cases of female supplication, nuptial scenes, or ritual bathing, all components of Phryne's narratives, as we will see in Chapters 4 and 5. However, the female participants in sympotic activities depicted on Attic red-figure *kylikes* intended to be used and viewed by men at the symposium are more likely to be associated with prostitution, whether represented as completely nude, fully clothed, forcibly engaged in sex acts, or in a less explicit, intimate scene. Within this category, the hetaera cannot with any certainty be distinguished from the brothel slave or other types of prostitutes, except for the *auletris* whose iconography and placement within the symposium give a clear indication of her identity. Like the authors of forensic speeches, Attic vase painters could exploit the ambiguous identities of such figures for their own economic, narrative, and visual purposes. The subject of the symposium as the primary domain of the hetaera will be considered in more detail in the next chapter. While most of these representations shed little light on Phryne as a historical figure, beyond illuminating how difficult it is to securely identify hetaeras in the artistic record, they nonetheless situate her within an artistic milieu in which explicit sexual activities associated with prostitutes eventually gave way to a more muted, respectable form of female nudity that coalesced around hetaeras in the fourth-century BCE and eventually generated her legacy in art.

Hetaera Names?

> The list of Athenian women who are known to us from
> literature is rather short . . . women are quite often mentioned
> in the extant private orations; but for all that, only a handful
> are known to us by name.[131]

The last debate about hetaeras to be examined in this chapter concerns the extent to which a hetaera can be identified by specific onomastic criteria. Phryne, for instance, allegedly answered to multiple names beyond the name Mnesarete assigned to her at birth. Some scholars persist in maintaining that it is possible to identify hetaeras in the historical record based on naming practices alone, while others argue that the names of hetaeras do not significantly deviate from those of citizen women in fourth-century Attic inscriptions and thus are not a reliable attribute.[132] The latter view has been most forcefully articulated by Claire Taylor, who asserts that there is no such thing as a "*hetaera* name."[133] Proponents of dedicated hetaera names rely on many of the same assumptions as the previous two scholarly controversies, namely, that historical hetaeras and their literary counterparts were clearly demarcated from free citizen women by the social and sexual terms that applied to them, their physical appearance, public notoriety, spatial mobility, and naming practices.

It has been well established that Athenian citizen women were to have no public presence, at least not until after death, as Pericles famously advises the widows in his audience, "great glory is hers who has the smallest reputation among men, whether for praise or blame."[134] In a foundational essay, David Schaps demonstrated that the Attic orators went to great lengths to avoid mentioning the names of citizen women, referring to them instead by the names of their male relatives. For example, the mother at the heart of the inheritance dispute in Demosthenes' *Against Boeotus I* and *II* is never named, but is identified at one point by seven distinct male relatives: her father, brothers, father-in-law, husband, and son:

> My mother, men of the jury, was the daughter of Polyaratus of
> Cholargos, sister of Menexenus and Bathyllus and Periander.
> Her father gave her in marriage to Cleomedon, son of Cleon,
> adding a talent as her marriage portion; and at the first she

54   Phryne of Thespiae

lived with him as his wife. She bore him three daughters and one son, Cleon.[135]

By naming only the woman's male relatives, the speaker signals her virtuous character and high status as a member of an illustrious family. In contrast, hetaeras occupied the discursive, rhetorical, and civic spaces avoided by citizen women: they were well-known public figures familiar to all, publicly named in both oratory and comedy. In the earliest literary account of a hetaera, we are told "all of the Greeks knew the name of Rhodopis by heart."[136] As we will see in Chapter 5, the women most frequently named in forensic oratory are thus unsurprisingly women of questionable origins and/or those associated with the speaker's opponents, such as Neaera and Phano in *Against Neara*. Apollodorus refers to Neaera by her name over fifty times in the course of his speech, while in contrast Demosthenes in his speech against Onetor alludes to his respectable sister twenty-two times, but never by name.[137] When Apollodorus describes Phrastor's marriage to Phano, he mentions the girl by name, but when he alludes to his remarriage, the name of the woman is omitted: she is simply called the legitimate daughter of Satyrus and the sister of Diphilus.[138] There is only one exception to this rule: free citizen women could be named without offense in oratory after their deaths or publicly commemorated with funerary monuments and inscriptions.[139]

The names of Greek hetaeras attracted much attention in classical antiquity, appearing frequently in Attic oratory and in fourth-century comic plays, in Alexandrian prosopographies and hetaera catalogues, and as a popular topic among Second Sophistic writers, Greek writers living in the Roman Empire during the second century CE.[140] The *Lexicon of Greek Personal Names* lists 162 names associated with hetaeras in literary texts, inscriptions from Attica and beyond, and late sixth-century vases.[141] The confusing jumble of birth names, nicknames, epithets, and homonyms associated with hetaeras from radically divergent genres and time periods that comes down to us, mostly from Athenaeus, makes it impossible to disentangle actual women from their fictive counterparts. As Cohen observes, "virtually all of the prominent hetaeras of the Greek literary tradition are homonymically shadowed by predecessors or successors of the same name."[142] Most of the exegeses on hetaera names in Athenaeus appear in the sections dealing with the *Chreiae* of Machon (c. third cent. BCE), Attic oratory, and hetaera

Precarious Lives, Unstable Identities   55

treatises.[143] They can be considered nicknames or professional names, as in the case of the hetaera Mania, who was originally called Melissa, a name that had been given to her in infancy.[144] Machon, as quoted by Athenaeus, acknowledges the confusion created by these two names, calling it unseemly for an Athenian woman, particularly a high-class hetaera, to bear a servile Phrygian name:

> A member of my present audience might perhaps be
> surprised—and reasonably so!—that any Athenian woman was
> ever addressed or known as Mania; for it is disgraceful for a
> woman from the heart of Greece to have a Phrygian name, and
> particularly a hetaera.[145]

The names attributed to Athenian hetaeras are difficult to classify and do not conform to any one overarching pattern: many derive from animals, like Corone ("Crow"), Leaena ("Lioness"), and Hys ("Sow"); others from plants, such as Ocimon ("Basil"), Corriano ("Coriander"), and Anticyra ("Hellebore"); commerce, including Obole and Clepsydra ("Water Clock"); place names, such as Cyrene and Sinope, female abstractions, such as Eirene ("Peace") and Opora ("Harvest"); or desirable female characteristics, like Hedeia ("Sweet One"), Thaleia ("Bloom"), and Sige ("Silence").[146] Athenaeus' remark that the hetaera accompanying Cyrus the Younger on campaign changed her name from Milto to Aspasia, possibly in emulation of Pericle's *pallake*, could be taken to mean that hetaeras adopted a new name when entering their profession.[147] Many involve derogatory meanings or puns that dehumanize the women, such as an unnamed hetaera who seems to have had two nicknames, Leme ("Runny Eyes") and Parorama ("Oversight"), and another named Phanostrate who went by Phtheiropyle ("Picking off Lice at the Door").[148] Some of these fanciful names may have been literary inventions assigned to fictive characters, but likely not all, given the frequency with which Attic comic genres target contemporary historical individuals, while others may have been professional names or epithets, especially when a primary name is given.

Then again both the birth name and the professional might be equally uncommon, such as one Synoris ("Pair of Horses") also known as Lychnus ("Lamp").[149] A consideration of the inscriptional record seems to confirm this. According to Athenaeus, the primary name (*to kyrion onoma*) of Clepsydra was Metiche; of Corone, Theocleia; of Hys,

56   Phryne of Thespiae

Callistion; and of Anticyra, Oia. These alleged birth names are either unattested in the fourth- and third-century Attic inscriptions, such as Metiche and Oia, or rare, as with Melissa and Theocleia, although they do occur with regularity outside of Athens, indicating women so named were of foreign birth. Conversely, names that sound like literary inventions, such as Ocimon, Opora, and Sige, are all attested at Athens, suggesting that real women could bear these names, whether as citizen daughters, freedwomen, or slaves, with many having origins outside of Athens. The same with Phanostrate and Callistion, which are both found in connection with free women of citizen status in late classical Athens. Indeed, over a hundred years ago, Schneider estimated that only 10 percent of the three hundred names included in his entry, "Hetaeras," in Pauly-Wissova's encyclopedia can be considered "Hetäresnamen."[150] Claire Taylor further argues that several names often associated with hetaeras by both ancient and modern scholars are also fairly frequently used for free Athenian women in the inscriptional evidence. The name Glycera ("Sweet One"), for instance, recurs both in Greek new comedy and in Alexandrian taxonomies as a hetaera name.[151] But Glycera is also a common female name, attested seventy times throughout antiquity, not counting the women mentioned in the literary record, and is the most recorded female name in the fourth century, occurring frequently in Attica. Women named Glycera dedicated in sanctuaries, commemorated after death within family groups, are mothers, wives, and daughters, and their social status that of citizens and metics.[152] Malthace ("Soft"), another name associated with hetaeras, is also a particularly Athenian name predominantly found in fourth- or early third-century Attic inscriptions. These women are recorded making dedications at Brauron and the Asklepieion at Athens, and at least one was a member of the Athenian elite.[153] The same goes for the name Aphrodisia, which is actually among the top fifteen most attested female names in the corpus of Greek onomastics, nor does it appear anywhere in Greek literature in connection with a hetaera, although it is inscribed on a sympotic cup.[154]

Beyond Attic inscriptions, another source to look for the names of "real" women who worked as hetaeras less likely to be highly fictionalized is in Attic oratory, where, presumably, such names would have alluded to historical women resident in Athens, whether citizens or metics, familiar to the jurors during the time of the trial, whatever their social status. Indeed, comic plays seem to have borrowed some of the more notorious figures from this genre, such as Phryne, whose impiety trial was remembered several decades later in Posidippus' *Ephesia*. Although Schaps does not analyze the types of names associated with the named women of oratory, he observes that most of them are associated with alien and low status, and are usually connected in some way to prostitution, including the other six girls raised by Nicarete, Anteia, Stratola, Aristocleia, Metaneira, Phila, and Isthmias; Antigona, "the cleverest hetaera of her age" and a *pornoboskousa* or procurer; Aristagora, who may have been charged with masquerading as a citizen although an alien, just like Neaera; and Phryne.[155] Although not hetaeras, two other alien women, Ninos and Theoris, who were tried and executed for impiety, are also alluded to by name.[156] To this list should be added Alce, the woman described as a former brothel slave, procuress, and quasi-wife of Euctemon, and Phile, a woman accused of being the daughter of a hetaera and therefore without claim to the estate of her father, Pyrrhus.[157] More will be said about the involvement of women in the Athenian courts in Chapter 5.

If we compare the names of the women in *Against Neaera* to the inscriptional record, we find the following names are unattested outside of literary sources: Neaera,[158] Anteia,[159] Strattola,[160] Metaneira,[161] Phila,[162] and Isthmias. Their absence does not conclusively show that these women did not actually exist. For instance, Metaneira is mentioned in three separate forensic speeches.[163] At least two comic plays, one by Antiphanes (c. 408–334) and the other by either Eunicus (third cent. BCE) or Philyllius (fifth/fourth cent. BCE), take their titles from the name Anteia.[164] Given the symbiotic relationship between comedy and oratory in the fourth century and their reliance on historical individuals, it does not seem a stretch to assume that these names would have been familiar to Athenian spectators and jurors during this period as actual people. The other three names mentioned in the speech are all attested, at least once, in fourth-century Attic inscriptions: Strybele,[165] Phano,[166] and Aristocleia, a common Greek female name that occurs eight times in Athenian inscriptions from the classical period, and multiple times in Attica and elsewhere in Greece.[167] Turning to the other speeches, Antigona seems to have been a common name, but all fifty-seven instances are non-Athenian except for one.[168] Aristagora is a predominantly Athenian name, occurring with frequency in fourth-century inscriptions. Ninos is unattested outside of oratory, and Theoris appears in one, possibly two, fourth- and third-century inscriptions.[169] Alce, with the accent on the ultima, is unattested at Athens, while Phile is frequently attested as the name of citizen women in third- and fourth-century Attic inscriptions.

By the time of Athenaeus, multiple authors, genres, and time periods had simultaneously preserved and obscured the names of hetaeras in the extant literary record; even historical figures had become embellished by anecdote and comic fiction, only to reemerge in authors like Lucian and Alciphron as fully realized literary tropes evocative of classical Athens and its cultural milieu. As Taylor explains, this process indicates "a development of a literary tradition surrounding *hetaeras* that is independent of the lives of women themselves."[170] Historical courtesans thus became occluded and erased by the tendency to assign to them nicknames and epithets and the frequent use of the same name for different women. Where does all this leave us? A few tentative conclusions: first, the public naming of a living woman in Attic oratory often denoted, or deliberately evoked, marginal and alien social status, often in association with prostitution. Second, whether hetaeras actually adopted more than one name or not, it was clearly an onomastic practice perceived to be linked to them. But it is also a convention associated with celebrated female figures more generally, such as Olympias, the mother of Alexander the Great, who bore multiple names, apparently without censure.[171] Many of the names of women listed as hetaeras in the *Lexicon for Greek Personal Names* are also found in Attic inscriptions from the classical period, accompanied by the names of male relatives such as a father or husband, indicating that they were free citizen women. Other names occur more frequently outside of Attica, which suggests that they were foreign names and the hetaeras who bore them resident. The names of famous hetaeras that regularly populate literary discourses, such as Rhodopis, Neaera, and Corone, seldom appear, if at all, in Athenian inscriptions from the fifth and fourth centuries. The fact that the names of these women are absent from Attic inscriptional records should not be taken as conclusive evidence that such women never actually existed, but rather that famous hetaeras carefully crafted their professional identities by adopting a secondary name, often unusual and foreign-sounding in order to set them apart from citizen women.

Such is the case with the subject of this book. The name Phryne appears only five times apart from Athenaeus in the *Lexicon of Greek Personal Names*. The first possible reference to Phryne as a proper name occurs in line 1101 of Aristophanes' comic play *Ecclesiazusae* (392 BCE), a genre that often alludes to contemporary figures and events. During

Precarious Lives, Unstable Identities   59

the scene in which three old women attempt, like prostitutes, to attract the attention of a young man, one is described as a "Phryne with white paint on her face."[172] Although the meaning of this line is much disputed, it suggests that Phryne, whether a proper name or noun, already had a specific association with hetaeras in the early fourth century, well before Phryne of Thespiae would have moved to Athens and taken up her profession. Inscriptional evidence places a "Phryne" at Athens in the early fifth century; other epigraphical instances of the name are from fourth-century Samos; Hellenistic Sinope; and Abella, an ancient city in Campania close to Nola, in connection with a freed woman, date indeterminate.[173] All other references to Phryne's name come from the first and second centuries CE. As we have seen, Plutarch believes that Phryne was a nickname and Mnesarete her real name. Mnesarete is attested as an Attic name for citizen women,[174] and a variant, Mnasareta, occurs in inscriptions mostly from fifth-century Thespiae, with scattered fourth- and third-century references at Messene, Phoinice, Larissa, Orchomenos, and Coroneia.[175] Athenaeus gives two versions of Phryne's name, one that agrees with Plutarch, for which he cites Aristogeiton's fourth-century speech, *In Defense of Phryne*, and an alternate account derived from Apollodorus' Hellenistic treatise, *On Hetaeras*. The latter states that Phryne was the name of two different prostitutes with the nicknames Klausigelos ("Laughing through Tears") and Saperdion ("Little Fish").[176] Athenaeus then identifies another Phryne found in Herodicus' Hellenistic prosopography and distinguished by the nickname Sestus ("Swindler/Sifter"), "because she sifted and stripped all who slept with her."[177] The identities of these women are unclear. Either there were four separate women named Phryne important enough to elicit comment in the Greek discourse on hetaeras, which may reflect the generic association of the name with hetaeras, or a composite figure evolved, incorporating the earlier nicknames and epithets.[178]

Wayward Lives

The vigorous debates about what constitutes a hetaera based on linguistic terms, iconographic attributes, or onomastic practices reflect the precarious lives of the women like Phryne who, while symbolically central, operated outside of the constraints, and protections, that governed citizen women in classical Athens. Whereas a freeborn daughter of a citizen father would have had close kinship ties that could be relied upon to safeguard her identity and to protect her body, as well as life stage rituals to which others bore witness, such as marriage and childbirth, and participation in public civic cults with other women, non-citizen or metic daughters had few external markers of social legitimation. Their freedom from social limitations could work to their advantage, potentially allowing them not only to escape the brothel and become prosperous businesswomen, but also to pass themselves off as legitimate wives, appropriating some of those prerogatives for themselves, as we saw previously in the case of Alce in Isaeus 6. Euctemon freed her and then put her in charge of one of his rental properties where he opted to take most of his meals, instead of at home with his wife and family, and eventually lived with her there fulltime. This arrangement encroached upon the category of legitimate citizen wife, emboldening Alce to request that Euctemon introduce her son in his phratry and to participate in the rituals of the Thesmophoria.[179] Neaera requires from Phrynion not only help in attaining her freedom, but also "love, obedience to her desires, and respect for her *persona*."[180] Even a *porne* could exert some influence over her relationships as indicated by a rare instance of quoted female speech in Attic oratory in which the unnamed woman at the heart of the ownership dispute between two men in Lysias 4 states that she wishes to be loved by both men.[181]

Although these women, whether *porne*, *pallake*, or free hetaera, could eventually become economically independent and even wield a certain amount of power over their male lovers and expect their protection in return for their companionship, their position was nonetheless tenuous and always contingent upon their male partners. As we have seen, the lives and social standing of Alce, Neaera, Chrysis, and other female prostitutes could change in an instant according to the needs and desires of their owners and lovers. When Neaera had lost her bloom, Nicarete sold her to two men who held her in common as their joint property and then abruptly jettisoned her once they reached the proper age for marriage. Although they offered Neaera the chance to buy her freedom at a reduced rate, she could have just as easily been returned to the brothel, if it had not been for the intervention of Phrynion, which turned out to be a mixed blessing.[182] At his hands, Neaera endured physical abuse, including compulsory carousing, humiliating public sex, and, ultimately, gang rape.[183] Sexual violence against hetaeras seems not to have been uncommon, albeit socially unacceptable and legally

Precarious Lives, Unstable Identities   61

actionable, according to a fragmentary speech of Lysias that accuses the Athenian citizen Philonides of raping Nais, an alleged hetaera, whose *kyrios* or guard was a man named Archias, possibly a *pornoboskos*, a case discussed in more detail in Chapter 5.[184]

Even a beloved hetaera living in a long-term relationship with a citizen man as his *pallake* could not count on her future social and economic stability. In Menander's *Samia*, Demeas, suspecting infidelity and disobedience, casts Chrysis out onto the street, where he imagines her bleak prospects as a hired prostitute:

> You think you're such a big deal! In town you'll see exactly
> what you are. The others of your type dash to their parties,
> where they charge a mere ten drachmas, and knock back
> strong wine until they die—or else they starve, if what they
> do's not quick and willing.[185]

The possibility of such a rapid status reversal, from protected, cherished *pallake* to indigent hetaera forced to charge by the sex act, underscores not only the economic precarity that women who trafficked in sex faced, even at the highest level, but also the multiple changes of social status they underwent during the course of their careers. A hetaera's independence was thus highly contingent, as the career of Neaera illustrates. Neaera was allegedly the property of four different individuals: the brothel-keeper, Nicarete; the two bachelors from Corinth who originally purchased her; and the Athenian citizen, Phrynion. Even when finally declared "mistress of herself," she remains under Stephanus' roof, where he serves as her *kyrios*, part putative husband, part *pornoboskos*, in what seems to have functioned as both a brothel and extortion factory. As Susan Lape so eloquently observes in her recent discussion of mobility and prostitutes, then as now, "unspoken legacies of displacement, economic migrancy, and the social and political systems . . . kept sexual laborers disadvantaged and marginalized . . . entangl[ing them] in webs of precarity."[186]

Conclusion

By examining three scholarly debates about terminology, iconography, and onomastic practices, this chapter demonstrates the difficulty of establishing reliable criteria for identifying hetaeras and distinguishing them from other types of prostitutes and even from citizen wives in fourth-century Athens. As applied to Phryne, it suggests not only that her elusiveness as a historical figure arises from her marginal and unstable social status, but also that the ways that such women entered into discursive history reflect male bias. The prosecution speech against Neaera demonstrates how the same woman could be interchangeably called a *porne*, a *hetaera*, and a *pallake*, depending on the rhetorical aims of the speaker. She could also successfully masquerade as a citizen wife and the mother of legitimate Athenian offspring, for decades, it seems, without attracting too much scrutiny, at least not until she was caught in the cross-hairs of an ongoing legal dispute between two men. This forensic speech and others like it underscore the ambiguous and unstable identities of women in classical Athens, particularly of aliens who lived outside of prevailing social and legal structures and the threats they posed to the social order. We will see a variation of this narrative in the accounts of Phryne's prosecution for impiety in Chapter 5.

Turning to representations of women on Attic vases, we find a similar lack of clear signifiers that differentiate the hetaera from other types of prostitutes, and again, from citizen wives and daughters. However, the female figures represented as engaging in explicit sex or sympotic activities, like the *auletris*, on sympotic cups are more likely to be prostitutes, although it is impossible to determine whether the male viewer would have labeled them hetaeras. At the same time, the display of the naked female body in Attic vase painting, while not always eroticized, foreshadows the development of "respectable" female nudity in art and the stories that begin to coalesce around Phryne and Praxiteles, discussed more fully in Chapter 4. And despite the many names associated with hetaeras that have come down to us, most cannot be verified as the names of actual historical women because of the widespread practices of aliases in addition to given names, homonyms, and the fact that so many are unattested in the inscriptional records of fourth-century Athens. Their absence suggests that most hetaeras from this period were metics, working under assumed names, as in the case of Phryne. This chapter has outlined the major obstacles to recovering the lives of prostitutes in classical Athens, even those of independent hetaeras, and the scholarly debates they have engendered. In addition to the social and political forces that conspired to erase these women,

evidentiary challenges involving terminology, iconography, and onomastic practices have further erased them. Although many of these
issues are insurmountable, the next takes chapter a closer look at the
fourth-century evidence for historical hetaeras in order to establish the
possibilities for fabulating a biography for Phryne.

64   Phryne of Thespiae

3

Sex and the Ancient City

Solon purchased women and placed them in brothels to meet
the needs of young men . . . and he was the first to found
a temple of Aphrodite Pandemos from the earnings of the
women in charge of the brothels.[1]

Whereas the previous chapter illustrated the challenges of identifying
hetaeras and other types of sexual laborers in the literary and historical
remains of ancient Greece, this chapter turns to the historical context in
which such women lived and worked, examining the traces of historical hetaeras in contemporary fifth- and fourth-century sources, such
as comedy and oratory, material evidence such as inscriptions and archaeological assemblages and structures, and the historical writings of
Herodotus, Thucydides, and Xenophon. The likelihood that a hetaera
actually existed increases with the number of cross-references to her
presence in a variety of sources, particularly in material evidence such as
inscriptions, as persons familiar to male jurors and spectators in oratory
and comedy, as interlocutors in Socratic dialogues, and their association
with specific events and individuals.[2] I argue that by drawing parallels
between what we know of Phryne and these contemporary sources, it
is possible to imagine her as a historical figure, not just a literary invention. I begin with a look at the mythic origins of prostitution and
its link to Athens' emergent democracy and the worship of Aphrodite.
I then consider the spaces in which hetaeras and other sexual laborers
moved and intersected with their clients, including brothels and private
residences, and their spatial mobility as migrants and metics. The economic aspects of commercial sex are then explored, including pricing,
taxation, and the potential for social mobility, independence, and wealth

Phryne of Thespiae. Laura McClure, Oxford University Press. © Oxford University Press 2024.
DOI: 10.1093/9780197580882.003.0004

as predominantly women-owned businesses. The chapter concludes with a discussion of a few historical hetaeras from the fifth and fourth centuries as a way of framing and imagining Phryne's biography.

Sex and Athenian Democracy

Prostitution in classical Athens was lawful, pervasive, and bound up with the polis from the archaic period onward. Comic writers portray brothel sex as a democratic and socially acceptable alternative to other forms of nonmarital sex. As quoted previously, the middle comic poet Philemon (368–264) and the Hellenistic author Nicander (fl. second cent.) credit the Athenian lawgiver Solon (c. 640–560) with the invention of state-subsidized brothels for the benefit of young men:

> You invented something everyone appreciates, Solon! For
> they say you were the first person to see this, something
> both democratic and conducive to health, by Zeus,—and it's
> fitting for me to say this, Solon—seeing the city crowded with
> youths who impelled by nature strayed where they should not
> have gone, you purchased women and set them up in spaces
> equipped and ready for all. The women stand there naked,
> so you can't be deceived. Look at everything! Maybe you're
> feeling out of sorts . . . The door's open! (It costs) one obol!
> Hop on in! There's no acting shocked, no chit-chat; she doesn't
> pull away. Instead, you immediately get the girl you want,
> however you want her. You leave—tell her to go to hell! She's
> somebody else's problem.[3]

Although this flagrant depiction of sex trafficking would offend most modern readers, for Philemon it is comic fodder, as he conflates Solon's democratic agenda, namely his reforms aimed at increasing the political and economic rights of non-elites, with the democratization of sex, embodied by the availability and affordability of female prostitutes for all Athenian men. In this cultural myth, the establishment of brothels coincides with, or rather facilitates, the foundation of the cult of Aphrodite Pandemos, the goddess "of the whole people." Although of dubious historicity, Solon may have established the site as part of his efforts to circumscribe the power of the aristocracy in public religion by establishing cults in which the *demos* ("the people") could participate.[4]

Prostitution nonetheless had very real democratic and political implications in fourth-century Athens, with both male and female prostitutes subject to the loss of rights essential to their civic status. Citizen men who sold their bodies were excluded from governance of the polis, while female prostitutes and their offspring could not marry citizen men or engage in civic ritual, and both were subject to public shaming in the law courts.[5] In Aristophanes' *Ecclesiazusae*, radical legislation engineered by the city's women similarly analogizes economic and sexual rights by dictating that all property belongs to the polis and sexual priority must be given to the least desirable women, that is, the elderly and the ugly. Solon's association with democratic sexual reforms may in fact derive from his modification of Draco's statute that justified homicide in cases of adultery, stipulating that such charges could not be brought against a man caught having sex with women "of the sort who sit in a brothel or work in the streets openly."[6] In reality, although Solon's laws related to the family and sexual mores were important to the legal definition and regulation of prostitution, they did not introduce commercial sex to Athens.[7] Rather, the transition from war captives, like those depicted in Homeric epic, to freelance hetaeras in the classical polis must have been a much more gradual process.

Under the Sign of Aphrodite

At first glance, Aphrodite might seem an unlikely candidate for Athenian worship, given her non-Greek origins; identification with desire, sexuality, and procreation; and the intrinsically personal nature of her worship, powerfully expressed in the poetry of Sappho.[8] Indeed, the goddess does not figure prominently in Athenian foundation myths, nor were her festivals on the same scale as other civic events like the Panathenaea.[9] In the earliest account of her birth, Aphrodite arises from the foam that coalesces around the severed genitals of the primordial sky god, Ouranos, and has as her portion "the whisperings and smiles and deceptions of maidens and sweet love and love-making."[10] In popular myth, she leads Helen to Paris, supplies Hera with a magical garment for seducing Zeus, cheats on her husband Hephaestus in their marital bed, abets Sappho's erotic pursuits, and punishes an acolyte of

Artemis for rejecting her.[11] Notably she is not associated either with polis formation or with prostitution in any of these accounts. Yet according to ancient authors, the cult of Aphrodite in her capacity as Pandemos had an important role to play in Athens as a symbol of political unity. According to Athenian mythology, the hero Theseus founded the cult to commemorate the synoecism of Attica.[12] However, the goddess was mostly likely consecrated in the archaic period "in a spirit that was in a broad sense political," but there is no concrete evidence for associating either Aphrodite Pandemos or any such cult with Solon himself or any other specific figure or century.[13] The cult of Peitho, an epithet that could refer both to rhetorical persuasion and erotic attraction, also had a place in the precinct of Aphrodite, further reinforcing her democratic associations.[14] Fourth-century texts articulate two separate cults of Aphrodite: that of Pandemos and that of Ourania, the first associated with the "common" love of men for women, and the second with the "higher" form of love between men.[15] Aphrodite Ourania may have received a public cult near the Athenian acropolis by around 500 BCE, where an offering box designed to accommodate premarital offerings of one drachma attests to her manifestation as a goddess of conjugal sex, but her forms of worship at Athens are otherwise unknown.[16]

Although Nicander identifies Aphrodite Pandemos as the patron deity of female prostitutes, there is no evidence for this relationship outside of the text. Literary sources from the fifth century do, however, establish a connection between such women and Aphrodite more generally. A famous passage from Herodotus frequently cited in support of the argument for the practice of ritual prostitution in antiquity stresses the association of prostitution with Aphrodite, identified by her Assyrian name, Mylitta:

> The foulest Babylonian custom is that which compels every
> woman of the land to sit in the temple of Aphrodite and have
> intercourse with some stranger once in her life . . . Once a
> woman has taken her place there, she does not go away to her
> home before some stranger has cast money into her lap and
> had intercourse with her outside the temple; but while he casts
> the money, he must say, "I invite you in the name of Mylitta."
> It does not matter what sum the money is; the woman will
> never refuse, for that would be a sin, the money being by this

act made sacred. So she follows the first man who casts it and rejects no one.[17]

Although Stephanie Budin has convincingly debunked the myth of sacred prostitution in the ancient Mediterranean world, this passage nonetheless stresses how intertwined were conceptions of venal sex, barbarian customs, and the worship of Aphrodite in the Athenian imaginary by the middle of the fifth century BCE.[18] A fragment of Pindar quoted by Athenaeus further corroborates this idea. He alleges that at Corinth—Neara's birth place famous for commercial sex and its large temple of Aphrodite—individuals promised to dedicate hetaeras to Aphrodite in exchange for success in their endeavors, citing a skolion, or song composed for the symposium, that celebrates the victory of a certain Xenophon in the Olympian games. Invoking the hetaeras as "hospitable girls, handmaids of Persuasion," the ode describes them as burning incense and offering prayers to heavenly Aphrodite, who has "permitted to pluck/ without blame in delightful acts of love/ the fruit of soft youth."[19] As Budin observes, the fragment does not directly refer to the women as hetaeras or other type of prostitute, nor does it mention any form of temple prostitution practiced at Corinth.[20]

The Ludovisi Throne (c. 460), most likely an altar front from a shrine of Aphrodite in South Italy, provides material evidence of Aphrodite's connection with prostitution from outside of Athens during the fifth century. The central relief (Figure 3.1) depicts the goddess rising from the sea wearing a transparent pleated garment, her hair loose along her neck and shoulders, and flanked by two female attendants, possibly the Horae, who hold out opaque drapery before her lower half. The left panel (Figure 3.2) shows a young, nude girl seated on a pillow with one knee crossed over the other, wearing a *sakkos*, a type of hairnet, and playing the aulos; based on vase parallels, she is probably meant to represent an *auletris*, a female musician and prostitute sometimes interchangeable with the hetaera, as we saw in the last chapter. On the other relief (Figure 3.3), a fully clothed, veiled woman, variously interpreted as a priestess or citizen wife, offers incense from an incense burner in her left hand.[21] While these sources confirm the importance of Aphrodite worship to prostitutes and citizen wives alike, they make no reference to civic engagement with prostitution at Athens and the cult of Aphrodite Pandemos. Rather, our primary and earliest Athenian account of prostitution, that of Herodotus, explicitly represents prostitution as an alien

Sex and the Ancient City   69

FIGURE 3.1 Aphrodite, Ludovisi Throne, Parian marble, c. 460 BCE. Rome, Terme National Museum 3, inv. no. 100.

cultural practice associated with the ancient Near East, as we saw in the Babylonian passage, as well as ancient Persia, where the Lydians trafficked their daughters to finance their dowries, and, finally, Egypt, where the hetaera Rhodopis made her wealth, discussed more fully at the end of this chapter.[22]

Hetaeras and other prostitutes were obviously identified with Aphrodite as exemplars of physical beauty and sexual allure. Indeed, Phryne's receptions depict her as the mortal embodiment of the goddess in narratives about art, particularly the creation of the *Cnidian Aphrodite*, and in accounts of her disrobing at her impiety trial, both of which will be explored in the next two chapters. The affinity of the deity with prostitution may have also arisen from the actual women themselves, who, as female economic migrants, may have brought their own religion with them to Athens in the late sixth and early fifth centuries. For example, a silver pendant with an image of Astarte, the ancient Near Eastern equivalent of Aphrodite, found in Building Z_3 in the Athenian Kerameikos, a structure widely identified as a brothel and dealt with more fully in what follows, suggests that the women who inhabited the space were foreign and worshipped their native deities in Athens.[23] Although the worship of foreign gods was not technically illegal in Athens, it was often

FIGURE 3.2 *Auletris*, Ludovisi Throne, Parian marble, c. 460 BCE. Rome, Terme National Museum 3, inv. no. 100.

viewed with suspicion and even fear, with the result that preconceptions about the alien nature of these practices may have motivated the various prosecutions of hetaeras, including that of Phryne, a topic to which we will return in Chapter 5.

FIGURE 3.3 Priestess or female worshipper, Ludovisi Throne, Parian marble, c. 460 BCE. Rome, Terme National Museum 3, inv. no. 100.

The Topography of Sex

Turning from the mythic origins of prostitution and its connection to Aphrodite, this section considers the spaces that hetaeras and other sexual laborers inhabited in the Athenian polis and how they distinguished them from citizen wives. Whereas the latter occupied the domestic space of the household, symbolized by the fixity, permanence, and purity of the hearth and where they underwent rituals of incorporation as brides and outsiders, rarely leaving home other than to participate in religious activities, women who sold their bodies moved freely about Athens, between households, and even between cities as female economic migrants.[24] Neaera not only left Nicarete's brothel to cohabit with her two lovers in a private residence in Corinth, she also accompanied Phrynion to Athens, ultimately leaving him for Megara until she finally resettled in Athens with Stephanus as his putative wife. Indeed, her prosecutor claims that she worked all over the Peloponnese, in Thessaly and Magnesia, in Chios, and through most of Ionian, rhetorically linking her extreme spatial mobility to her sexual promiscuity.[25] Although an exaggerated claim, it nonetheless points to the reality that many immigrant women may have come to Athens seeking to support themselves in the sex trade, a trope also employed by Greek new and Roman comedies.[26] Other examples include Rhodopis, who was born in Thrace and then brought from Samos to Egypt to work as a hetaera; Sinope, who moved from Thrace to become a hetaera on Aegina, but ultimately moved her practice to Athens; and Pythionice, who worked as a hetaera in both Corinth and Athens.[27] Hetaeras and concubines customarily followed armies and accompanied generals on campaigns throughout Greece and to foreign lands.[28] Phryne's narrative follows a similar trajectory: born in Thespiae, she purportedly migrated to Athens where she moved freely about the city, accompanying her clients to dinners, drinking parties, and religious festivals, extending her symbolic reach as far as Thespiae and Delphi where tourists could view her remarkable portrait statues.

The Athenian spaces occupied by prostitutes varied according to their social and economic status. Enslaved prostitutes solicited customers from brothels on the city's streets under compulsion, although some may have been able to rent out a room where they received their clients for a higher fee. Wealthy hetaeras entertained men in their own sumptuous homes or joined them at dinner parties and symposia hosted by their patrons. The majority, however, probably worked out of brothel, a public venue that could assume a variety of forms but does not seem to have been a purpose-built structure like the Lupanar at Pompeii.[29] Indeed, a diversity of settings accommodated the wide range of activities associated with prostitutes and the varied forms prostitution could take, with the result that brothels were not segregated but rather intermingled with business and residential buildings throughout the city, although they were especially prevalent in the Kerameikos and

Sex and the Ancient City   73

the Piraeus.[30] According to Xenophon, the streets of Athens were full of prostitutes and sex stalls known as *oikemata*.[31] For the orator Aeschines (390–c. 322), the activity defined the space rather than the other way around:[32]

> For it is not the lodgings and the houses which give their names to the men who have lived in them, but it is the tenants who give to the places the names of their own pursuits. Where, for example, several men hire one house and occupy it, dividing it between them, we call it an "apartment house," but where one man only dwells, a "house." And if perchance a physician moves into one of these shops on the street, it is called a "surgery." But if he moves out and a smith moves into this same shop, it is called a "smithy"; if a fuller, a "laundry"; if a carpenter, a "carpenter's shop"; and if a pimp and his sex workers from the trade itself it gets its name of "brothel."

Here a *porneion* or brothel is defined by the presence of a *pornoboskos* ("pimp") and the enslaved prostitutes he controls. The more general term *oikema*, a room or holding pen, could also designate a brothel, particularly when used in the formulaic phrase "to sit in an *oikema*," while *egasterion*, workplace, was the legal term for brothel.[33] Brothels were frequently incorporated into establishments that offered food, wine, or shelter, like inns and taverns, or even bakeries, but they "could appear anywhere and even be a temporary setup."[34] Women could also work out of a *sunoikia* or private apartment complex, such as that owned by Euctemon in the Kerameikos and managed by the retired sex worker, Alce, where inexperienced young slave prostitutes serviced their customers in individual stalls.[35]

The archaeological remains of Building Z_3 in the Kerameikos, which consists of several small rooms large enough to accommodate only one or two couches organized around a central courtyard, may have served as a brothel at least at one point in its history.[36] Both the location of the building and the assemblages found inside point to this interpretation. The site is located within the city walls in the Kerameikos close to the Sacred Gate, a district that had numerous brothels of various grades and yet was not considered an especially disreputable area of the city. In addition to copious fineware for the serving and consumption of food and drink, many of the finds indicate that that the occupants were women

74   Phryne of Thespiae

of foreign birth, including small ceramic vessels such as *pyxides* and *lekythoi* used for cosmetics and perfume, a bronze mirror, and a miniature bronze chest for jewelry.[37] Votive deposits, such as iconic images of Cybele/Astarte in the form of a silver pendant or marble statuette, and Aphrodite/Selene, point to the foreign origins of the residents and their worship of a non-Greek incarnation of Aphrodite.[38] The presence of oil lamps and coinage in small denominations is further indicative of sex trafficking. Spindle whorls and other implements used for textile production and the concern for water supply needed for preparing wool and perhaps flax suggests that the space could serve a variety of functions, "from residential to commercial, accompanied by eating, drinking, weaving, and whoring."[39]

In most cases, however, the spaces of Athenian commercial sex are difficult to differentiate from domestic structures in the archaeological record, since identifying features such as courtyards, wells, sympotic ware, and loom weights are found in both types of buildings.[40] Further, prostitutes often inhabited the same space in which they worked. To return to previous examples, Alce lived in the same building as the brothel slaves she sold, while Neaera cohabitated with Stephanus in his private residence where they jointly ran her sex business.[41] Very wealthy hetaeras could entertain men at their private residences, allowing exclusive access to select "friends."[42] Theodote, for instance, owned a well-appointed house financed by the gifts of her wealthy admirers.[43] The hetaera Gnathaena occupied a well-known residence together with her daughter, Gnathaenion ("Little Gnathaena"), also a hetaera, where she dined and drank with her lovers and became famous for her witticisms.[44] These were not brothels, exactly, but rather private spaces in which one woman, or a mother-daughter pair, could command a high fee for her services while retaining an air of respectability and, more importantly, financial control.

Drinking with Men, "As a Hetaera Would"

Hetaeras were synonymous with sympotic celebrations. Since most did not possess enough wealth to entertain out of their own homes, they traversed private male domains as dinner guests, symposiasts, performers, komos-revelers, and sexual companions. The word *symposium* simply means "drinking together" and applies to a specific form of communal drinking that the ancient Greeks practiced from the eighth century BCE onward. In its archaic and classical form, it consisted of a small group of men who gathered in the house of a friend for an evening of drinking.[45] Sometimes a meal or *deipnon* preceded it, but the main event was the drinking of copious amounts of wine, usually diluted by half with water, in an elaborately ritualized procedure.[46] This all-male event took place in a purpose-built room called the *andron* ("men's room"), a space, as indicated by the name, associated with men, but perhaps not exclusively used by them.[47] Extant architectural and decorative features that signify an *andron* include mosaic floors, off-center doorways to accommodate the couches upon which the symposiasts reclined, easy access to the street, but separated from the more private areas of the house.[48] During the party, participants reclined on couches, leaning on their left elbows, as they drank, sang lyric poetry, played music, and conversed about various topics.[49] This form of commensality forged ties between men and reinforced their social identity as equals, becoming increasingly democratized by the classical period.[50] The andron was thus not simply a private space but rather "a civic space that admitted civic life, including civic sexuality, across the threshold of the oikos."[51]

Whether a dinner or full-blown symposium, these parties regularly featured female symposiasts in the form of hetaeras, female entertainers, and *pornae*, but never wives.[52] As Isaeus unequivocally asserts, the latter did not "accompany their husbands to dinners or think of feasting in the company of strangers, especially unexpected guests," although they may have helped with preparations before retiring to the women's quarters.[53] In contrast, Phrynion's outrageous treatment of Neaera included a demand that she join him in his excessive partying: he brought the hetaera along with him to dinners "all over the place," where he drank and joined in komastic festivities with her.[54] Hetaeras and female performers were thus stock components of any drinking party, as crucial to its success as comfortable furniture, garlands, and delicious food, as this passage from Aristophanes suggests, "Everything else stands ready: couches, tables, cushions, mattresses, garlands, perfume, tasty tidbits; *pornae* are there, cakes, pastries, sesame crackers, rolls and dancing girls . . . pretty ones!"[55]

But in contrast to their patrons, hetaeras and other sexual laborers were only temporary occupants of these spaces, injecting noise, drunken revelry, and disruption into otherwise quiet city streets:

76   Phryne of Thespiae

That the woman, whom the defendant has deposed that he gave in legal marriage to our uncle, was a hetaera who gave herself to anyone and not his wife, has been testified to you by the other acquaintances and by the neighbors of Pyrrhus, who have given evidence of quarrels, serenades, and frequent scenes of disorder which the defendant's sister occasioned whenever she was at Pyrrhus's house.[56]

Spatial transience thus distinguished the hetaera from the other residents of the oikos, since the woman in question did not in fact live continuously at Pyrrhus' house, but rather visited him on a recurring basis.[57] Neaera, we might recall, lodged at the home of Ctesippus when she attended the Panathenaea as a young girl, and subsequently lived in various houses owned by men in Corinth, Athens, and Megara.[58]

Whereas vase representations frequently depict nude or partially clothed women engaged in graphic sexual activity with the male symposiasts, our two most detailed literary accounts of the symposium make no mention at all of sex with the female participants.[59] Xenophon's *Symposium*, for instance, describes feasting, laughter, drinking, and singing before the evening's entertainment is introduced, but not sex, "He had with him a fine piper girl, a dancing girl—one of those skilled in acrobatic tricks,—and a very handsome boy, who was very good at playing the kithara and at dancing . . . They now played for the company, the piper girl on the pipes, the boy on the kithara."[60] In a reversal of sympotic protocol, Socrates dismisses the flute girl at the beginning of Plato's *Symposium* with the words, "Let her play to herself, or if she wishes, to the women within."[61] The departure of the flute-girl signifies a shift to serious and sober conversation, while the presence of another, who accompanies the drunken Alcibiades and his companions in a *komos* at the end, marks the restoration of normal sympotic festivity.[62]

Phryne would have been a regular presence on the fourth-century Athenian sympotic circuit where she honed her biting wit during rounds of drinking, according to Athenaeus and his sources, Lynceus and Machon.[63] Although the point of many of these jokes is obscure, several revolve around verbal puns that assert her discursive dominance over her interlocutors. For instance, when a client balked at paying at the high price of her sexual services, one mina, or one hundred drachmas, complaining that she had charged a previous lover only two gold coins, or forty drachmas, Phryne contemptuously replied, "Well you can hang around until I'm horny again—and then I'll take the two gold coins!"[64] At dinner with a foul-smelling man, she picked up a piece of pig hide and said: "Take this and eat it!," or "Take this, too, old goat!," a type of joke that seems to have made the rounds, since a similar insult is attributed to the hetaera Thaïs.[65] When another customer sent her a small amount of good wine and told her that it was ten years old, she jested, "It's small, for being that old!"[66] Asked why wreathes are hung up at the symposium, she remarked, "Because they evoke the souls of the dead."[67] In response to a male slave, called a *mastigias* (literally, "someone who deserves to be beaten"), who boasted that he had slept with a number of women, she scoffed, "I am angry at you for having so many!," a pun that plays on the number of his lashings and his amorous conquests.[68] A very late text attributes to her the following quip: "The hetaera Phryne said of a young man who had lost his field and was pale on account of sickness, 'Boy, why are you pale? You've not eaten your land?'"[69] As this banter indicates, Phryne and many other hetaeras were active participants at dinner parties and *symposia*, known not only for eating and drinking in the presence of unrelated men, but also for their verbal dexterity, coarse sexual humor, and savage mockery of their male clients. Not only did hetaeras occupy the civic spaces that excluded citizen women, it seems they could speak openly and even insultingly to men in open defiance of the code of silence that governed citizen women.

The Business of Sex

Although much of the work on Athenian prostitution in recent decades has stressed that hetaeras operated mainly within a gift economy, Phryne's joke about her sliding scale reminds us that this work was very much a business in classical Athens. It is thus important to situate prostitution within the larger economic framework of the polis, as Edward Cohen has brilliantly done in his book, *Athenian Prostitution: The Business of Sex*. Cohen argues, perhaps a bit too optimistically, that Athenian prostitution was not differentiated "either structurally or linguistically" from other types of labor as a business and skill and that within this system female entrepreneurs could operate independently, more or less on the same level as male tradesmen and retailers.[70] By the fourth century BCE, when references to hetaeras begin to proliferate in the literary sources, Athens was the dominant

78   Phryne of Thespiae

commercial center of the eastern Mediterranean, and its economy relied on various trades and entrepreneurial enterprises, many of them owned and operated by metics. Nonetheless, traditional aristocratic values denigrate paid labor while exalting agriculture as the proper economic endeavor for the free citizen man.[71] Free individuals nonetheless could respectably engage in "liberal professions" such as making shoes, selling fish, or even sitting in a brothel, if undertaken on one's own behalf rather than under compulsion.[72] Indeed, free Athenians avoided at all costs working in a slavish way for another person, since, according to Aristotle, "The nature of the free man prevents his living under the control of another."[73] The pervasive use of slaves in Athenian society made the presence or absence of supervision and control a key factor in attitudes toward paid labor.[74] If the level of control was more important than the type of labor performed, then it follows that the prostitution of hetaeras did not substantively differ from other types of labor as a business and skill in the minds of the Athenians.[75]

There has been much speculation about the wages of commercial sex, with reliable figures elusive.[76] The evidence, mostly from comic sources, indicates that charges could vary considerably for both male and female prostitutes, reflecting not only government edict but also the parties' situation, needs, desires, and capacity.[77] The lowest price mentioned for a single act by a female prostitute is one obol, or one-sixth of a drachma, for a woman, presumably a slave, working in a brothel, as indicated by the fragment of Philemon discussed previously. William Loomis argues that most of the references to the cost of prostitution are exaggerated, either upward or downward, for comic effect.[78] He estimates that the going rate for an average prostitute fell somewhere between three and five obols, or one-half to almost one drachma. For comparison, the stone workers constructing the Erechtheion in 409–407 BCE earned one drachma per day, while soldiers and sailors the same period were paid three obols, meaning that the cost for a single sexual encounter was approximately equivalent to one day's labor.[79] At the other end of the spectrum, a high-cost and more socially acceptable hetaera could command between 100 drachmas or 1 mina, like Phryne, or as much as 10,000 drachmas or 100 minas, like Lais.[80] Menander's *Samia* speaks of hetaeras attending dinner parties for a mere ten drachmas, while elsewhere a *pornoboskos* charges a "foreign client" the exorbitant amount of three minas or three hundred drachmas for a certain hetaera per night, a sum he describes as ten times the usual fee of other high-priced women.[81] We might recall that Stephanus and Neaera also directed their extortion scheme toward unsuspecting foreigners.[82] The variable prices for prostitutes implies that charges were neither standardized nor regulated but rather depended on the "attractions of the prostitute and the resources and urgency of the customer," as well as the sexual position desired.[83] A hetaera or her pimp could command much more for long-term cohabitation, as in the case of Neaera, who cost her lovers 3000 drachmas, or 30 minas, the equivalent of a dowry or a very fancy house in a desirable area of Athens.[84] It seems clear that even hetaeras at the low end of the pay scale could far exceed the amounts that might be earned in other pursuits by relatively well-compensated, self-employed males.[85] And those at the top were fantastically rich, able to afford lavish lifestyles featuring large houses, numerous servants, and costly clothing and jewelry. Only the most affluent men could have afforded to maintain such hetaeras—the expenses incurred by Demeas to fund his liaison with Chrysis, for instance, were a drop in the bucket compared to the tax levied on his extraordinarily rich family, the financing of a tragic chorus. Together with outfitting a naval trireme, this was a form of taxation known as a liturgy that applied only to the wealthiest 1,200 Athenians, whether citizens or metics. But such extravagant pleasures also threatened to bankrupt the men who indulged in them.[86]

Although those who worked in the trades and professions paid no tax, all persons who sold their bodies for sex were subject to a special a tax called the *pornikon telos*.[87] The official tax register, now lost to us, annually delivered detailed data on individual prostitutes to private tax collectors, who did not have to guess but apparently "knew exactly" who they were and where to find them.[88] The inscription of their names on the registry would have constituted concrete and visible evidence of their profession and could be used against them in court.[89] Failure to pay the tax could result in seizure of property, as in the case of two *pornae*, whose furniture was illegally seized by Androtion even though they owed no tax.[90] Some well-to-do hetaeras were forced to pay a recurrent "extraordinary" tax, or *eisphora*, on property, imposed only on the several hundred persons purported to be the richest inhabitants of Attica.[91] Such women would have been incentivized to cultivate a façade of "gifts" and "friendship" instead of dealing in cash transactions in order to evade this tax.[92]

Woman-Owned

After hearing the facts from both parties and the woman
herself, they announced their decision . . . that the woman was
to be free and her own mistress.[93]

When Timanoridas of Corinth and Eukrates of Leukas offered Neaera
the chance to buy her freedom for the reduced cost of twenty minas on
the condition that she no longer work in Corinth, she seems to have
entered into an enforceable contractual agreement with them. The subsequent transaction could be interpreted as the straightforward sale of
the woman to Phrynion rather than a manumission since she was unable to come up with the full amount on her own.[94] He would then have
had just cause for trying to reclaim her when she left him (not to mention the stolen furniture) while the hetaera herself later acknowledges
that she had acted unjustly in her treatment of him.[95] When Phrynion
attempted to seize her as his slave, Stephanus challenged him in a private arbitration, alleging that she was in fact a free woman. Acting on
her own behalf, Neaera reached an agreement with her two clients that
required mutual consent for any change in the terms regarding property
and maintenance in exchange for sexual services to both.[96] Although
the details remain murky, Neaera seems to have possessed the ability to
negotiate on her own behalf, even when enslaved, to enter into viable
contracts, and to earn her freedom as her own legal guardian (*kyria*)
and owner of her own body. Free hetaeras like Neaera and Phryne could
thus function independently, were not under control of another person,
and could enter into binding contractual arrangements with their
lovers.[97] Similarly, when Demeas seeks to end his relationship with the
free hetaera Chrysis in Menander's *Samia*, the property settlement he
proposes, that she retain not only her own property but also servants
and possibly her gold jewelry similarly points to a prior understanding
that may have taken the form of a legal contract.[98]

Written arrangements for the sale of sex seem to have been commonplace and complex contracts for erotic services so widespread that the
phrase "hetaera under written contract" had become widespread in legal
discourse by the fourth century.[99] These contracts suggest the reciprocal
nature of the commitments undertaken by the two parties, allowing the
hetaera to assert conditions and thus exert some degree of control over

Sex and the Ancient City   81

the relationship. Cohen argues that such arrangements, whether written or oral, were legally binding at Athens, and that "even persons ordinarily lacking legal capacity as a *kyrios*, such as women or slaves," might in business contexts enter into agreements enforceable in the courts, even for prostitution.[100] On the other hand, mutually binding agreements were not without risk for prostitutes, since they often removed the signatories from supportive social networks and resources that might defend them against abuse and enslavement and/or involved unreasonable demands, effectively erasing their agency and autonomy. According to Susan Lape, a contract could also function as "a tool that grants politically and socially marginalized prostitutes an illusion of free choice and autonomy."[101]

In addition to entering into exclusive contracts with male clients, independent hetaeras could support themselves through trafficking other women, presumably without male interference in their compensation or business activities.[102] Since this type of prostitution often took place within the oikos, as we saw with Stephanus and Neaera, it could have been seen as a particularly discrete, readily accessible, and lucrative form of female entrepreneurship.[103] Female control and management of sex businesses parallels and fits within the larger framework of the household in which women supervised economic activities.[104] Apollodorus gives a good idea of how such businesses operated in his description of Nicarete, original owner of Neara. A former slave, Nicarete had to find a source of income when freed by her master, Charisios, and turned to the trafficking of girls. This profession required the ability to identify beauty in young girls and expertise in training them. By calling them "daughters" and rearing them to act like free women, she could charge the highest possible price for their services, and once she had exhausted their revenue potential, she sold them off.[105] Possibly Nicarete had once been a hetaera herself, like Antigona, who had been the most powerful hetaera of her day before running a brothel as a *pornoboskousa*.[106] When she received a commission of three hundred drachmas from selling a retail operation dealing in fragrances, she set aside the money for the purchase of a girl.[107] Theodote manages a household of attractive and well-dressed young women, who may well have been prostitutes.[108] Isaeus alludes to several women who managed brothels at Athens, in particular the previously mentioned female entrepreneur, Alce, who ran a brothel in the Piraeus, where she kept a group of slave girls.[109]

The woman-owned brothel is really a variant, or perversion, of the traditional oikos model whose functioning relied on female management,

82   Phryne of Thespiae

economic productivity, and generational continuity centered around the residents of the household. But in this economy, the primary generational tie is not that of father and son but rather of mother and daughter, a relationship reflected in onomastic practices. Phano, a daughter who resides in a "home that was really a brothel" is consistently referred to as "the daughter of Neaera," allegedly her hetaera mother.[110] Inscriptional evidence also seems to indicate matrilineality among hetaeras: because women are rarely identified by their mothers' names, many of the matronyms found in funerary inscriptions may be explained as referring to hetaeras or other types of sex workers, with their fathers unknown.[111] One inscription identifies Callistion, a well-known fourth-century hetaera, as the daughter of Nichomache, a popular Athenian name, but possibly also Corone mentioned by the comic poet Machon in his *Chreiae* recorded by Athenaeus.[112] Similarly, Malthace is identified by the matronymic "daughter of Magadis," and another woman, Galene, is called "the daughter of Polycleia."[113] Another inscription records "Aspasia daughter of Mania."[114] In Athenaeus, mother-daughter heteara pairs abound while Lucian's *Dialogues of the Courtesans* imagines their dual-purpose brothel households as residences and businesses where servants expedite sales and services and hetaera mothers rigorously train their daughters into their trade, and are clearly in control, such as Crobyle/Corinna and Daphnis/Lyra.[115]

Although the literary record makes no reference to Phryne's trafficking in women, nor to her mother or any daughter, there are repeated allusions to the enormous wealth she earned with her body, which would have allowed her not only to be selective about her clients but also to engage in public benefactions. In one of the jokes discussed prior, Phryne rejects a lover for refusing to pay her asking price of one hundred drachmas while elsewhere, a comic character similarly complains, "But unlucky me, I fell in love with Phryne in the days when she was gathering capers and did not have as much property as she does now, and even though I spent enormous amounts, whenever I visited, her door was locked."[116] She even joked that in her advancing years she got a better price for the "dregs" of her body.[117] While presumably fictitious, or at least highly exaggerated, these anecdotes portray Phryne as the *kyria* of herself, as a female entrepreneur not under the control of men, able to choose or reject her customers at will. From the profits of these commercial activities, we are told, she was able to offer to rebuild the walls of Thebes, with the stipulation that the citizens acknowledge her as their public benefactor, "Alexander tore them down, but Phryne built them up again."[118] To Thespiae, her hometown, she dedicated its most famous tourist attraction, a statue of Eros by the sculptor Praxiteles.[119] In return, the Thespians dedicated a gilded statue of the hetaera at Delphi, also wrought by Praxiteles. Both statues will be considered in greater detail in the next chapter. Female prostitution, as it turns out, could be extremely lucrative in the democratic polis, enabling an impoverished girl of alien origins to move within the most powerful political and economic networks in the classical polis and even to become a formidable public benefactor and international celebrity. Sex, as it turns out, has everything to do with the city.

Fourth-Century Hetaeras

Having traced the various ways in which hetaeras and other types of prostitutes may have traversed and negotiated the Athenian polis, let us move beyond Neaera to three other examples of historically attested hetaeras as a way of imagining a history for Phryne. Importantly, most of our accounts of these women come from evidentiary sources potentially more credible than comedy and oratory: historical and philosophical writings, both of which deal with contemporary historical figures. We start with Rhodopis, who lived in the first half of the sixth century BCE and is the first woman to be called a hetaera in the sense of female prostitute in the Greek literary tradition. Our only account of this hetaera comes from Herodotus' *Histories*, which serves as the basis of most Second Sophistic and Roman references to her.[120] In contrast to Phryne, Rhodopis' reception remains undeveloped in the later tradition, probably because her story does not appear to circulate beyond Herodotus. Thracian by birth, Rhodopis began her life as the slave of Iadmon of Samos and fellow slave of the storyteller Aesop.[121] Brought by the Samian Xanthus to Naucratis, Egypt, a city known for prostitution, she was freed by Charaxus, the brother of the poet Sappho.[122] This woman is presumably the Doricha of Sappho's poems, although little more than the name survives.[123] Herodotus situates her within an illustrious literary circle, that of Aesop and Sappho, which would have been well known to his Athenian audience. As a free woman, she worked for herself, amassing great wealth from her body.[124] She is credited with financing a small Egyptian pyramid, erroneously in Herodotus' view, as she had enough wealth "for a Rhodopis (e.g. a hetaera), but not for

84   Phryne of Thespiae

the building of such a pyramid."[125] In reality, she spent one-tenth of her earnings on a dedication at Delphi, consisting of a large number of iron spits for roasting sacrificial meat:

> For Rhodopis desired to leave a memorial of herself in Greece, by having something made which no one else had contrived and dedicated in a temple and presenting this at Delphi to preserve her memory; so she spent the tenth part of her substance on the making of a great number of iron ox-spits, as many as the tithe would pay for, and sent them to Delphi; these lie in a heap to this day, behind the altar set up by the Chians and in front of the shrine itself.[126]

Herodotus had evidently witnessed these spits at Delphi, and the base of the monument inscribed with the words "Rhodopis dedicated" has survived today, attesting to the hetaera's historical presence and agency over a hundred years after her death.[127] As the first hetaera narrative, this account establishes several characteristics that the Greeks of the archaic and classical periods associated with hetaeras: servile origins, spatial and social mobility, foreign birth, migrancy, physical beauty, wealth, notoriety, and large-scale public benefactions.

The second example is Aspasia, a woman who lived around the time Herodotus put Rhodopis' story into circulation. Although her actual sexual and social status is unknown, Aspasia's literary reception assumes that she was a hetaera.[128] Athenaeus refers to her as one, including her among the other famous Athenian hetaeras of book 13.[129] Yet as the "wise" and "Socratic" Aspasia, renowned for her intelligence and political acumen, as well as for instructing Pericles and Socrates in rhetoric, she stands apart and should perhaps be grouped within the female philosophic tradition.[130] In fourth-century texts, however, she is notably never called a hetaera. The comic poet Cratinus (519–422 BCE) in *Chirons* refers to her as a "dog-eyed *pallake*" and Eupolis (c. 446–11 BCE) in *Demes* as the *porne* mother of Pericles' bastard son.[131] Whatever her true status, her fluid social identity as a female economic migrant would have allowed her to be refashioned to fit the rhetoric, and the jokes, of the literary sources.

As with Phryne, there is very little contemporary biographical data for Aspasia, and the main account of her life comes from a Second Sophistic source, Plutarch's *Life of Pericles*.[132] Material evidence in the

Sex and the Ancient City   85

form of a funerary stele from the harbor town of Piraeus inscribed with the names Axiochos, Alcibiades, Aspasia, and Aspasios has led to the speculation that she was born around 470 BCE in the Miletus, a wealthy city in Asia Minor, to a man named Axiochos. She probably came to Athens around 450 as a fatherless refugee of marriageable or nearly marriageable age and may have been related by her sister's marriage to the Athenian Alcibiades, grandfather of the notorious Alcibiades.[133] Ostracized in 460 BCE, the elder Alcibiades may have spent his exile in Miletus, where, as Peter Bicknell proposes, he may have married a daughter of Axiochos and by her had two sons, Axiochos (b. c. 458 BCE) and Aspasios (b. c. 456 BCE). Aspasia would have been the younger sister of this Milesian wife. In Athens, Aspasia made the acquaintance of the recently divorced Pericles, perhaps through the elder Alcibiades, as early as 452/1.[134] Although she may be tentatively identified as the dependent relation of an Athenian aristocrat, Aspasia was nonetheless a metic whose arrival coincided with Pericles' legislation that restricted citizenship only to sons born of Athenian mothers. Previously, aristocratic Athenian men often married foreign women, such that distinguished politicians like Themistocles, Cimon, and Cleisthenes all had foreign mothers.[135] Thus when Aspasia gave birth to her son, Pericles junior, he was presumably a bastard until he was exempted from the provisions of this law when it was modified in 430/29.[136] After Pericles' death in 429, Aspasia married the sheep dealer Lysicles, and presumably became eligible for lawful marriage at the same time as her son received citizen rights.[137] As this narrative indicates, Apasia's biography more than any other historical hetaera is closely entwined with fifth-century Athenian politics, contemporary anxieties about citizenship and immigration, and democratic ideology.

Several contemporary sources portray Aspasia as actively engaged in Athenian politics, where she often serves as a target of attacks, as in a joke from Aristophanes' *Acharnians* (525 BCE) that blames the outbreak of the Peloponnesian War on her:[138]

> But then some tipsy, cottabus-playing youths went to Megara
> and kidnapped the *porne* Simaetha. And then the Megarians,
> garlic-stung by their distress, in retaliation stole a couple of
> Aspasia's *pornae,* and from that the onset of war broke forth
> upon all the Greeks: from three sluts (*laikastrion*)! And then
> in wrath Pericles, that Olympian, did lighten and thunder and

stir up Greece, and started making laws worded like drinking songs, that Megarians should abide neither on land nor in market nor on sea nor on shore.[139]

The humor operates on multiple levels. First, it constructs a negative portrait of Aspasia as a brothel-keeper and purveyor of *pornae* of the lowest order, a viable profession for a retired hetaera, as we have seen.[140] It also parodies Herodotus' account of the sequence of events that led to the Trojan War, the retaliatory abductions of various women, culminating in Paris' seizure of Helen, the supreme symbol of female promiscuity.[141] It further plays on a tradition that Pericles proceeded with a war against the Samians on the advice of Aspasia.[142] Just as in oratory, the figure of the hetaera in comedy could be weaponized to defame a male opponent or controversial contemporary figure, in this case, Pericles and his military policies, reflecting Athenian prejudices against foreign women. Like Phryne, Aspasia was also allegedly charged with impiety by the comic poet Hermippus, who further accused her of procuring "free-born women into a place of assignation for Pericles," although there is no contemporary evidence for this trial.[143] The susceptibility of hetaeras and foreign women to charges of impiety is addressed more fully in Chapter 5.

Another near-contemporary source also represents Aspasia as deeply engaged in the political ideology of the polis as a teacher of rhetoric, speech writer, and interlocutor of Socrates. Plato's *Menexenus*, an early dialogue with a dramatic date of 386 BCE, is the only one of three extant ancient dialogues concerned with Aspasia, and she is the only provably historical woman given a speech in his entire corpus.[144] Socrates seems to have engaged in frequent conversations with Aspasia, consulting her as an authority not only on politics and rhetoric, but also on love, marriage, and the training of young wives.[145] The dialogue features an exchange between Socrates and a young man called Menexenus who tells him that the political body known as the Boule has decided to solicit a speaker to deliver a funeral oration for Athenian soldiers killed in battle.[146] When Menexenus expresses skepticism that anyone could compose the speech on such short notice, Socrates responds that Aspasia had rehearsed a similar speech the day before, extemporizing and inserting sections from previous speeches she had composed, including Pericles' famous funeral oration, and then proceeds to recite the speech.[147] Read as an intertextual engagement with

Sex and the Ancient City   87

Pericles' famous funeral oration, the speech plays on his closing admonition to the widowed wives of the Athenian War dead to be "least talked about among men whether for praise or blame."[148] Aspasia, a woman, a foreigner, and the mother of a bastard son, not only contravenes this advice as a public celebrity and political content creator, but is allowed to speak publicly, albeit as ventriloquized through Socrates, who delivers a patriotic address that valorizes the war dead and the land they defended. These two political speeches, according to Socrates, belong to a much larger corpus of political speeches that he proposes to share with Menexenus at a later date. According to Madeleine Henry, Plato assigns this speech to Aspasia in order to critique the epideictic genre of the funeral oration by exploiting Aspasia's alien status and drawing on her negative comic portrayal as a *porne* and the monstrous progenitor of a bastard son. Perhaps the main point, however, is not that Aspasia is being vilified and mocked, but rather that she was so deeply embedded in the intellectual and political imaginary of classical Athens as to make this dialogue plausible, even in its irony, to an Athenian audience .

Our last example of a historical hetaera is Theodote of Athens, a figure who also converses with Socrates as depicted in Xenophon's *Memorabilia* (c. 370 BCE). Like Rhodopis, she appears in no other extant contemporary text, although the name is recorded in a few fourth-century Attic inscriptions in connection with citizen women.[149] Nor does she share in a robust literary reception, in contrast to Aspasia, but rather survives into the Second Sophistic period mainly through Xenophon's account.[150] The euphemistic exchange never uses the word hetaera of Theodote, nor any other term for prostitute, rather, she is introduced as "a beautiful woman in the city, whose name was Theodote, the kind of woman who consorts with anyone who persuades her."[151] The explicit reference to the woman by her name rather than by that of her male kin suggests that we are to understand her as a hetaera. The flirtatious exchange between the philosopher and hetaera constructs their dialogue as a form of transactional exchange that revolves around the act of viewing and seduction.[152] Indeed, her exceptional beauty attracts Socrates, who wishes to experience it first-hand, and artists seeking to paint her portrait. Theodote manipulates this culture of erotic viewing by "showing only as much as appropriate," meaning only her breasts and chest, as Athenaeus later tells us, a "respectable" form of nudity associated with hetaeras and a topic to which we shall return in the next chapter.[153] From the perspective of art history, this comment suggests that the representation of full female nudity—with the exception of sexual activity on Attic pottery—had not yet fully evolved. Theodote profits from the men who view her, whether in person or in art, because they draw more customers to her by spreading news of her beauty, while they, in turn, longing to touch her, go away aroused, and become her admirers.[154] This visual economy has endowed Theodote with great wealth: she and her mother wear costly clothing and jewelry; maintain a retinue of attractive, well-cared for handmaids; and inhabit a beautifully furnished house.[155] Asked how she can afford such luxury, whether by owning a farm, a house, or artisans, Theodote evasively responds, "If one of my friends wishes to be generous, that's my livelihood."[156]

Noting the precarity of this arrangement, Socrates proceeds to advise her as to how she might achieve a more sustainable revenue stream through the systematic pursuit of wealthy benefactors with an eye for beauty.[157] By analogizing the art of seduction to the aristocratic pursuit of hunting, Socrates imbues it with a sense of propriety. To attract and retain "friends," it is necessary to use pleasing glances and gentle conversation, to receive readily an eager customer while rejecting a fickle one, and to convince them not just by words but by deeds.[158] Most importantly, she should not gratify a friend too readily, but rather "behave as a model of propriety, by a show of reluctance to yield, and by holding back until they are as keen as can be."[159] Although Theodote, like Aspasia, converses with Socrates, she does not belong to the female philosophic tradition; rather, she is depicted as a shrewd businesswoman "pursuing an erotic métier in a fashion appropriate to a free woman" and careful to conform to the values of free Athenian labor.[160] The dialogue thus allows us a glimpse into the workings of a high-earning hetaera who operates her own business at home, working together with her mother, and possibly also offering her "handmaids" for sale. By carefully curating appearances, not only her own, but that of her mother, her servants, her home, and even her conversation, Theodote maintains a veneer of respectability while at the same time reaping huge profits off her customers. She clearly runs this business independently, without the intervention of men, inviting Socrates by the end of the dialogue to become her "partner in pursuit of friends."[161]

Toward a Biography of Phryne

The fragmentary traces of Phryne found in the quotations of Athenaeus and allusions in other Second Sophistic texts do not contradict but rather intersect with many aspects of contemporary accounts of hetaeras and prostitutes in classical Athens. If we take seriously the idea of Phryne as a historical figure who actually lived and worked in Athens during the fourth century BCE, as do Antonio Corso, Esther Eidinow, and Konstantinos Kapparis, we can critically imagine the following biography.[162] Phryne would have been born in the late 380s/early 370s in Thespiae, a city in Southern Boeotia. Her original name, Mnesarete, combined with the patronymic, daughter of Epicles, suggests she was originally a free-born citizen rather than a slave and perhaps the descendant of an aristocratic family.[163] Her identification with her native city of Thespiae reinforces her status as an outsider and metic resident of Athens, but also perhaps indicates that she was a person of some renown, like Aspasia of Miletus.[164] Like many other hetaeras, she left her native city and immigrated to Athens, probably as a refugee of war. As Thebes moved to conquer Thespiae in the 370s, destroying its walls, large numbers of its citizens fled to Attica, many of them women.[165] Funerary inscriptions of Thespians in Athens, in which women outnumber men, attest to their metic presence during this period. When Thespiae was completely destroyed not long after 371 BCE, many stayed on for several years, or even took up permanent residence, judging by the evidence of wealthy Thespian women in the Hellenistic period involved in land leasing and endowments.[166] If we are to believe that Phryne was born in Thespiae before it was ravaged by the Thebans and fled to Athens after the purge of 373 BCE, we might imagine that she fled the city in the late 370s when still a child.

How and when she became involved in prostitution is impossible to know. But drawing on parallel narratives of historically attested hetaeras, we may imagine, as a freeborn woman, she probably did not start in a brothel, like Neaera. Rather, she resided in Athens as a metic and worked independently, free from male intervention, like other celebrated hetaeras. Perhaps she adopted the name of Phryne, a name that may have been a slang term for prostitute, once she took up her profession and gradually become more well known, attending dinners and symposia, by turns conversing with and mocking her male companions. A lucrative, presumably contractual, liaison with Praxiteles may have followed, allowing her economic security and social mobility. Antonio Corso proposes that she had a prior connection with Praxiteles through another sculptor, Cephisodotus the Elder, who had worked on two groups of Muses for the sanctuary on Mt. Helicon under the control of Thespiae, a point to which we will return in the next chapter.[167] In his view, she became the lover of Praxiteles in the mid-360s, around the time he created his Eros of Thespiae, and subsequently served as a model for the body of *Cnidian Aphrodite*, probably around 364–61 BCE. Around 350, she took up with the orator, Hyperides, who defended her against charges of impiety, sometime in the 340s. A little time later, she returned to Praxiteles and he modeled another Aphrodite for the Spartans after her.[168] In the 330s, she inspired Apelles' painting, *Aphrodite Rising from the Sea*. Like Theodote, she controlled who could see her body while at the same time allowing select artists to reproduce her form in painting and sculpture, further enhancing her celebrity.

Although resident in Athens as a metic, Phryne nonetheless continued to maintain close ties to her native city. From the profits of her entrepreneurial activities, Phryne dedicated the statue of Eros given to her by Praxiteles to her native city and was rewarded in return with an honorific portrait statue at Delphi. Finally, in her old age, she offered to fund the rebuilding of the walls of Thebes at her own expense, and she had the autonomy, and audacity, to demand that the citizens acknowledge her as their public benefactor. These public gifts recall Rhodopis' pyramid and the spits she dedicated at Delphi, stressing the role of the wealthiest hetaeras as civic patrons and philanthropists. The next two chapters will address Phryne's artistic and forensic legacies, the two strands of her biography that are most frequently recounted by later authors and are also the most fictionalized. A close examination of these narratives within their historical contexts indicates that they could arguably have had some basis in reality and may in fact have influenced each other.

Sex and the Ancient City 91

4

Phryne's Receptions in Greek Art

> At the Eleusinia and Posidonia festivals, with all Greeks
> watching, Phryne took off her robe, let down her hair, and
> entered the sea. Apelles drew the inspiration for his painting
> Aphrodite Anadyomene ("Rising from the Sea") from her. So
> too the sculptor Praxiteles, who was in love with her, used her
> as the model for his Cnidian Aphrodite . . . He also gave her
> a choice of his statues, letting her decide whether she would
> like to have the Eros or the Satyr that stood in the Street of
> Tripods, and she chose the Eros and dedicated it in Thespiae.
> The people who lived in the area had a gold statue made of
> Phryne herself and dedicated it, mounted on a column of
> Pentelic marble, in Delphi; Praxiteles produced it.[1]

Just as Phryne became a subject of fascination in late nineteenth- and
early twentieth-century art, so, too, she inspired various connections
to artworks and artists in antiquity, as detailed by Athenaeus previously. Although Phryne is probably best known today as the model
for *Cnidian Aphrodite* by the Greek sculptor Praxiteles (active 70–30
BCE), the first monumental female nude in Western art, Athenaeus is
the only extant source to make this claim.[2] The ancient sources more
frequently refer to the two other art objects mentioned in the prior epigraph, neither of which survives today: Praxiteles' stone statue of Eros,
the god of desire, which the hetaera purportedly dedicated to her native city of Thespiae, and her gilded portrait statue at Delphi.[3] Praxiteles
also crafted two other portraits of Phryne, one fashioned out of marble
that stood next to the Eros at Thespiae and another of bronze called the
Happy Hetaera, perhaps originally located near the theater of Dionysus

Phryne of Thespiae. Laura McClure, Oxford University Press. © Oxford University Press 2024.
DOI: 10.1093/9780197580882.003.0005

in Athens.[4] According to these receptions, not only did Phryne inspire these important sculptures, she was also a public benefactor, dedicating Praxiteles' triad to her native city.[5]

First put into circulation around the first century BCE, these stories likely developed out of a desire to explain and embellish the history of authentic Greek monuments and inscriptions or in response to a poetic tradition that celebrated them. Literary accounts linking Phryne to these artworks most likely did not precede them, but rather the monuments themselves, publicly displayed and viewed by thousands of citizens and tourists alike, along with copies that circulated widely throughout the ancient world, likely generated numerous stories about their creation.[6] For instance, the heightened fascination with the *Cnidian Aphrodite* at the end of the second century BCE as travel, trade, and tourism increased dramatically in the Mediterranean, spurred on by Roman expansion, inspired numerous epigrams about the statue and her creator.[7] Several others triangulate the Thespian Eros, Praxiteles, and Phryne, celebrating a fictitious love affair between artist and hetaera.[8] In turn, these accounts influenced Second Sophistic discourse on Athenian hetaeras and their lovers. For this reason, Havelock argues that Phryne is largely a fictitious character and her liaison with Praxiteles a fantasy concocted well after the sculptor's death.[9]

This chapter, however, attempts to offer a more nuanced exploration of the evidence, distinguishing the portrait statues of Phryne from her associations with the Eros and Cnidia. I argue that the portraits were probably authentic and thus help to make the case that a fourth-century hetaera named Phryne from Thespiae plausibly existed. For this reason, the first part of the chapter considers the form and meaning of both private and public portrait dedications of women in Greek sanctuaries during the late classical period. I then turn to Praxiteles' Thespian triad, which placed Phryne's image between two deities, Eros and Aphrodite, followed by discussions of the two other portrait statues, the Happy Hetaera and the portrait statue at Delphi. In the second half, I briefly examine constructions of idealized, "respectable" female nudity in Greek art and literature as precedents for the historical emergence of the *Cnidian Aphrodite*, particularly the so-called kneeling bather scenes found on late fifth-century Attic red-figure vase painting and how Phryne came to be associated with this artistic milieu.

Phryne's Receptions in Greek Art   93

Female Portrait Statues and Dedications

Since many of the statues associated with Phryne belong to the portrait genre, this section lays out a brief history of portrait statues placed in Greek sanctuaries and the role of women as dedicants and honorands within this religious and civic system. The practice of setting up statues of individuals, both male and female, in sanctuaries as gifts to the gods originated in the archaic period with the development of the genre of marble statues known as the male *kouros* and female *kore*. The physical characteristics, pose, and proportions of these figures were generalized and closely adhered to established convention, rather than representing the individualized features of the subject. The stone bases on which they were mounted have survived in far greater number than the figures and give the name of the dedicator, the divine recipient, and sometimes the name of the sculptor. The absence of a name for the image has made it difficult to determine the identities of these *korai*, whether they represent priestesses, female votaries, or even images of Athena.[10] Whatever the case, non-specific votive images of women were a common feature of the sacred landscape at Athens and elsewhere in Greece from the archaic period onward. Moreover, women could make such dedications on behalf of themselves, as in the case of Nicandre, the earliest attested *kore* figure (c. 640–630 BCE) from the sanctuary of Artemis in Delos and possibly a priestess.[11] The inscription indicates that she dedicated the statue herself, as well as identifying her through her relationships with three different male relatives, "Nicander dedicated me to the goddess, far-shooter of arrows, the daughter of Deinodicus of Naxos, distinguished among women, sister of Deinomenes and wife of Phraxus."[12] Although this statue importantly indicates that elite women from the earliest period of Greek history could dedicate monuments on their own behalf, they were rare, accounting for fewer than 10 percent of the statue dedications on the Athenian acropolis in the archaic and early classical periods.[13] At the sanctuary of Apollo at Delphi, the site of Phryne's most famous statue, only a handful of statues or statue groups from the archaic to Hellenistic periods were set up by women.

By the fifth century, a revolution in sculpture led to two major developments that influenced the development of the portrait genre: the creation of life-sized painted bronze votives depicted in naturalistic poses, with realistic proportions and individualized features, and honorific portraits of famous men, designated by the Greek term *eikon*,

94   Phryne of Thespiae

representing historical figures such as Themistocles and Pericles, cultural heroes, and poets, most of which were set up posthumously.[14] Soon thereafter honorific portrait statues of living individuals were publicly dedicated to commemorate major civic events such as a military victory or civic benefaction. By the beginning of the fourth century, the genre of portrait sculpture, previously confined to honoring important men, began to be used for representations of private Athenian citizens, many of them women, that were often placed as votive dedications in sanctuaries.[15] Female portraits, however, differed from those of men in several important ways. First, most known female portraits set up in Greek sanctuaries tended to be private, commissioned by relatives, and usually situated within the larger family group. Second, the faces of female figures were less individuated than their male counterparts and their features confined to a narrow representational range defined by ideals of physical beauty embodied by Aphrodite.[16] Representations of mortal and divine women are thus often difficult to distinguish based on appearance alone for both ancient viewers and modern scholars. The fungibility of Phryne and Aphrodite perhaps reflects and expands upon the artistic practice of likening ordinary women to images of the goddess. Third, female figures were adorned with lavish, but modest, clothing painted in a dazzling array of colors and patterns—including red, blue, bright pink, mauve, yellow, and green—that conveyed the individuality and social status of the honorand.[17] Crucially, the main evidence for the individual woman comes from the inscribed stone base that supported the statue. It was an essential component of portrait statues, elevating the figure above its surroundings as well as separating it from nearby monuments. The base also provided valuable information not evident from the figure itself, such as the woman's name, her family members, religious activities, the dedicator of the statue, the divine recipient, and the sculptor.[18]

From the fourth century onward, women increasingly made dedications of portrait statues in sanctuaries, actively participating in setting up images of their family members and themselves, usually within the family group but sometimes apart. A hundred years later after Phryne dedicated her statue at Delphi (c. 335 BCE), a woman named Aristaeneta dedicated her own elegant and costly private monument near the entrance to the Temple of Apollo. The group consisted of two tall Ionic columns on a stepped foundation that supported an elaborately decorated architrave, on top of which stood portrait statues of the

Phryne's Receptions in Greek Art   95

woman, her son, and her parents, about thirty feet above the ground.[19] This dedication demonstrates that a woman could commission and display her own elaborate portrait statue but was more likely than a man to situate it in a family group.

Occasionally women dedicated single images of themselves, particularly if they were female civic benefactors, priestesses, lesser sacred personnel, or initiates.[20] Although these statues stood alone, their dedicatory inscriptions reflect a family orientation. In contrast, male portrait statues often make little reference to relatives, but rather give the name of the honorand in the nominative, without the demotic or patronym, allowing "the subject to exist in the absolute, an autonomous actor."[21] A single votive statue of a woman, Archippe from Axione, carved by Praxiteles, an artist widely known for his skill at individual portraits, and placed on the Athenian acropolis in the late fourth century, offers a rare example of a woman functioning as a sole dedicant:

> [The statue of daughter] Archippe [daughter] of Cleogenus
> of Axione mother Archippe [daughter?] of Couphagorus
> dedicated. Praxiteles made [it].[22]

This inscription indicates that a mother, Archippe, commissioned a statue for her daughter, Archippe. Although both women are identified by their male relatives, as the daughters of Couphagorus and Cleogenus, respectively, their special bond as mother and daughter is highlighted. No divine recipient is named, and it is unknown whether the honorand was a priestess or initiate, whether she was alive at the time of the dedication, or the occasion for it. Another example, the portrait of a priestess called Simo from Erythrae in Asia Minor, similarly identifies the dedicator with her male kin:

> [S]imo, wife of Zoilos, priestess of the city, daughter of
> Pancratides, set up this image (*eikon*) of beauty and example of
> virtue and wealth, for Dionysus as an eternal memorial for my
> children and ancestors.[23]

Although Simo made the dedication on her own behalf, to advertise her civic importance as a priestess and to immortalize herself and her family, she nonetheless defines herself by her male family members,

96   Phryne of Thespiae

reflecting the tendency of female dedications to situate their public images within a familial context.[24]

In addition to dedicating statues of themselves and their loved ones, women could also be the subjects of public honorific portrait statues dedicated by a civic body, although these were rare before the late Hellenistic period. When they were so honored, it was usually because of their participation in important local cults as priestesses. The earliest and most famous such monument is that of Lysimache, who served as priestess of Athena Polias for over sixty years, and her image possibly dedicated by the Athenian citizens.[25] Her assistant, Syeris, also had a statue, made by the sculptor Nichomachus and later viewed by Pausanias, which bore the inscription, "This portrait image is a clear likeness; my deeds, too, and my soul now live clearly for all."[26] From this brief overview, it is evident that women could and did participate actively in the public display of dedications in Greek sanctuaries, both as the subjects of private votive offerings set up by themselves and their families and of public dedications by civic bodies commemorating their service as priestesses and benefactors. In contrast to male portrait statues set up by men, female images continued to be more generalized and were more likely to be incorporated into a larger family group, and/or identified by their male kin in their dedicatory inscriptions. Nonetheless, the presence of such portraits within the sacred and urban landscape of Athens offers valuable documentation that historical women could influence their communities as cultic personnel and civic benefactors and appropriately commemorate their accomplishments with dedications intended to be seen by all.

Praxiteles' Portraits

Almost all the artworks that figure in Phryne's receptions were attributed in antiquity to the Athenian sculptor Praxiteles. He was born around 395 BCE, presumably to Cephisodotus, also a sculptor, who had worked for the Thespians in the early fourth century as one of three sculptors involved in creating a statuary group of Muses for the sanctuary of the Muses on Mt. Helicon, attesting to an early link between his workshop and the city, as we saw in the last chapter.[27] Praxiteles inherited such extensive property holdings from his father that he was obligated to pay a liturgy or special wealth tax in the form of financing a tragic chorus, a public benefaction commemorated by a monument in his honor from the 360s.[28] Only men of such financial means, we might recall, were among the select few able to afford the expensive luxury of a hetaera. Praxiteles appears to have been active from the 370s to the 320s BCE, roughly equivalent to the date Pliny the Elder (23–79 CE) assigns to his floruit of 364–361, a period associated both with the influx of metics and an intensification of interest in hetaeras in the literary tradition.[29]

Although the extant literary tradition identifies Praxiteles as a sculptor of gods and satyrs, the material evidence for his work in the form of seven extant inscribed statue bases indicates that the artist, along with his father and his two sons, Timarchus and Cephisodotus the Younger, produced a number of private portrait statues commissioned by their family members.[30] Indeed, Quintilian praises Praxiteles for his faithfulness to the natural and places him in the company of two other artists whose activity as portrait painters was well attested, Demetrius Alopece (early fourth cent. BCE) and Lysippus (c. 370–300 BCE).[31] All of the bases that contain Praxiteles' name supported votive portrait statues of family members, and all of the votives involve women as either dedicants or honorands.[32] A base that displayed a bronze portrait statue of a man, Thrasymachus of Thespiae, dedicated by his sister and son, further attests to an early connection between the sculptor and Pryne's native city:

Archais [son of] Thrasymachos Wanaxareta [daughter of]
Charmidas [the statue of] Thrasymachos son of Charmidas
dedicate to the gods. Praxiteles the Athenian made [it].[33]

According to Aileen Ajootian, Praxiteles' extant statue bases demonstrate his active participation "in an artistic trend catering to and sustained by wealthy Athenians and others who created a public image of their family's enduring vitality through portrait statues and inscriptions."[34] Viewing Praxiteles as a portrait sculptor, along with his contacts with Thespiae, helps to authenticate his three images of Phryne dedicated in Athens, Thespiae, and Delphi, as actual monuments and further substantiates the claim that a powerful and socially consequential hetaera named Phryne probably existed during his floruit.

98   Phryne of Thespiae

The Thespian Triad

Situated at the foot of Mt. Helicon, to the southwest of Thebes, Thespiae, a relative backwater in Boeotia, was the only city in Greece to honor Eros with an important cult.[35] According to Pausanias (c. 110–180 CE), the original cult statue was very old and hewn out of rough stone.[36] By the second century BCE, the god was celebrated every four years in the festival of the Erotideia, in association with an earlier established festival, the Mouseia, honoring the Muses at nearby Helicon.[37] His worship seems to have been further bound up with Aphrodite, both of whom figured in Praxiteles' triad, along with Phryne, who stood between the two, all three carved out of Parian marble. The group stood in some sort of sacred enclosure, probably in a sanctuary of Eros.[38] By the Roman period, the triad was purported to have been dedicated by Phryne to commemorate an unknown occasion.[39] Although all three images have been lost, a portion of the triad is possibly represented on a coin struck during the reign of Domitian (81–96 CE) that shows an image of Aphrodite holding an object, either a mirror or apple, in her left half and extending her right arm in a gesture of protection over a smaller, female figure at her feet that has been interpreted as Phryne.[40] On the basis of this coin and other material evidence, Corso believes that Praxiteles' Thespian Aphrodite was the earliest nude representation of the deity, preserved in subsequent iterations as the half-draped Arles type (Figure 4.1) and reworked as Aphrodite/Phryne at Delphi.[41] She follows conventions of fourth-century idealized female nudity, her lower body modestly draped, so that she, like Theodote, "shows only as much as proper."[42] An inscription on a fourth-century Thespian dedicatory relief depicting Aphrodite bears the words, "Lovely voiced Pedagenes to Aphrodite ready to listen," further stressing the importance of the goddess to the city.[43] Pausanias states that there was also a sanctuary of Aphrodite Melainis worth seeing at Thespiae, as well as a theater and agora. Since Aphrodite is the primary female deity associated with this city, it is possible to interpret the female face featured on Thespian coins minted between 386 and 374 BCE as images of the goddess.[44]

Like Apelles' Anadyomene, the Eros was wildly popular with the Romans and the only major tourist attraction at Thespiae. According to Cicero (106–43 BCE), the Thespians refused to give their Eros to anyone else because it was so important to their local economy, "there being no other reason to go there."[45] Indeed, [Lucian], *Amores*, an erotic dialogue

FIGURE 4.1 Arles type Aphrodite, Hymettan marble, late first century BCE. Paris, Louvre, Ma 439.

of unknown date, possibly as late as the late fourth or early third century CE, locates Thespiae and Cnidos as the two major centers of erotic art in the ancient Mediterranean, anchored by the twin deities Eros and Aphrodite as the respective embodiments of homoerotic and heterosexual love.[46] By the time of Strabo (64/3 BCE–24 CE), tourists had abandoned the city and Pliny and Pausanias report that the statue was taken by the emperor Caligula to Rome then returned by Claudius and removed once again by Nero who placed it in the portico of Octavia, where it was destroyed by fire in 80 CE.[47] Coincidentally, neither the Aphrodite of the Thespian triad nor Phryne's portrait statue seem to have made it to Rome.[48] An extant statue base that dates to early imperial times discovered reused in the walls of Thespiae reveals that a new Eros by Menodorus had replaced the original statue plundered by Nero. It bears an inscription composed in hexametric verse by a female poet, Herennia Procula, a member of a wealthy Roman family resident at Thassalonica, "This Eros has taught desire. Aphrodite herself said: where did Praxiteles see you with me?"[49] The couplet employs a trope of Greek epigram, that of the goddess looking at her own statue and her surprise that a male viewer could have contrived to see her naked.[50] Significantly, the inscription makes no mention of Phryne, suggesting either that her portrait was longer on display, or that the main focus was on the figures of Eros and Aphrodite, and the importance of romantic love to sexuality, rather than on the hetaera.[51]

The fame of Praxiteles' Eros during the Hellenistic era and its connection to Thespiae probably inspired stories of a romance between Praxiteles and Phryne that became wildly popular in both her ancient and modern receptions. Greek epigram celebrates the statue as the concrete embodiment of their love and as a generalized symbol of human desire. Athenaeus states that an Eros by Praxiteles, probably the same statue that was later transferred to Thespiae by Phryne, stood in the theater at Athens and bore the inscription previously quoted in the introduction:[52]

Praxiteles perfectly portrayed that Love he suffered, taking the model from his own heart, giving me to Phryne in payment for myself. But I give birth to passion no longer by shooting arrows, but by darting glances.[53]

This epigram, and others like it, locates the object within an economy of gift exchange, as a payment, or *misthos*, for the hetaera's favors, playfully as "the Eros for *eros*," a "reward for loving," and the "recompense for desire."[54] But Phryne is not just an object of erotic exchange in these vignettes: she is also a public benefactor who uses the profits of her trade to benefit her community:

> Phryne dedicated to the Thespians the winged Love beautifully
> wrought, the price of her bed. The work is the gift of Cypris, a
> gift to envy, with which no fault can be found, and Love was
> a fitting payment for both. I praise for two forms of art the
> man who, giving a god to others, had a more perfect god in his
> soul.[55]

If a hetaera named Phryne really did set up Praxiteles' statue of Eros, let alone an entire triad, as a votive offering at Thespiae, the benefaction indicates that she would have been in command of the kind of economic means only available to the wealthiest Athenian men.

Although most literary sources focus exclusively on the triad's Eros, a striking fragment from Alciphron includes a statue of Phryne in the group. Borrowing from epigram the trope of a romance between sculptor and hetaera and the portrait subject's appraisal of her own statue, it imagines Phryne speaking in two voices, as a living woman writing to her beloved and as a statue to her creator:

> Have no fear; for you have made a very beautiful thing, such
> as no one, in fact, has ever seen before among all things that
> have been made by hand, having set up your own mistress in
> the sanctuary. I stand in the middle by Aphrodite and your
> Eros too. Do not begrudge me this honor. For those viewing us
> will praise Praxiteles that people praise when they have gazed
> at me; and because I am born from your skill the Thespians
> will not condemn me for being placed between gods. But one
> component of your gift is still missing, that you come to me, so
> that we may lie together with each other in the sanctuary. For
> we will not defile the gods we ourselves have made. Farewell.[56]

The fragment has obvious affinities with popular stories of the male creation of an idealized female form embodied by Ovid's Pygmalion.[57] Phryne, as ventriloquized by Alciphron, gives no details about the

102   Phryne of Thespiae

appearance of the statue, particularly whether it was clothed or un-clothed, but the context of erotic viewing and the invitation to have sex in the sacred precinct conflate her image with that of the Thespian or Cnidian Aphrodites, reinforcing that she is the mortal embodiment of the divinity. The scene evokes and inverts epigrams in which Aphrodite visits her shrine at Cnidus to view her statue, echoed by Herennia Procula's verse above, "Cypris, seeing Cypris in Cnidus, said, 'Alas! alas! where did Praxiteles see me naked?'"[58] But why does Praxiteles fear his creation? Corso argues that the sculptor worries that placing a hetaera next to two divinities might be considered blasphemous.[59] But during the fourth century, the setting up of both private and honorific portrait statues of wealthy and important women within Greek sanctuaries, such as priestesses and benefactors, in the proximity of images of deities, was not in and of itself transgressive, nor were the dedicatory offerings of hetaeras.[60] Rather the poem situates Phryne's statue, like that of the Cnidia, within a context of sacred viewing that inspires fear and awe, much like the effect of Phryne's naked torso on the male jurors at her trial, as we shall see in the next chapter.

The Happy Hetaera

From Pliny we hear of another portrait statue of Phryne modeled by Praxiteles, the Happy Hetaera (*meretrices gaudentis*), one of a pair that included the Weeping Matron (*flentis matronae*), neither of which survives today:

> Also two of his statues expressing opposite emotions are admired, his Matron Weeping and his Merry Courtesan. The latter is believed to have been Phryne and connoisseurs detect in the figure the artist's love of her and the reward promised him by the expression on the courtesan's face.[61]

Pliny follows the epigram in emphasizing the transactional nature of the relationship between artist and hetaera: Praxiteles transmits his love to the statue as payment (*mercedem*) for Phryne's sexual services promised, or received, by the expression on her face. The pair embodies the two dominant emotions of ancient theater, tragedy and comedy, represented by the twin theatrical masks of laughter and sorrow, as well

Phryne's Receptions in Greek Art 103

as reflecting the pervasive presence of hetaeras as characters in middle comedy. Corso speculates that the group was originally set up near the Theater of Dionysus in Athens, near Praxiteles' Satyr and Eros, in order to celebrate a comic or choregic victory.[62] Since Pliny includes these artworks in his catalogue of bronze masterpieces, many of which had been removed from their Greek cities, the two statues likely made it to Rome where they may have decorated the new theater of Pompey placed between portraits of poets and hetaeras.[63] There Tatian the Assyrian presumably encountered the statue around 170 CE and identified Phryne as the subject of the portrait, "Praxiteles and Herodotus made the courtesan Phryne for you."[64] Little is known about this Herodotus. He may have been Praxiteles' pupil, specializing in the statues of young women, especially hetaeras and actresses, like Argia and Glycera.[65] Another copy of a statue of a hetaera by Herodotus is known from a Roman inscription.[66] Lastly, a very late source, Choricius of Gaza (491–518 CE), informs us that Praxiteles made a statue of Aphrodite based on Phryne for the Spartans, probably conflating his Cnidia with his other Phryne statues.[67]

Phryne's Portrait Statue at Delphi

> The people who lived in the area had a golden statue (*andrianta . . . khruseon*) made of Phryne herself and dedicated it, mounted on a column of Pentelic marble, in Delphi; Praxiteles produced it. When the Cynic Crates saw it, he called it a monument to Greek depravity. This statue (*eikon*) stood between those of Archidamus, the king of Sparta, and Philip son of Amyntas (Philip II of Macedon) and carried the inscription "Phryne the daughter of Epicles of Thespiae."[68]

Like her statue at Thespiae, Phryne's portrait at Delphi was also a votive offering and the only female portrait in the sanctuary attested by literary and epigraphical sources that did not form part of a mixed male and female family group prior to the Roman period.[69] Next to the Eros, it is the second most frequently cited statue by Praxiteles linked to the hetaera and sometimes the subject of extended ancient comment.[70] Excavations at the sanctuary have failed to recover either the statue or the base, and the exact location of the monument remains unknown.[71] Probably dedicated around 335 BCE, the dedication was composed of a

104   Phryne of Thespiae

high column of Pentelic marble with a female figure mounted on top, according to Alcestas, the mid-Hellenistic writer of Delphic antiquities, quoted by Athenaeus above.[72] The statue itself is variously described as an *agalma* or divine image, an *andrias* or human subject, and an *eikon* or portrait.[73] Whatever the term, all of the ancient writers identify it as a portrait of Phryne, except Diogenes Laertius, who states that Phryne dedicated not an image of herself at Delphi, but one of Aphrodite.[74] On this basis, Corso argues that the statue conflated the two: the real subject was Aphrodite with Phryne serving as "the mundane filter, the earthly medium" of the deity.[75] In his view, the statue was a reworking of the Thespian Aphrodite or Arles type (Figure 4.1), perhaps intended as a symbol of Thespian independence after the city had been liberated from Theban rule.[76]

The presence of similar types of dedications at Delphi from the same period, however, point to the authenticity of both the monument and of the portrait statue.[77] Another column of Pentelic marble, also created by Praxiteles' workshop and known as the Acanthus Column (Delphi Archaeological Museum 1584), celebrating the Athenian victory over Sparta at Alyzia in 375 BCE, supports a group of three graceful, dancing girls, presumably female chorus members, but possibly dancers. Portraits of gilded bronze elevated by columns were also popular during the fourth century in the form of dedications of important political and intellectual figures, such as Gorgias of Leontini, the orator Isocrates, the king of Sparta, Archidamus III, and Philip II. According to Alcetas, Phryne's portrait was a public dedication made by *hoi perictones*, or "those who live in the area," a phrase that has been variously interpreted as the Thespians, the people of Delphi, or the Delphic amphictyony, a league formed to support the temple of Apollo at Delphi that numbered the Boeotians among its twelve founding populations.[78] The latter two civic bodies were known for setting up honorific portrait statues in the sanctuary at Delphi.[79] Other sources state that Phryne set up the statue herself.[80]

Dedications of portraits and other objects by hetaeras in Greek sanctuaries do not appear to have been particularly uncommon or transgressive in the ancient world. For example, the hetaera Cottina dedicated an *eikonion*, a small portrait of herself, at Sparta.[81] Rhodopis' spits discussed in the last chapter offer an immediate precedent for the practice of hetaeras making prominent dedications in the sanctuary at Delphi.[82] Although Rhodopis' and Phryne's dedications took very different forms,

Phryne's Receptions in Greek Art   105

both functioned as costly memorials to themselves. Rhodopis' monument has more claims to authenticity than most monuments associated with Greek hetaeras if we accept the restoration of Rhodopis' name on a small archaic marble fragment, possibly from around 530 BCE, found built into the walls of a church near the site. The dedication consisted of a pile of iron spits, *obeloi*, representing one-tenth of the hetaera's net worth.[83] Though fragmentary and reworked, the inscribed statue base upon which the objects rested does not contradict the form, size, and appearance of the monument as described by Herodotus.[84] Although we only have the first five letters of the inscription, Mastrokostas offers a convincing restoration, *anetheke Rhodopis*, "Rhodopis dedicated," based on the widespread use of the verb in connection with dedications, the relative rarity of names and other words in Greek beginning *Rho-*, and the presence of hexametric verse.[85] The enduring legacy of Rhodopis' dedication in the northeast area of the Temple of Apollo may have legitimated the placement of Phryne's portrait.

By all accounts, Phryne's portrait statue was physically imposing in its medium, location, and size. It was either fashioned of solid gold or, more likely, of gilded bronze, in contrast to the more common material of marble.[86] Gilding distinguished the portrait from most other monuments in the sanctuary since only three other examples are known before the Hellenistic period, two of which predated Phryne, a gilded portrait Alexander I of Macedon dedicated to himself and another by the sophist Gorgias of Leontini.[87] As Dillon observes, "a gilded portrait of a human subject is an extravagant dedication not only because of the added cost, but also because gilding emulated the precious material that tended to be reserved for statues of the gods."[88] The elevation of the portrait high above the ground on the top of a tall column would have further likened the figure to a divinity, much like a *deus ex machina* at the end of a tragic play, making it clearly visible throughout the sanctuary.[89] The figure was also strategically placed near the entrance to the temple of Apollo, between portraits of two powerful male rulers, also most likely fashioned out of gilded bronze, Archidamus III, king of Sparta, and Philip II, king of Macedon, and not far from Rhodopis' dedication.[90] The statue of Philip II was likely to have been set up between the Third Sacred War (346 BCE) and Philip's death in 336 BCE, a period that overlaps with Praxiteles' attested sculptural activity.[91] The conspicuous location and towering visibility of Phryne's statue lend credence to the theory that it was an honorific portrait statue dedicated by a

106   Phryne of Thespiae

civic body rather than an individual dedication.[92] The inscription on the statue base, "Phryne, daughter of Epicles, of Thespiae," probably further specified the dedicators, beyond their identity as *hoi perictiones*, as well as identifying the sculptor, since Athenaeus includes this information in his account. Importantly, the extant inscription situates the hetaera within a familial context, as the daughter of Epicles, following the dedicatory norms for women discussed previously.[93]

Single dedications made by women, like that of Phryne, were extremely rare and anomalous in the sanctuary at Delphi.[94] Moreover, monuments dedicated by or on behalf of hetaeras were often criticized by ancient writers as an infringement upon male public space. For instance, the hetaera Pythionice's funerary monument, commissioned by her lover, Harpalus, was so visually impressive and strategically situated on the road from Athens to Eleusis that it could have been mistaken as that of an Athenian general or other famous individual.[95] Her memorial was considered transgressive in part because the honor of public commemoration properly belonged to men. The main criticism, however, had to do with the expense of not only the monument but also her lavish funeral procession, which consisted of an enormous chorus and various musical groups.[96] Phryne's monument at Delphi similarly affords the Cynic philosopher Crates to condemn it as an excessive display of wealth and power as well as a symbol of uncontrolled lust: "Look up there and behold among the generals and kings Mnesarete wrought in gold, who, as Crates said, stands as a trophy to the licentiousness of the Greeks."[97] To make this point, moral discourses typically stress the column's height and the costliness of the portrait fashioned out of solid gold rather than gilded bronze, as well as emphasize the similarly expensive and vainglorious portraits of men, and even women that surrounded it, "kings and queens" and important individuals such as Gorgias of Leontini.[98] Phryne's portrait statue at Delphi, I would argue, is problematic not because it commemorates a hetaera or because it occupies sacred space that is properly the province of men, but rather because it embraces and asserts the values of wealth, power, and fame antithetical to Cynic philosophy, regardless of gender. The fact that a woman could indeed plausibly be numbered among such figures is a testament to the extensive material resources, religious and economic agency, and political clout that hetaeras at the upper echelon of Athenian society could wield. They not only dedicated portrait statues and other objects in sanctuaries, but they were also civic benefactors and philanthropists. The Athenian hetaera and *auletris*, Lamia, for instance, is said to have sponsored the construction of a painted colonnade for the city of Sicyon.[99] Not to be outdone, Phryne offered to restore the walls of Thebes destroyed by Alexander the Great on the condition that they included the following inscription, "Alexander tore them down, but the hetaera Phryne built them up again."[100] The walls of Thebes, the Thespian Triad, and the portrait statue at Delphi, identify Phryne as a wealthy and powerful public benefactor who made costly dedications not only to her native city and region but to all Greece in the panhellenic sanctuary of Apollo at Delphi. Examples of benefactions by wealthy hetaeras like Phryne in the literary record may well have influenced, or been inspired by, patterns of female euergetism in the Hellenistic world and beyond, like that of Arsinoe II, who dedicated the Rotunda on Samothrace, and other Ptolemaic queens.

Phryne and the Invention of the Female Nude

Chapter 2 touched briefly upon the subject of female nudity in Attic red-figure vase painting and middle comedy as an index of prostitution, especially in contexts of explicit sexual activity in the symposium and brothel. This section turns to "respectable" or idealized forms of female nudity, in particular, bathing as a pretext for the display the female body and as a prototype for Praxiteles' *Cnidian Aphrodite*. As discussed previously, archaic and classical art usually stresses the modesty of its female subjects through elaborate, multi-colored, and multi-layered garments, from the early *korai* statues of adolescent girls to the fourth-century portrait statues of historical women. Although rare, archaic literary texts allude to erotic but respectable forms of bathing by prenuptial girls and married women. For instance, the adolescent Nausicaa washes her clothing and bathes her body outdoors in the "lovely streams of the river" in preparation for her wedding, while an unnamed pre-nuptial girl in Hesiod's *Works and Days* is also described as bathing and anointing her tender skin indoors during the winter.[101] Preparations for sex frequently involve bathing, as when Hera washes herself before donning the magical *kestos* or sash of Aphrodite in order to seduce her husband Zeus.[102] Bathing and water in particular are associated with Aphrodite, and with sexual activity more generally, beginning with her birth from the sea, her toilette before her sexual encounter with Anchises, and after her adulterous liaison with Ares, when the goddess returns to the Island of Cypris and is bathed and anointed by the Graces.[103] Because washing and intercourse were so connected, archaeological evidence for a brothel from the classical period usually includes ample access to water.[104]

Although these literary scenes do not depict graphic sexual activities, they are undeniably erotic, expressing the irresistible power of female beauty and sexuality. At the same time, they discretely avoid explicit references to the nakedness of these women or their undressing, but rather focus on their elaborate, shimmering garments and intricate, golden jewelry:

> Anchises gazed and took stock of her, wondering at her
> appearance, her stature, and her shining garments; for she
> wore a dress brighter than firelight, and she had twisted
> bracelets and shining ear buds. Round her soft neck there were
> beautiful necklaces of gold, most elaborate, and about her soft
> breasts it shone like the moon, a wonder to behold. Anchises
> was seized by desire.[105]

Here, and in other scenes of dressing and adornment, desire and beauty reside in the material objects—the garments, necklaces, earrings, and other accoutrements—lavished upon the female body and vividly described by the poet. Indeed, references to the physical attributes of women engaged in literary scenes of bathing and seduction are almost entirely absent, with the exception of Aphrodite, whose neck and breasts are repeatedly isolated as characteristics of her beauty.[106] Euripides' plays on this form of erotic viewing when he describes Menelaus' dropping his sword at the sight of Helen of Troy's naked breasts.[107] And the hetaera Theodote, we might recall, also displayed her upper body to admirers, a gesture that was described as a respectable form of erotic display by Xenophon.

In vase painting, bathing scenes featuring naked women of uncertain social status begin to proliferate on Attic pottery during the last three decades of the sixth century, more than half on drinking cups associated with the symposium, and some with overt pornographic intent, along the lines of those discussed in Chapter 2.[108] Such scenes were obviously intended for the male symposiasts who drank from the vessels that these female bathers adorned. But around 430 BCE, the bathing motif underwent a radical change with the introduction of the kneeling female bather, one of the most important figural inventions of the classical period.[109] A faded, red-figure terracotta pyxis dated to circa 420–400 BCE showing the stages of preparations for a wedding offers a good example of this type (Figures 4.2–3). The frieze begins with the bathing of the bride who crouches at left as Eros, the personified deity of desire, empties an amphora filled with water over her head (Figure 4.2). Avoiding full-frontal nudity, the painter depicts the naked torso of the bather, but fully conceals her pubic region. Other women carry ribbons to adorn a large loutrophoros, a ritual vessel containing water for the nuptial bath, and to bind their hair. Inside the house, a woman sits with an Eros on her lap while a crowned, and clothed, Aphrodite and an attendant look on (see Figure 4.3 drawing). The kneeling bather motif quickly enters the visual repertoire of nuptial vases, unambiguously defining its subjects as respectable by the presence of wedding accoutrements and of divinities associated with love, desire, and female beauty, such as Eros, Pothos, Aphrodite, and Eucleia, as, for example, portrayed on a red-figure lekythos attributed to the Shuvalov Painter in the Hermitage Museum.[110] Significantly, these representations reached a new, female audience, more frequently decorating pots used by women such as cosmetic jars, *epinetra* for working wool, and nuptial shapes, rather than sympotic ware.[111] According to Robert Sutton, the classical kneeling bather represented on these and other vases points to a "transformation of the naked bather into a noble heroic or divine nude, even as she remains powerfully erotic, bathed by Eros himself."[112] The motif further indicates a new conceptualization of the nude female body as a source of aesthetic beauty rivaling that of the male body in art, foreshadowing Praxiteles' creation of the *Cnidian Aphrodite* and other female nudes. And because these are nuptial vases, they demonstrate the integral role of Aphrodite in instilling beauty and sexual allure in women, whether brides or hetaeras.

Around the time the kneeling female bather begins to appear in Attic vase painting, we find the earliest reference to a hetaera serving as the model for a work of art. As examined in the previous chapter, when Socrates visits Theodote at her residence, he finds her posing for a portrait by one of a steady stream of artists who regularly sought to render her likeness.[113] The use of live models seems to have coincided not only with a new interest in the respectable female nude, but also with a turn to portraiture more generally, especially of women in both painting and sculpture. Socrates for instance comments that he prefers

FIGURE 4.2 Red-figure pyxis with nuptial scene, c. 420–400 BCE. New York, Metropolitan Museum, 1972.118.148.

FIGURE 4.3 Drawing of the frieze decorating the red-figure pyxis in Figure 4.2. New York, Metropolitan Museum.

Phryne's Receptions in Greek Art 111

to contemplate the virtues of a living woman over a painted one, not even if "Zeuxis showed me a portrait of a beautiful woman painted by his own hand."[114] Very little reliable information on the Greek painter Zeuxis has survived, and most of it is late.[115] He worked throughout the Greek world, arriving in Athens as a youth in the late 430s and early 420s.[116] Although none of his work is extant, he was known in antiquity for his paintings of women, above all for his famous nude rendering of Helen of Troy.[117] According to ancient accounts, Zeuxis chose as models for his Helen not one beautiful adolescent girl, but five, incorporating the best features of each, "so that true beauty may be transferred from the living model to the mute likeness."[118] The story of Zeuxis' rendering of Helen later became a favorite motif among classical history painters from Angelica Kauffmann onward, who interpreted it as a statement about the relationship of art, and nature, as very briefly touched upon in the introduction. In contrast to Polycleitus, who believed ideal artistic forms derived from numerical proportions, Zeuxis reimagined the figure of Helen through direct observations of living models.[119] According to Valerius Maximus and Aristides, the painter inscribed two famous lines from the *Iliad* as an epigram to the painting, "Surely there is no blame on Trojans and strong-greaved Achaians if for a long time they suffer hardship for a woman like this one."[120] These lines both identify the subject of the painting as Helen as well as inviting the viewer to contemplate the image as an idealized depiction of female beauty and a serious piece of art. Unlike earlier images of female nakedness, such as Cassandra at the altar (Figure 2.3), Zeuxis' nude Helen is not a figure of pathos, nor does her lack of clothing convey violation and transgression, but rather represents "a noble display of female beauty."[121] The painting, in Sutton's view, probably led to a "revolutionary redefinition" of the female nude in Greek art, influencing the development of the kneeling female bather beginning around 425 BCE, and opening the way for the convention of female nudity and semi-nudity in the fourth century.[122] This form of idealized female beauty became fused with the figure of the hetaera as illustrated by Aelian's comment that the painting later became known as *The Hetaera* because Zeuxis charged a fee for viewing it.[123]

Numerous post-classical sources, foremost among them Pliny the Elder, similarly depict hetaeras as the models for famous painters. Pausias (c. mid-fourth cent. BCE) painted a portrait of his lover and fellow resident of Sicyon, Glycera.[124] The Theban painter Aristides the Younger (c. fourth cent. BCE) created a famous image of Leontion, the hetaera associated with Epicurus.[125] As discussed in the introduction, Apelles fell in love with the mistress of Alexander the Great, Pancaspe/Campaspe, while painting her portrait, as well as drawing inspiration from the sight of a young Lais drawing water from the Peirene spring in Corinth.[126] Although this evidence is late, the material from Xenophon suggests that a close connection had already been forged between the emergent genre of portrait painting, the development of the heroic female nude, and the use of living women as models, particularly hetaeras, in the early fourth-century imaginary, inaugurating a tradition that would become elaborated and romanticized by later authors.

By the time of Athenaeus, Phryne's mythology incorporates aspects of the fourth-century culture of erotic viewing, artistic mimesis, and idealized female nudity, as well as reflecting later discourse about hetaeras as models for famous art works. Like Theodote, Phryne is portrayed as following conventions of respectable female nudity, hiding from view the lower, and inappropriate, part of her body, and controlling when and how men could see her:

> The parts of Phryne's body that were not seen were actually
> the most beautiful. As a consequence, it was not easy to get a
> glimpse of her naked, because she used to wear a tunic that
> clung to her body, and avoided the public baths.[127]

Phryne purportedly only displayed her fully nude body before the assembled Greeks at the Eleusinia and the Posidonia, two festivals that may have been associated with hetaeras and famously combined in Siemiradzki's painting, *Phryne at the Posidonia in Eleusis*, as discussed in the introduction:

> But at the Eleusinia and the Posidonia festivals, with all the
> Greeks watching, she took off her robe, let down her hair,
> and entered the sea; Apelles drew the inspiration for his
> Anadyomene (Aphrodite Rising from the Sea) from her. So too
> the sculptor Praxiteles, who was in love with her, used her as
> the model for his Cnidian Aphrodite. (Ath. 590f–591a)

Not to be confused with the more famous Eleusinian mysteries held in honor of Demeter, the Eleusinia was a festival of games that featured athletic and music competitions and was second only to the Panathenaea in importance. Little is known about the Posidonia festival held on the island of Aegina other than that it may have been associated with hetaeras since Aristippus is said to have spent two months there annually attending the festival with the hetaera Lais. [128] To return to Phryne, waiting for the moment when her entrance would have commanded the most attention, the hetaera enacts Aphrodite's birth from the sea, recalling the image of the goddess on the Ludovisi throne examined in the last chapter (Figure 3.1). This part of Athenaeus' account follows post-classical narratives surrounding the Cnidia that identified Phryne as the preferred model among fourth-century Greek painters who used the hetaera "in her bloom" for their images of Aphrodite.[129]

The most famous ancient painting associated with Phryne was Apelles' Anadyomene. Although it was well known by the time of the early Roman Empire, the original work has not survived, nor is it mentioned in extant fourth- or third-century BCE literary sources.[130] Much of our knowledge about Apelles, active around 300 BCE, comes from Pliny, who praises his paintings for their charm and realism and states that he surpassed all ancient Greek painters before and after him, not only because of his artistic productivity but also for his theoretical writings on painting.[131] The Anadyomene was so renowned that the emperor Augustus removed it from the island of Cos and shipped it to Rome, where he dedicated it to the divine Julius Caesar, although he makes Pancaspe/Campaspe instead of Phryne the model for this painting.[132] A mural from a villa in Pompeii (Figure 4.4) is probably based on this painting, attesting both to its popularity among the Romans as well as its subsequent influence on Western art as the inspiration for Botticelli's *Birth of Venus*. Phryne's identification with Apelles' Anadyomene is likely the product of the same literary revival advanced by dedicatory epigrams that immortalized Praxiteles' *Cnidian Aphrodite* and conflated statue, goddess, and mortal woman.[133] Indeed, the work inspired an epigram by Antipater of Sidon:

> Look on the work of Apelles' brush: Cypris, just rising from
> the sea, her mother; how, grasping her dripping hair with her
> hand, she wrings the foam from the wet locks. Athena and
> Hera themselves will now say, "No longer do we enter the
> contest of beauty with you."[134]

As described by the epigram, the image bears the traces of fourth-century conventions of heroic female nudity, conveying the beauty

114   Phryne of Thespiae

FIGURE 4.4 Fresco featuring a Roman version of the Aphrodite Anadyomene motif, first century CE, House of Venus, Pompeii. Adam Harangozó.

and erotic power of the female subject at her bath. As Pliny himself observes, by his time the Anadyomene has become "eclipsed, yet made famous by the Greek verses which sing its praises."[135] Whereas Phryne's dedications attest to her prestige and economic agency both in her native city of Thespiae and throughout Hellas, her association with painted and plastic representations of Aphrodite stresses the provocative sexual power of the hetaera as her mortal embodiment, a point that comes to bear on her notorious trial, as we shall see in the next chapter.

Phryne and the Cnidian Aphrodite

Despite the possibility that Phryne, if she actually existed, could have known Praxiteles and even served as his model, as Corso has argued, her ancient receptions must be viewed as literary fantasies generated by celebrated artworks familiar to Greek and Roman readers and tourists alike, most of which were associated with Aphrodite.[136] The narratives explored in this chapter repeatedly link Phryne to well-known images of the goddess, as the inspiration for Apelles' Anadyomene, in the Thespian triad that triangulates her with Eros and Aphrodite, at Delphi, where at least one source states that she dedicated a golden statue of the deity rather than a self-portrait, and as the model for an unattested statue of Cypris at Sparta. As an artistic precedent, Praxiteles may have modeled the Cnidia on his earlier representation of a half-draped Aphrodite at Thespiae, which has survived only through extant copies of the Arles Aphrodite (Figure 4.1), and may have been inspired by Zeuxis' famous painting of the nude Helen and the kneeling bather motif it inspired.[137] This discourse most likely generated the conflation of Phryne with the statue of Aphrodite of Cnidos found in Athenaeus as well as underlying the joke he records that she was "Praxiteles' little Aphrodite."[138] The fourth-century interest in rendering the idealized female form, embodied by the figure of Aphrodite (whether in painted portraits and statue dedications of women), the use of living models (many of them hetaeras), and the introduction of heroic female nudity in red-figure vase painting are among the cultural forces that seem to have influenced Praxiteles' creation of the monumental sculpture Aphrodite of Cnidos (c. 364–1 BCE; Figure 4.5), one of the most viewed statues in all of antiquity.[139]

According to Pliny, Praxiteles originally created two statues of the goddess for the art market, one draped, as was customary in Greek art of the period, and the other completely unclothed.[140] Coincidentally, Cos, the same city that commissioned the Anadyomene, chose the clothed version "as the only decent and dignified course of action," while the Cnidians purchased the shocking nude version of the statue, which ultimately made the city famous. The figure was placed in the center of an open, colonnaded building, high on a cliff at Cnidos, with a commanding view of the sea, allowing visitors to view it from all sides.[141]

> The shrine in which it stands is entirely open so as to allow
> the image of the goddess to be viewed from every side, and
> it is believed to have been made in this way with the blessing
> of the goddess herself. The statue is equally admirable from
> every angle. There is a story that a man once fell in love with it
> and hiding by night embraced it, and that a stain betrays this
> lustful act.[142]

In a more detailed account of the man who had sex with the Cnidia, an Athenian tourist, eager to get to Thespiae and see the homoerotic Eros, concludes that he must have been making love to a boy, from behind, because the blemish was located at the back of the statue, allowing him to avoid the female parts.[143] Although Pliny and pseudo-Lucian stress the erotic effect of the statue on her male viewers, whether their preferences were for women or men, Havelock argues that fourth-century Greeks would have perceived the statue as an object that inspired religious awe rather than lust, meant to be viewed in the round, like a votive offering encouraging viewers to experience the sculpture as a form of divine epiphany.[144] According to Larissa Bonfante, the full frontal nudity of ancient Near Eastern goddesses such as Astarte and Ishtar and the Greco-Roman Aphrodite and Venus signifies fertility, fecundity, and power, rather than immorality and disgrace.[145] As with Phryne's public display of her body at the Eleusinia, Posidonia, and in the Attic law court, Aphrodite's statue at Cnidos perhaps invited a form of sacred viewing appropriate to a powerful goddess of female beauty, sexuality, and eroticism.

Not only did Praxiteles introduce the female nude as a subject in art, his work inspired countless variations of the goddess that were in turn adopted by the Romans and then disseminated far and wide.[146] Although the original Aphrodite of Cnidos has not survived, these copies, both large and small, of clay, bronze, and stone, were found all over the Mediterranean world, while images of the goddess persisted on Roman coins into the third century CE, inspiring artists of Renaissance Italy and northern Europe.[147] Because these replicas are so divergent, it is difficult to reconstruct the exact features of the original statue, although they are divided into two categories: the Belvedere, which most closely resembles the figure on Cnidian coins, and the Colonna.[148] Coins struck by the emperor Caracalla and his wife Plautilla (211–18 BCE) bearing the image of the original Aphrodite provide the most reliable evidence for her pose, as seen in the drawing below (Figure 4.6). As the marble figure shows (Figure 4.5), the sculptor borrowed earlier conventions of idealizing, heroic nudity in his representation of the goddess: she is depicted at her bath, clutching a garment that she has just removed, which falls gently down her left side, coming to rest on a vessel that presumably contains water for her bath, like the hydria Eros holds over the bather in Figure 4.2. Although her breasts are fully exposed, she modestly covers her pubic region with her right hand, as she turns her head to the left, averting her gaze in another gesture of modesty. According to Pliny, the statue was so realistically painted that it produced the illusion that the goddess was almost a real woman. Praxiteles may have

FIGURE 4.5 Restored Roman copy of Praxiteles' Aphrodite of Cnidos, c. fourth century BCE. Rome, Museo nazionale romano di palazzo Altemps, Inv. 8619.

FIGURE 4.6 Engraving of a Roman coin featuring a version of the Cnidian Aphrodite from Paul Carus, *Venus of Milo: An Archaeological Study of the Goddess of Womanhood*. Chicago and London: Open Court Publishing, 1916, p. 162.

collaborated with the Athenian painter, Nicias, another artist known for his detailed portraits of women.[149]

Although not mentioned in any extant contemporary source and ignored or unknown to philosophers, dramatists, and poets of the fourth century and early Hellenistic period, the statue became the subject of numerous poems and literary accounts, but only in late Greek antiquity.[150] The first securely dated literary reference is that of Cicero around 70 BCE, but most are found almost two hundred years later among the same authors that reference Phryne, such as Pliny, Pausanias, Lucian, and Athenaeus.[151] In the view of Havelock, there appears a "new and intense interest" in Praxiteles' statue around 100 BCE as travel throughout the Mediterranean increased under Roman expansion. The rediscovery of another Aphrodite sculpture with the same distinctive hand gesture, the right hand covering her pubic area, dedicated on the island of Delos as part of a sculpture group together with Pan and Eros (150–100 BCE), perhaps also made by Praxiteles, may have

Phryne's Receptions in Greek Art   119

further contributed to the widespread popularity of the Cnidia during this period.[152] Like the Eros, the sculpture soon became a subject for the epigrammatists, eleven of which are extant.[153] Significantly, none of these poems make any reference to Phryne; the only possible connection occurs in one by Antipater of Sidon (second cent. BCE) that references the Thespian Eros:

> You will say, when you look on Cypris in rocky Cnidus, that
> she, though of stone, may set a stone on fire; but when you see
> the sweet Love in Thespiae you will say that he will not only
> set fire to a stone, but to cold adamant. Such were the gods
> Praxiteles made, each in a different continent, that everything
> should not be burnt up by the double fire.[154]

If a tradition linking the hetaera and statue had already been established by this period, it seems that the poet would have referred to it. Several other epigrams imagine the deity traveling to Cnidos to view her image and her surprise at the accuracy of Praxiteles' representation, reiterating the question, "Where did Praxiteles see me naked?":

> Paphian Cytherea came through the waves to Cnidus, wishing
> to see her own image, and having viewed it from all sides in its
> open shrine, she cried, "Where did Praxiteles see me naked?"
> Praxiteles did not look on forbidden things, but the steel
> carved the Paphian as Ares would have her.[155]

The question plays on the history of female bathers in Greek literature and art, in which the male viewer gazes at what he should not while at the same time gesturing to the modesty of the female subject, who does not wittingly allow herself to be seen. Praxiteles, the epigram concludes, does not actually view what is not right, but rather his chisel does.[156] Alciphron borrows from the epigram the motif of the subject viewing her own statue in the fictional letter addressed from Phryne to Praxiteles, discussed in the previous and next chapter, that conflates the more famous statue of Aphrodite at Cnidos with the image of Phryne at Thespiae, but does not directly identify her with the Cnidia. The statue is mentioned in two of the longest and most complete discussions of a single art object in ancient literature, one by Pliny and the other by pseudo-Lucian, as follows:[157]

120   Phryne of Thespiae

In the midst [of the temple] sits the goddess—she's a most
beautiful statue of Parian marble—arrogantly smiling a little as
a grin parts her lips. Draped by no garment, all her beauty is
uncovered and revealed, except in so far as she unobtrusively
uses one hand to hide her private parts. So great was the power
of the craftsman's art that the hard unyielding marble did
justice to every limb.[158]

This extensive account nowhere mentions Phryne as the subject or
model of the Aphrodite at Cnidos but does bring up Thespiae as the
home of the other most famous statue of Praxiteles worth seeing and
as examples of two sexual polarities, heterosexual and homoerotic love.
The only distinguishing facial characteristic, her smile, recalls both
Sappho fr. 1, in which the goddess smiles as she addresses the poet,
and Praxiteles' portrait of Phryne as the Happy Hetaera.[159] These details
further support the view that Phryne's association with the statue of
Aphrodite at Cnidos was a late fiction with little basis in reality, other
than that she had been a well-known figure in late classical Athens, the
subject of portraits by the artist, and part of his longstanding identification with Thespiae.

Conclusion

This chapter explored the authenticity and meaning of artworks
connected with Phryne, particularly Praxiteles' three portrait statues of
the hetaera, the Thespian Phryne, the Happy Hetaera, and her image
at Delphi, as well her dedication of the Eros at Thespiae. It further
considered her various links to other representations of Aphrodite, including Apelles' Anadyomene and a lost Spartan statue of the goddess.
Based on parallels with female portraits dedicated in Greek sanctuaries
and extant statue basis, the chapter argues that Praxiteles plausibly
could have created Phryne's portrait statues at Thespiae and Delphi, and
that the hetaera could have made these dedications on behalf of herself. From the fourth century onward, they became important public
monuments much sought after by Greek and Roman tourists, who
traveled to the hetaera's native city to marvel at the famous Eros and to
Delphi to look up at her gilded portrait surrounded by images of famous
men and not far from Rhodopis' dedication. The enduring presence of

her monuments in these sanctuaries allowed Phryne to be later written into the history of Greek art objects, votive dedications, and important sacred and urban spaces.

From these sources, the picture of Phryne that emerges is of an independent, influential, and enormously wealthy hetaera who made costly gifts to her native city, region, and panhellenic Greece as a public benefactor. But as time elapsed, the historical basis of her narrative gradually became erased and subsumed by a process of literary embellishment, invention, and fantasy, probably around 100 BCE, as the fame of Praxiteles and the *Cnidian Aphrodite* began to circulate throughout the ancient Mediterranean world. Genres such as epigram and epistolary fiction were instrumental in inventively reading into the Eros of Thespiae a romance between Phryne and Praxiteles, and eliding or conflating her with Aphrodite, ultimately leading Athenaeus, or his source, to claim that the sculptor based his Cnidia on her. The late tradition linking Phryne to the Anadyomene and the Cnidia was thus reverse engineered to suit imperial literary tastes that incorporated a nostalgia for fourth-century Athens with an interest in heterosexual love and famous Greek artworks. The proliferation of stories that developed around the statues of Phryne and her dedications very likely influenced subsequent accounts of her notorious trial, the subject of the next chapter.

122   Phryne of Thespiae

5

The Prosecution of Phryne

When Hyperides accomplished nothing, and the jurors
seemed likely to convict Phryne, he brought the woman out
in public, and after tearing off her garments and exposing her
naked breasts, he concluded his speech with piteous wailing at
the sight of her, causing the jurors to feel a superstitious fear
of this interpreter and temple-attendant of Aphrodite, and to
yield to pity rather than put her to death. Afterward, when she
had been acquitted, a decree was passed to the effect that no
speaker was to lament on another person's behalf, and that no
accused man or women was to be put on display while their
case was being decided.[1]

We turn now to the most important strand of Phryne's biography, her
notorious trial for *asebeia* ("impiety"), and her instant acquittal brought
about by the spectacle of her naked body, as recounted by Athenaeus
above, and famously re-imagined centuries later by Jean-Léon Gérôme
(Figure I.1). This memorable event introduces and frames the subject of
her public nudity at the Eleusinia and Posidonia as the inspiration for
Apelles' Anadyomene and Praxiteles' *Cnidian Aphrodite*, and her dedication of the Eros at Thespiae.[2] Athenaeus' framework indicates how
the fourth-century narrative of Phryne's trial, probably the most reliable
strand of her biography, gradually became closely intertwined with her
artistic receptions not only in antiquity but also in the post-classical period as explored in the introduction.[3] According to ancient accounts,
the charges were brought against Phryne by a former lover, the orator
Euthias, while her current lover, the orator Hyperides, came to her
rescue and defended her. The two speeches, defense and prosecution,

Phryne of Thespiae. Laura McClure, Oxford University Press. © Oxford University Press 2024.
DOI: 10.1093/9780197580882.003.0006

were well known in antiquity and preserved into the Byzantine period. This chapter argues first for the historical authenticity of the trial by examining parallels of litigation involving women in forensic oratory, the legal meaning of *asebeia*, and examples of this type of trial, mostly famously that of Socrates, and the cultural mindset of suspicion that fostered this type of allegation during the fourth century. New forms of worship, whether informal *thiasoi*, bands of worshippers that sang and danced in honor of traditional gods, or foreign ecstatic cults, many associated with women, may have motivated the charges against Phryne. By situating the disrobing within fourth-century Athenian legal and religious practices together with a close reading of Athenaeus' language, I show that the disrobing had multiple cultural associations from the late classical to Second Sophistic period, suggesting its original intent was not erotic but rather a form of emotional appeal intended to elicit sympathy in the jurors. To this narrative, Athenaeus adds the language of sacred viewing used to describe encounters with the *Cnidian Aphrodite* and Phryne's Thespian statue by pseudo-Lucian and Alciphron respectively to evoke the powerful erotic effect of encounters with images of female divinity.

Women and the Athenian Legal System

To understand the historical significance of Phryne, it is necessary to examine first the Athenian legal system and the ways in which women intersected with it. The exercise of political rights, whether participating in the assembly, holding political office, or serving on a jury, were the exclusive domain of adult citizen males over the age of thirty in the classical polis. The cornerstone of Athenian democracy were the popular courts, the *dikasteria*, which heard the majority of trials from the fifth century onward, with the exception of homicide, intentional wounding, and offenses against sacred olive trees.[4] At the beginning of each year, the state empaneled a pool of 6,000 volunteer jurors who swore an oath to vote in accordance with the laws and decrees of the Athenian council.[5] By the fourth century, jurors in the popular courts received three obols, or the equivalent of a day's pay for a manual laborer working on the Athenian acropolis in the years 409 to 407 BCE, or the price of a low-end sex worker.[6] Those who presented themselves for selection as jurors were randomly allotted to trials, with the size between 201 to 501 members, depending on the type of case.[7] The legal process was overseen by a chief magistrate, known as an archon, from a board of nine, who held preliminary hearings, assigned cases to law courts, and formally presided over trials, although did not vote on them.[8]

Athenian law distinguished between a public offense, or *graphe*, which could be prosecuted by any willing adult male or in some cases metic, and a private case, or *dike*, that could be undertaken only by a party to the suit.[9] In a major public suit, like that of Phryne, juries could number into the thousands. Another distinguishing feature of a public litigation was that the potential penalty that the prosecutor could incur if he secured less than 20 percent of the jurors' votes or dropped the case before it went to trial, a fine of one thousand drachmas and sometimes a ban on any further public litigation. The purpose was to discourage sycophancy, the introduction of malicious or baseless claims at trial to damage a personal enemy or to extort payment for dropping the charges.[10] Public lawsuits lasted an entire day, allowing each litigant to deliver one lengthy speech, starting with the prosecution. Immediately after, without any deliberations, the jury voted by secret ballot with the outcome determined by a simple majority.[11] In both types of trials, litigants were responsible for providing evidence, determining the legal violations, deciding on the charges, and summoning witnesses.

To initiate a procedure, the prosecutor needed to determine the appropriate magistrate and then issue an oral summons to the defendant and, in the presence of one or more witnesses, to appear before the relevant magistrate at a specified date and time, before the case proceeded to court.[12] At the meeting, the prosecutor presented a written statement of the charge, and the magistrate determined whether he could proceed and scheduled a preliminary hearing. There the defendant submitted a written response, and each litigant swore an oath attesting the veracity of their statements, at which point the case went either to arbitration or to trial. In the case of the latter, a public notice stating the charge, the penalty, a sworn denial, and the date, time, and location of the proceeding was posted in the agora on the railings of the enclosure around the Eponymous Heroes of Athens.[13] In the fifth and fourth centuries, most of these cases were tried in the popular courts, also located near the agora. The magistrate who heard the initial pleading presided over the trial, not as a judge but rather in the capacity of an administrator. All upcoming cases and the individuals they involved thus would have been widely known to the general public. Moreover, the final verdict would have been entirely dependent on the reaction of the individual jurors to the speeches set before him rather than from group deliberation, meaning that any surprise maneuver, like Phryne's disrobing, would have had an immediate impact on the decision.

The role of women in the male domain of law was obviously limited. Women could not directly initiate legal proceedings, speak in court either as witnesses or litigants (not even on their own behalf), or sit on a jury.[14] Despite these limitations, forensic speeches depict citizen and metic women interacting with the legal system surprisingly often during the fourth century, both as subjects and objects and in a number of ways.[15] Although rare, they could be prosecuted for a crime, as in the case of Neaera, but had to rely on male representatives to defend them in court, whether by their *kyrios*, or *prostates* in the case of a metic, in a private suit and by any interested adult male citizen in a public case.[16] A woman could also work behind the scenes to protect her family, rights, and property through a male representative, as in the case of Cleoboule, the mother of Demosthenes, who seems to have instigated a prosecution to recover his patrimony from his dishonest guardians. [17] She could also indirectly bring charges by making a complaint to the relevant magistrate or by giving evidence before an arbitrator.[18] Although women could not act as witnesses, a speaker could have them swear in a pretrial oath and then informally insert their testimony into the narrative.[19] A defendant's female kin along with his children might even occasionally appear in court as a rhetorical device to arouse pity in the jurors and win acquittal, as will be discussed more fully later.[20]

Among the extant fourth-century forensic speeches and their fragmentary remains, Kapparis has identified twenty-eight trials involving female litigants, whether citizen women, metics, or hetaeras.[21] Since orators went to great lengths to avoid naming respectable women in their speeches, as we have seen, it is highly likely that titles referring to women by the names of their male relations indicate their status as citizen women. Whereas cases involving men frequently centered on homicide, wounding, battery, and sexual offenses, such as seduction and rape, those related to women mainly revolved around disputes over social status, dowries, and inheritance. One type of case concerned the transmission of patrimonial property to a daughter or daughters in the absence of sons, known as an *epikleros*, a term that means "transferred with the estate." After her father's death, the *epikleros* was subject to the guardianship of his closest male relative who could claim her hand in

126   Phryne of Thespiae

marriage and then manage the estate until a son born to them survived two years beyond puberty, at which point he inherited the estate.[22] Examples include Isaeus 3, *On the Estate of Pyrrhos*, an inheritance dispute between the sister of the deceased Pyrrhos, the adoptive father of her son, and his *epikleros* daughter, as well as Lysias 32, *Against Diogeiton*, also an inheritance matter in which a widowed *epikleros* attempts to defend her property interests on behalf of her children.[23] The transmission of maternal wealth in the form of a dowry could also be a source of conflict, as in Demosthenes' *Against Boeotos II: Regarding His Mother's Dowry*. In this bitter and protracted legal battle about claims to the estate of the wealthy Athenian, Mantias of Cholargus, his son, Mantitheus, demands that his half brothers repay his mother's dowry. They counter with the claim that their own mother, Plangon, brought to the household an unusually large dowry in excess of one hundred minas, while his mother contributed nothing (Dem. 40.20–21). These cases illustrate how pivotal a role wealthy citizen women played in legal dramas because of their ability to transmit property and their connection to large assets in the form of dowries, even though they could not directly own property or engage in large commercial transactions.

Free women could also be subjected to religious prosecution, as evidenced by two other trials, [Dinarchus], *Dispute between the Priestess of Demeter and the Priest*, and Lycurgus, *On the Priestess*, about which next to nothing is known.[24] A handful of cases prosecute women for acts of violence and even homicide. In one extraordinary speech, Lysias, *On the Abortion*, a husband alleges that his wife committed homicide by inducing a pharmaceutical abortion, thereby depriving him of fatherhood.[25] The argument, that a fetus should be considered a living human being prior to birth, or what today is known as fetal personhood, seems to have been a novel one in the Athenian courtroom. In Antiphon's *Against the Stepmother for Poisoning*, the only homicide case brought against a woman in extant Attic oratory, the defendant, the prosecutor's stepmother, stands accused of lethally poisoning the victim, her husband, with the help of a female slave, who had already been tried and executed. The prosecutor is the victim's son and stepson of the defendant, who is represented by her two sons, the speaker's half brothers.[26] From these examples, it is clear that Athenian citizen women could be active parties in private lawsuits, mainly in questions of inheritance, but also in religious matters, and even violent crimes, although they remained anonymous and were compelled to work behind the scenes through male intermediaries.

Among the cases discussed by Kapparis, a remarkable number feature hetaeras and free metic women as plaintiffs and defendants. This simple but important fact underscores that the prosecution of such women was not an uncommon phenomenon in fourth-century Athens, meaning that Phryne's trial would not have been anomalous and could have plausibly occurred.[27] Because they could not lawfully marry male citizens and bear legitimate children, hetaeras were not subject to litigation related to dowries or property transmission, in contrast to citizen wives and daughters. Rather charges against them focused most frequently on citizenship and immigration violations, and, occasionally, religious offenses, all of which were felt to threaten the stability and integrity of the polis. The two most important cases involving hetaeras and other types of prostitutes that have survived from antiquity include [Dem.] 59, *Against Neaera*, a speech that has been critical to this study across all chapters, and Aeschines 1, *Against Timarchus*, the prosecution of an important Athenian politician on charges of debauchery and sex for pay. As we have seen, the main charge against Neaera was not that she had sold her body, but rather that she had falsely passed herself off as the lawful wife of a citizen man and as the mother of legitimate children, although an alien.[28] If convicted, metics like Neaera who disguised their status, failed to pay the metic tax, or lived with a citizen as a spouse faced enslavement. But Neaera's profession as a hetaera was not a criminal offense. Aeschines' *Against Timarchus* shows us that a male citizen could suffer grave consequences if convicted on a *graphe hetaireseos*, or charge of prostitution, for which the penalty was political disenfranchisement. Such a man could not participate in the assembly, hold political office, speak in the law court, or serve on a jury. He was further barred from entering the agora and all sacred spaces.[29]

Another common type of indictment involving hetaeras and female metics involved immigration violations, known as a *graphe aprostasiou*, a process employed for the prosecution of metics living in Attica who failed to register with the state, procure a sponsor, or pay the requisite tax. The Corinthian hetaera Aristagora may have suffered such a fate, judging by Hyperides' pair of speeches, *Against Aristagora*, which most likely arose in response to a *graphe aprostasiou*. Aristagora, along with Myrrhine, Phila, and Phryne, was one of several hetaeras kept by Hyperides and lodged in various parts of Attica.[30] In the second version of the speech,

128   Phryne of Thespiae

Aristagora appears together with several other famous, fourth-century hetaeras, "Hyperides also mentioned [Ocimon] in the second speech *Against Aristagora* saying the following: 'Lais who appeared to be the most beautiful woman ever, and Ocimon and Metaneira.'"[31] Elsewhere we hear of two sister hetaeras, Anthis and Stagion, nicknamed Aphyai ("Sardines"), because they were pale and thin, and had large, dark eyes.[32] References to contemporary hetaeras in prosecutions of their peers may have been a common topos designed to establish a rapport between the speaker and the jurors, who would have been familiar with such women and possibly had even patronized them.[33] For instance, Apollodorus mentions Anteia, Stratola, Aristocleia, Phila, and Isthmia as the companions of Neaera at Nicarete's house, while Lysias in his lost speech, *To/Against Lais*, evokes a similar circle of hetaeras, including Philyra, Scione, Hippaphesis, Theocleia, Psamathe, Lagisca, Anteia, and Aristocleia.[34] Such allusions could have been used to prove a woman's status as a hetaera by association. Other immigration cases that may have involved hetaeras include Hyperides, *Against Demetria*, and Dinarchus, *Against Hedyle*, although we have no information about either woman.[35] Very little is known about other cases probably associated with hetaeras based on explicit references to their names, including Lysias, *To/Against Lais* and *For Nichomache*, and Hyperides, *In Defense of Mica* and *To Timandra*.[36] The involvement of Hyperides in a significant number of these cases may suggest that hetaera trials may have been something of specialty for the orator or simply reflect his reputation for philandering.

One last case involving a hetaera deserves special mention. Lysias, *Against Philonides for Rape*, is our only example of the prosecution of a man for a crime of sexual violence against a woman to have survived from classical Athens.[37] The largest fragment is preserved by Athenaeus:

> Lysias in the speech *Against Philonides for Rape*, if it is
> authentic, says that this Nais had been a mistress of Philonides
> in these words: There is a woman, a hetaera, called Nais, whose
> *kyrios* or guardian is Archias, while Hymenaius is her friend,
> and Philonides claims that he is in love with her.[38]

Despite the confusion between Lais and Nais in the manuscript tradition, Attic old comedy, a genre famous for allusions to contemporary individuals and events, mentions a woman by that name involved in an affair with Philonides: "Isn't Nais in love with Philonides

The Prosecution of Phryne   129

because of you?."[39] Nais is also mentioned in Lysias, *Against Medon*, in Aristophanes' lost play, *Gerytades*, and as a toothless old woman in the *Huntress* by the middle-comic poet, Philaeterus (c. mid-fourth cent. BCE).[40] Philonides is possibly Philonides of Melite, the father of Onetor, one of Demosthenes' guardians, who was born around 420 and died around 366 BCE.[41] He was frequently the butt of comic invective, mocked for his large size, sexual excess, and boorishness.[42] Whatever the underlying motives for these proceedings, they attest to the widespread presence of hetaeras and other non-citizen women in the Athenian legal system not only as defendants, like Neaera, but also as plaintiffs protected under law from the violation of their bodies. Such women and their contemporaries were clearly historical figures well known to the Athenian jurors, whose unusual activities and lack of conformance to citizen norms may have aroused suspicion, rendering them vulnerable targets of legal abuse or vehicles of political retaliation.

The Graphe Asebeias

We turn now to the last type of indictment on a public charge involving hetaeras, the *graphe asebeias*.[43] Although no precise legal definition of the term exists, the wide variety of attested prosecutions for impiety suggest that it generally refers to the neglect of sacred duties or improper ritual conduct, and/or lack of reverence toward and profanation of sacred spaces, monuments, religious festivals, and rituals.[44] It also concerns violations against the dead, parents, or the fatherland.[45] Examples include "wrongdoing concerning a festival," temple robbery, "theft of sacred money," and offenses against sacred olive trees.[46] The variety of offenses covered by *asebeia* suggests that it was clearly an extremely fluid and capacious charge that in part reflects the nature of Athenian legal system that offered litigants flexibility in the interpretation of law and the procedure adopted. It further indicates a widespread concern with the protection and conservation of traditional ritual activity, much of which fell under the control of women.[47] Sacred transgressions such as the worship of new gods not approved by the Athenian state or the profanation of the Eleusinian Mysteries, secret rites in honor of Demeter and Persephone, were perceived to endanger the well-being of the entire city.[48] Profanation of mysteries thus frequently appears in connection with impiety trials, starting with the scandal of the herms in the summer of 415 BCE, during preparations for the Athenian invasion of Sicily. On the nights of June 6/7, the vast majority of the city's herms (rectangular blocks of stone topped with the head of the god Hermes and bearing an erect phallus in the middle) that stood before houses and temples suffered mutilation, to both faces and genitalia.[49] The ensuing investigation further revealed that the Eleusinian Mysteries had also been profaned. Based on testimony in the herms proceedings, the general and politician Alcibiades (c. 450–404 BCE), and the lover of the hetaeras Timandra and Theodote (Ath. 535c), was charged with parodying the Mysteries by a sacrilegious private performance of their secret rites, probably at a symposium.[50] These two trials were well attested in contemporary sources such as Thucydides and Xenophon, both of whom use cognates of *asebeia* in reference to this crime.[51] The charges in both cases were originated by individuals, Pythonicus and Diocleides, and sent to the popular courts, suggesting they were public *graphai*. All of this came about as a result of denunciations made by citizens, metics, and slaves, and most of those convicted were sentenced to death and their property confiscated.[52] The orator Andocides (c. 440–post-391 BCE) was also implicated in the scandal: he was arrested, imprisoned, and released once he agreed to serve as an informer in exchange for immunity.[53] Fifteen years later (c. 399 or 400), he was prosecuted again for violating a decree introduced by Isotimides in 415 that prohibited an individual who had admitted to committing impiety from entering sacred spaces, a crime punishable by death.[54] Andocides' trials illustrate several types of *asebeia* that the Athenians found dangerous to the public and worthy of prosecution: the defacing of sacred objects, the exposure of religious secrets in a secular place, and the transgression of sacred space.[55] Other attested cases of impiety, most of which involved men, indicate the range of potentially impious acts and the variety of procedures available to address them, including failure to acknowledge the gods, illicit astronomy, violation of a decree on honoring the gods, assault and battery of cultic personnel, association with a parricide, introducing new gods and assembling unlawful religious groups, improper ritual procedures, sorcery or witchcraft, composition and performance of apparently impious poems, and verbally insulting the cult statue of Athena in the Parthenon.

A Climate of Suspicion

Continued social, political, and economic upheavals at Athens in the waning years of the Peloponnesian War only served to intensify the culture of rumor mongering, mistrust, and denunciation set in motion shortly after the herms and profanation of the Mysteries scandals that ultimately led to an increase in impiety trials in the fourth century, starting with Socrates. During this time, Athens swung back and forth between democratic and oligarchic regimes, starting with the revolution of 411 when a group of four hundred oligarchs seized the power for five months, followed by a larger, more moderate group of 5,000 who reigned until democracy was restored in 410. After their capitulation, Athens became subject to yet another oligarchic party installed by Sparta, consisting of thirty tyrants, known as the Thirty, who were in power for eight months in 404/3, until democracy was re-established, initiating a period of legal reforms. Athenians also faced the socio-economic fallout from the Peloponnesian War, including demographic changes, economic deprivation, and perceptions of its impact, including the precarious relationship of the community to supernatural forces.[56] After narrowly avoiding the destruction of the city and the enslavement or annihilation of its residents, Athens moved from democratic to oligarchic regimes and back again. The loss of the war, on an ideological level, suggested not only that Athens could be beaten on the battlefield but also that democracy itself could be weakened and destroyed.[57] Moreover, by the end of the fifth century, Athens had lost nearly half its male citizens, not only from deaths in battle, but also from disease and immigration.[58] Literary accounts of the period contain increased references to poverty due to these factors, as well as the disruption in the mining of silver at Laurion, which was not fully restored until the middle of the fourth century.[59]

These years proved particularly challenging for women, who without the protection of male kin struggled to survive, often seeking asylum in new cities, particularly Athens. Writing about the Plataeans, who were expelled by the Thebans in 374 BCE and found refuge in Athens, the orator Isocrates describes children reduced to slavery, neglected parents, wives separated from husbands, and daughters from mothers, people being forced to work as manual laborers, and "the rest procuring their daily livelihood as best each one can, in a manner that accords with neither the deeds of their ancestors, nor their own youth,

132   Phryne of Thespiae

nor their own self-respect."[60] Elsewhere he relates the movement of another family, consisting of Thrasylochus, his mother, and his sister, from Siphnos to Troezen, eventually settling in Aegina.[61] Large numbers of these displaced individuals were women, "so many refugee sisters and nieces and female cousins," with widows and orphans being pervasive and vulnerable.[62] The risk of destitution led to the crossing of social boundaries and eroded distinctions between citizen and non-citizen women: the poor could be bribed to take on non-citizens as relatives or adopt them, which may have been the goal when Stephanus married Phano to Phrastor and Theogenes.[63] Unmarried women might have turned to menial labor or even prostitution. Apollodorus fears that citizen women might turn to prostitution if Neaera is acquitted, while the comic poet Antiphanes claims that a citizen girl without a guardian had been compelled to work as a hetaera.[64]

Against this backdrop occurred the most well-documented and thoroughly discussed *graphe asebeias*, the trial of Socrates (c. 470–399 BCE).[65] Much has been written about Socrates, and it requires only a brief consideration here. His prosecution took place in 399, either just before or after Andocides' second trial. The charges included corrupting the youth and "not acknowledging the gods whom the polis acknowledges, and introducing new divinities," in the form of the *daimonion* who spoke to him.[66] This charge followed the precedent introduced by the seer, Diopeithes, around 430 that called for the public prosecution of "those who did not acknowledge the divine or who taught doctrines about things in the sky," which was specifically intended to target Pericles' association with the pre-Socratic philosopher Anaxagoras.[67] Tried in the popular courts before a jury of around 500, Socrates was convicted by a narrow majority, sentenced to death, and executed by self-administered hemlock.

The trumped-up nature of the charges against Socrates reflects widespread anxieties about political and social stabilities and the spread of new ideas that moved away from Greek religious orthodoxy. For instance, corrupting the youth was not an illegal offense but rather a veiled reference to the fact that Socrates had instructed Critias, the leader of the extremist faction of the Thirty.[68] More importantly, there is no evidence for a law that prohibited the introduction of "new" or foreign gods in Athens.[69] Not only was Athens known for its hospitality to divine as well as mortal immigrants, religious innovation was a "conspicuous phenomenon" in the fifth century.[70] "New" or "foreign" could refer

The Prosecution of Phryne   133

to divinities known in other Greek communities but not yet established in Athens, as well as to non-Greek gods. Athens had well-established procedures for sanctioning new cults at Athens, while some gods designated as "new," like Pan and Bendis, were already being worshipped by groups or individuals before being institutionally recognized.[71] Introducing new gods into their city thus seems to have been standard practice for the Athenians, "they might stay the same or be transformed; remain the concern of subgroups or be absorbed into pantheon of the city."[72] Socrates' trial would provide a template for subsequent impiety prosecutions that also involved suspicious activities and strange new gods.

Women and Impiety

Phryne's trial reflects the early fourth-century culture of displacement, precarity, and mistrust, as one of a series of genuine, threatened, or alleged prosecutions for impiety directed against women in the fourth century.[73] Indeed, Kapparis argues that "at no other point in Athenian history is there such a concentration of impiety prosecutions brought against women."[74] Legal actions against women for impiety begin with Aspasia in the late fifth century and continue with Ninos, Theoris, and Phryne, whose public naming may suggest they were hetaeras, and two unnamed women, the sister of Lakedaimonios, and possibly the daughter of Phrynichos.[75] Likely all but the unnamed women were likely foreigners, as indicated by charges or implications of servile origins, sexual and social promiscuity, orgiastic cults, fraudulent claims to citizenship, drug trafficking, and magic.[76]

Esther Eidinow has characterized these trials as "witch-hunts" that arose from a climate of gossip, envy, and fear.[77] The increase in the number of alien cults with strange customs in Athens and other Greek cities during the fourth century may have also been a contributing factor.[78] Many of these unofficial, private cults seem to have attracted marginalized members of the community, such as women, metics, slaves, and prostitutes, in greater numbers, which may in part explain while impiety trials after Socrates' death predominantly targeted women. In the opening of Aristophanes' *Lysistrata*, the title character refers to several such cults when she bemoans the truancy of her compatriots: "If anyone had summoned them to a Bacchic rite, or to Pan's shrine, or to

134   Phryne of Thespiae

Cape Kolias, or to Aphrodite Genetyllis, you wouldn't have been able to get through for the mass of cymbals."[79] Together with the mourning of Adonis, these private celebrations overseen by unofficial cultic personnel seem to have involved ecstatic revelry, drinking, and the worship of deities concerned with female sexuality and childbirth.[80] Indeed, they were so popular that the deme of Piraeus had to pass a law forbidding unauthorized individuals from assembling *thiasoi* in its Thesmophorion (Parker 1996: 162). Another example is Sabazius, a Phrygian deity similar to Dionysus and later conflated with him, introduced to Athens in the late 430s as the object of private mysteries involving intoxication.[81] The earliest mention comes from a conversation between two tipsy slaves in Aristophanes' *Wasps*.[82] In *Lysistrata*, the worship of Sabazius is blamed for inciting female licentiousness.[83] A particularly rancorous passage of Demosthenes' *On the Crown* accuses the orator Aeschines of participating in ecstatic rites in honor of the god by helping his mother, Glaucothea, with her preparations and by leading ecstatic groups of worshippers:

> On arriving at manhood you assisted your mother in her
> initiations (*te metri telouse*) . . . . At night it was your duty to
> mix the libations, to clothe the initiates in fawn-skins, and
> perform lustrations . . . . During the day you led your lovely
> *thiasoi* through the public streets, their heads garlanded with
> fennel and white poplar; and, as you went, you squeezed the
> fat-cheeked snakes, or brandished them above your head, now
> shouting your sacred words.[84]

Although technically not a priestess, Glaucothea oversees the rites of initiation in the cult of Sabazius, which seem to have consisted of both men and women, given that mother and son worked together to arrange them. The fact that Demsothenes not only publicly names Aeschines' mother, but also adds that she was universally known by her nickname, Empousa, and that she was a musician, a *tympanistria* or player of the kettle drum, implies that she worked as a hetaera.[85] Although Demosthenes no doubt exaggerates Aeschines' involvement as part of his invective, or possibly even makes it up, his description nonetheless suggests that alien religious practices were commonplace, particularly associated with women and the lower classes, and likely to be viewed quite negatively by male Athenian jurors. At the same time,

The Prosecution of Phryne   135

the notoriety of these women points to the agency and influence they exerted over the public imaginary, even if they did not wield actual religious and social power.[86]

The broad spectrum of religious infractions embodied by the *graphe asebeias* made it a flexible medium for prosecuting infamous individuals who aroused public suspicion and mistrust, like Socrates. It may not be a coincidence that the earliest recorded impiety case against a woman is that of a member of his circle, Aspasia.[87] If authentic, Aspasia's trial would have preceded that of Socrates by around four or five decades, and that of Phryne by almost a century. According to Plutarch, our most extensive source for the trial, Hermippus (c. 440 BCE), a poet of old comedy, brought a public charge against Aspasia not only of impiety but also for pandering:

> About this time also Aspasia was put on trial for impiety,
> Hermippus the comic poet being her prosecutor, who alleged
> further against her that she received free-born women into
> a place of assignation for Pericles. And Diopeithes brought
> in a bill providing for the public impeachment of such as
> did not believe in gods, or who taught doctrines regarding
> the heavens, directing suspicion against Pericles by means of
> Anaxagoras. The people accepted with delight these slanders.[88]

The basis of the impiety charge is unknown. As written, the passage confuses it with pandering, an allegation that echoes a passage from Aristophanes' *Acharnians* that blames the outbreak of the Peloponnesian War on the retaliatory abduction by the Megarians of "two *pornae* who belonged to Aspasia," insinuating that Aspasia ran a brothel.[89] As with impiety, any male or female convicted on a charge of pandering a free woman or child, known as a *graphe proagogieias*, could be punished by death.[90]

Citing Aeschines as his source, Plutarch reports that Pericles interceded, winning her acquittal by supplicating the jurors with copious tears and entreaties *on her behalf*.[91] Weeping and supplication were common amateur ploys in the Attic law courts aimed at eliciting pity and ultimately acquittal. Socrates describes this topos as follows, "[the defendant] asked and beseeched the jurors, weeping copiously and marching his children up here to win as much pity as he could, and also many other relatives and friends," stating that he refuses to use such contemptible tactics himself.[92] But these performances typically fell to litigants rather than the orator. Pericles, like Hyperides at Phryne's trial, was perhaps compelled to make this display instead of Aspasia because as a woman she would not normally be allowed to speak in court. Madeleine Henry, and more recently Jakub Filonik, have argued that Aspasia's trial is a fantasy generated by comic invectives against the hetaera.[93] Mary Lefkowitz goes so far as to state that all accounts of impiety trials, and Aspasia's above all, are the invention of the Hellenistic biographical tradition, all of which are modeled on the prosecution of Socrates.[94] Kapparis accepts the suit as authentic, proposing that Aspasia served as a vehicle for a targeted attack against Pericles, much like Neaera was used against Stephanus.[95] For Eidinow, however, the historical accuracy of the passage is less important than what it says about the ways in which gossip and slander shaped the Athenian legal process as an illustration of "the malicious dynamics that could surround and support a public charge of impiety."[96]

In a trial that appears to have been well known during the fourth century, probably held around 362–358 BCE, a woman named Ninos was prosecuted on a *graphe asebeias*.[97] To return to Demosthenes, *Against Boeotus I* and *II*, two speeches related to an inheritance dispute, as we saw in Chapter 2, Menecles was the man who prosecuted and secured her conviction.[98] Another forensic speech reiterates that Menecles brought the impiety charge against her and that her son subsequently retaliated.[99] In *On the False Embassy,* Demosthenes again accuses Aeschines' mother, Glaucothea, of leading *thiasoi*, and then comments that the activity had earlier led to the death of a priestess.[100] A scholion to this passage identifies this woman as a priestess, *hiereia*, named Ninos, and further specifies that she was indicted for witchcraft in the form of casting love-charms on youths:

> For which another priestess was put to death> For these drugs (*pharmakois*) another priestess (*hiereia*) was also put to death. He means the so-called Ninos. Menecles charged her that she was making love-philtres (*philtra*) for young people.[101]

Another scholion specifies that an unnamed woman, also called a *hiereia*, and thus probably Ninos, was indicted on the charge of mocking and profaning the Eleusinian Mysteries, and condemned to death.[102]

From the outset they considered that the rites were a mockery (*gelota*) and an insult (*hybrin*) against the true Mysteries (*mysterion*), and this is why they put to death the priestess; after that because the god gave an oracle that these rites ought to continue to be held, they allowed the mother of Aeschines to initiate people.[103]

Although Ninos appears to have served in a sacred capacity, we have no information about either the deity or cult with which she was involved. In reality, little is known about this woman. Much of the evidence is late and unreliable, while the classical sources are vague on the reasons for her prosecution and punishment. Kapparis argues that Ninos was an Athenian citizen because the term *hiereia* is applied to her, but the strangeness of her name, which is not attested in Attica outside of forensic oratory, implies that she may have been a metic involved in some sort of foreign cult.[104] Indeed, Josephus states that the Athenians "put Ninos the priestess to death because someone accused her of initiating people into the mysteries of foreign gods," which he claims was forbidden by law and punishable by death.[105] Again it is claimed that introducing the rites of unknown or foreign gods in the city was a capital offense, despite all evidence to the contrary.[106] The underlying concern, however, appears to have been an attempt to stop the spread of controversial ideas that could have an adverse moral impact on citizens, especially those propagated by women because of their claim of access to a supernatural power unregulated by the Athenian state.[107]

Another woman who faced a charge of impiety at Athens during the fourth century was Theoris. Little is known about either the woman or her trial.[108] The name Theoris is found in two contemporary Attic inscriptions in connection with citizen women, while in the literary tradition it is attributed to a fifth-century hetaera patronized by the tragic poet, Sophocles.[109] Our primary source for her trial is a reference from Demosthenes, *Against Aristogeiton I*, a politician on trial as a state debtor:

It was this brother—I pass over the other facts—who got possession of the drugs and charms (*ta pharmaka kai tas epodas*) from the servant of Theoris of Lemnos, the filthy sorceress (*pharmakis*) whom you put to death on that account with all her family. She gave information against her mistress,

138   Phryne of Thespiae

and this rascal has had children by her, and with her help he plays juggling tricks and professes to cure fits, being himself subject to fits of wickedness of every kind. So this is the man who will beg him off! This poisoner, this public pest, whom any man would ban at sight as an evil omen rather than choose to accost him, and who has pronounced himself worthy of death by bringing such an action.[110]

Demosthenes describes Theoris as a *pharmakis*, a purveyor of drugs, which was considered a form of witchcraft. The fact that she came from Lemnos suggests that she may have been a metic.[111] She was brought to trial for supplying *pharmaka* intended to kill to an Athenian citizen, convicted, and executed, along with her entire family (*to genos hapan*), for unknown reasons. Interestingly, the same social mechanism of denunciation involved in the convictions for the profanation of the Mysteries is also at work here, since the disclosure of her maid is what triggered the investigation. As Kapparis notes, possessing or selling potions, philtres, or other magical objects was not a legal offense in classical Athens. What may have been at issue, rather, was their potential abuse, allowing women and foreigners to gain control over their victims through deceit and mental confusion.[112] Another version of the trial makes no mention of drugs, but rather refers to Theoris as a *hiereia*, like Ninos, and situates her within a larger network of wrongdoing, among which is a specific charge of "teaching slaves to deceive."[113] Here Theoris is again called a priestess or *hiereia*, although it is unclear in what capacity. The final accusation mentioned by ancient sources comes from the lexicographer Harpocration (c. second cent. CE), who implies that Theoris was tried for impiety and put to death because she was a *mantis* or prophetess.[114] The vague nature of Theoris' religious activities suggests that her trial may have resulted from an atmosphere of increased suspicion and fear regarding foreign cults, strange customs, and unknown drugs that could change an individual's behavior and put him/her under the control of a social inferior.

Two other cases that seem to have involved citizen women because the orators have avoided publicly naming them may also have been the result of impiety charges.[115] The first is the prosecution of an unnamed citizen woman, the sister of the aristocrat Lacedaemonius. According to Demosthenes' *Against Euboulides*, Euboulides brought the charge against the woman but failed to receive one-fifth of the jurors' votes, thereby incurring a fine of one-thousand drachmas.[116] This detail, among others, implies that the charges may have been frivolous and politically motivated.[117] Harpocration makes reference to another trial, Lysias' *On the Daughter of Phrynichos*, in his discussions of cultic terminology concerned with the dedications of young women to Artemis at Brauron before marriage.[118] The case may have involved a religious offense related to the cult of Brauronian Artemis, although it may have been an inheritance dispute that highlighted the distinguished cultic service of a young woman of aristocratic birth. It is impossible to know. Women like Theoris and Ninos were perceived to be dangerous because of their ambiguous social status, their unique access to supernatural powers, and their involvement in surreptitious and suspicious activities. Because the Athenian state could not adequately regulate unofficial types of worship, the women led in these rites, and encouraged others to do so, increasingly became targets of prosecution as a means of restricting, or eliminating, their autonomy and influence over a populace perceived to be vulnerable to their influence.

Hyperides' In Defense of Phryne

The foregoing overview of the Athenian legal system, in particular the *graphe asebeias* as a mechanism for prosecuting suspect individuals, particularly marginalized women, establishes a baseline for evaluating and interpreting the surviving remains of Phryne's trial, including the legal mechanisms, distortions, and gender dynamics that shaped it.[119] Of the three women accused and brought to trial for impiety in the fourth century BCE, Phryne was the only one to be acquitted, thanks to Hyperides' defense speech, and rogue legal move, if we are to believe later literary accounts. Almost none of the speech having survived, it was much praised in antiquity, becoming one of the few Attic lawcourt speeches translated into Latin. Quintilian tells us that the great Roman orator Messala Corvinus lost none of the subtlety nor delicacy of the original Greek in his rendition, while Longinus calls the speech beyond even the skill of Demosthenes.[120] The trial itself may have taken around 350–40 BCE, approximately fifty years after that of Socrates, and one hundred years after Aspasia.[121] All of the evidence for the event, however, is quite late, leading many scholars to conclude that the trial and the events surrounding it were largely fictional, especially the love

140   Phryne of Thespiae

triangle between the hetaera and the two orators and the disrobing incident.[122] But several have argued that the prosecution of Phryne actually had a historical basis, that the defense speech was authentic, and the events were inferred from Hyperides' original text.[123] In support of this view, a fragment from Posidippus' *Ephesia*, discussed more fully in the following, indicates that the procedure against Phryne was well known among comic audiences by the early third century CE. As we have seen, these two genres have historical value because of their engagement with the contemporary social and political landscape and the ways they reflect the Athenian imaginary.[124]

Posidippus does not specify why Phryne was put on trial, only that she "did terrible damage to people's lives."[125] The harm she caused others presumably refers to the impiety charge, but no information about the motive, trial date, or specific offense is given. Not until late antiquity do we learn about the legal basis for the prosecution, as summarized by a late anonymous rhetorical treatise from the second half of the third century CE: [126]

> Phryne was charged with impiety, for she participated in a
> *komos* ("revel") in the Lyceum, introduced a new (*kainon*)
> god, and led *thiasoi* of men and women in song and dance.
> (Euthias) "I have shown that Phryne is impious because she
> joined in a shameless *komos*, introduced a new god, and led
> unlawful *thiasoi* of both men and women."[127]

The text identifies the charge as a *graphe asebias* and then specifies three separate components: participation in a socially unacceptable type of *komos* or revel, the introduction of a new god, and the leading of mixed-gender *thiasoi* or ecstatic groups. The reference to a *komos* perhaps carries the implication of corrupting the youth, since the space where the gatherings took place was originally a sanctuary dedicated to Apollo Lyceus, a place to gather for military or civic purposes, likely to be frequented by youth.[128] The presence of both genders engaging in ecstatic song and dance may have also been problematic. More likely we are meant to think of the private, ecstatic gatherings of initiates that evaded state oversight like those organized by Aeschines and his mother. But the god worshipped in this case was not Sabazius, but Isodaites:

> (Isodaites) Mentioned by Hyperides in his oration for Phryne.
> Some foreign god (*xenikos daimon*) for whom common

The Prosecution of Phryne 141

women and those with questionable morals (*ta demode gynaia kai me spoudaia*) she used to perform rites (*etelei*).[129]

Not much is known about Isodaites apart from this passage. It describes him as a minor or semi-divine foreign god worshipped by "common" women, presumably prostitutes. The name is a Greek word ("dividing equally," "giving to all alike") that occurs as an epithet of Dionysus and Pluto in later sources.[130] But Isodaites does not appear to be a new or even foreign god nor his assemblies a rare occurrence during the fourth century.[131] Following the example of Glaucothea, the term for "performing rites," *etelei*, suggests an independent ritual practitioner not associated with a fixed sanctuary or official state cult. Terms related to the revelatory aspects of the Eleusinian Mysteries found in two other fragments of Hyperides' speech recorded by Harpocration may refer to their profanation, whether by the hetaera, or her prosecutor, Euthias.[132] Of course it is impossible to know the actual allegations in this case and the sacrilegious conduct that led to them. The main charge, leading *thiasoi* in honor of a foreign god, resonates in particular with the prosecution of Ninos, who was also accused of this activity, and may well suggest that Phryne was involved in initiating people into the mysteries of foreign gods and even serving in some capacity as its *hiereia*.

Moving now to the trial, according to the third-century grammarian and biographer Hermippus as paraphrased by Athenaeus, Euthias successfully indicted Phryne, and when he lost the case he was so incensed that he never went to trial again.[133] We know virtually nothing about this man. From what little remains, he seems to have been a shady character. He was apparently prosecuted by Lysias over something having to do with confiscated goods that perhaps rendered him a public debtor.[134] He was also among a group of individuals accused of sycophantic activities.[135] A fragment of the defense speech makes Euthias a previous lover of Phryne and asserts that Hyperides distinguished himself from his opponent by saying "it is not the same when one man will go to any lengths to save her, while the other to kill her."[136] Alciphron re-creates this love triangle in his fictional letters by hetaeras, none of which, unsurprisingly, have anything good to say about him, as the prosecutor of one of their friends: he is described as a corrupt and stupid man ultimately jilted by Phryne and later taken up by the gullible Myrhinna:

142   Phryne of Thespiae

We hetaeras are all grateful to you, and each one of us is just as grateful as Phryne. The suit, to be sure, that was brought by that worthless Euthias involved Phryne alone, but it meant danger to us all: for if we ask our lovers for money and don't get it, or if we find paying customers and then face prosecution for impiety, it's better for us to be done with this way of living.[137]

But even Euthias' authorship of the lost prosecution speech is open to question, since Athenaeus tells us that Anaximenes may have composed it.[138]

The ancient sources have obviously much more to say about the orator Hyperides (390–322 BCE). He was the son of Glaucippus, from the deme Collytus. His enormously wealthy family owned houses in Athens and Piraeus, estates in Eleusis, and tombs in front of the Hippades Gate. In 340 and 339 BCE he performed three extensive liturgies, meaning that his family belonged to the highest class of Athenian society, like Praxiteles and the fictional Demeas in Menander's *Samia*. His affluence explains the frequent association of the orator with profligacy in the form of costly hetaeras, whether as personal companions whom he either supported or purchased outright, including Myrrhine, Aristagora, and Phila, or as litigants he either defended or prosecuted in court, or sometimes both.[139] Indeed, Hyperides admits, presumably early in the defense, to a sexual relationship with Phryne: "I have been associated with her in the past and I am still associated with her now."[140] Because of this affair, Plutarch tells us, the orator agreed to serve as Phryne's advocate.[141] Elsewhere Athenaeus claims that Hyperides and Phryne were known to be connected, since other enemies of Hyperides brought cases against Phryne, such as Aristogeiton (second half of the fourth cent. BCE), a notorious sycophant and public debtor punished with political disenfranchisement, much like Euthias.[142]

The Disrobing

For the sake of clarity, I begin with excerpts from each of the five extant, late accounts of Phryne's disrobing, quoted in English translation (please see endnotes for the Latin and Greek originals). The earliest examples are from the first century CE, the Latin text of Roman educator and rhetorician Quintilian, and that of the Greek author Plutarch.

The other three are Greek texts from around the third century CE by the physician Sextus Empiricus, Athenaeus, as quoted at the outset of this chapter, and Alciphron.

1) *Quintilian* (c. 35–100 CE)
   Antonius, defending Manius Aquilius, tore open his client's clothes and disclosed the scars he bore in front, earned in his country's service, and thus, instead of relying on his own eloquence, delivered a shock to the eyes of the people of Rome, who, we are led to believe, were chiefly moved to acquit him by the mere sight. And a speech of Cato's, as well as other records, is evidence that Servius Galba escaped condemnation solely through the pity he aroused by not only exhibiting his own little children before the assembly, but also carrying in his arms the child of Sulpicius Gallus. So also, it is thought, Phryne was saved from danger not by Hyperides' pleading, admirable as it was, but by the sight of her lovely body, which she had further uncovered by undoing her tunic.[143]

2) *Plutarch* (c. 45–120 CE)
   And, as it is indeed reasonable to suppose, it was because he had also associated with Phryne the hetaera that when she was on trial for impiety he became her advocate; for he makes this plain himself at the beginning of his speech. And when [Phryne] was about to be convicted, he led the woman out into the middle of the court and, tearing off her clothes, displayed her breasts. When the judges saw her beauty, she was acquitted.[144]

3) *Sextus Empiricus* (c. late second/early third cent. CE)
   So the elders of the people in Homer's *Iliad*, although exhausted by war and wholly estranged from Helen as the cause of their woes, are yet persuaded by her beauty, and at her approach they address one another as follows, "Surely there is no blame on Trojans and strong-greaved Achaians if for a long time they suffer hardship for a woman like this one." When Hyperides was pleading for her and she was on the point of being condemned, Phryne, too, as they say, tore asunder her garments and with her breasts bare flung herself at the feet of the judges, and because of her beauty had more power to persuade her judges than the rhetoric of her advocate.[145]

144 Phryne of Thespiae

4) *Athenaeus* (late second/early third cent. CE)
When [Hyperides] accomplished nothing, and the jurors seemed likely to convict [Phryne], he brought the woman out in public, and after tearing off her garments and exposing her naked breasts, he concluded his speech with piteous wailing at the sight of her, causing the jurors to feel a superstitious fear of this interpreter and temple-attendant of Aphrodite, and to yield to pity rather than put her to death. Afterward, when she had been acquitted, a decree was passed to the effect that no speaker was to lament on another person's behalf, and that no accused man or women was to be put on display while their case was being decided.[146]

5) *Alciphron* (late second/early third cent. CE)
For I believe that your trial has actually brought you good luck; that scene in court has made you famous not only in Athens but also throughout Greece . . . . when people tell you that, if you hadn't torn open your shift and shown the judges your breasts your advocate would have been of no avail, don't believe them. As a matter of fact it was his pleading that gave you the opportunity to do that very thing at the right moment.[147]

By the time of Quintilian and Plutarch, Phryne's disrobing at the culmination of her trial had become the most celebrated event of her biography and continued to elicit comment over the next two hundred years, using many of the same tropes: the recalcitrance of the jurors, the leading of the hetaera into the courtroom, the rending of her garments, the public display of her breasts rather than her entire body, and the persuasive effect of the spectacle on the male jurors, whether because of admiration, shock, or religious awe. Although Quintilian does not specify which part of Phryne's body was exposed, only that the jurors reacted to the sight of her body (*conspectu corporis*), the parallel he draws with Manius Aquilius—whose advocate, Marcus Antonius, stripped off his tunic to reveal the battle wounds on his chest (*pectore*)—suggests that he had in mind her upper torso.[148] The first three passages represent the disrobing as the triumph of beauty and sex over rhetoric, although Quintilian does group it together with the pity topos. Sextus Empiricus compares the power of Phryne's naked breasts to the mythological exemplum of Helen, citing the same lines from Homer's *Iliad* about her blameless beauty that Zeuxis' inscribed on his famous painting.

The Prosecution of Phryne   145

The reference may also implicitly allude to the story that Menelaus, conquered by Aphrodite, threw away his sword at the sight of Helen's naked breasts.[149] The passages differ, however, with respect to agency, as to whether Hyperides or Phryne tore the tunic off her body, with three ascribing the move to the hetaera. Athenaeus' version is the most elaborate, introducing a few features not found elsewhere. Instead of delivering closing arguments, the orator introduces piteous laments in response to the sight of Phryne's naked body. Further, the author deploys religious language of the dramatic moment describing the hetaera as a *hypophetis* and a *zakoros* of Aphrodite. Athenaeus ends his account by stating that Hyperides' unprecedented move resulted in two changes to the Athenian legal system, a ban on speakers lamenting on another person's behalf and the display of accused individuals in the courtroom before the verdict.

Although most scholars, even if they agree about the authenticity of the trial, believe the disrobing never occurred, I argue that the reported conduct of both Hyperides and Phryne hews in some respects to cultural norms, although the extant texts reflect numerous distortions introduced by later authors, possibly influenced by the fame of the *Cnidian Aphrodite*.[150] Let us start by considering the earliest, non-forensic reference to Phryne's trial, Posidippus' fragment, quoted here in full:

> Before our time, Phryne was far and away the most famous
> courtesan there was; because even if you're younger than
> that, you've heard about her trial. Although seeming to have
> corrupted a greater part of the citizens, she won the court
> contending for her life; and by taking the jurors' hands
> (*dexioumene*), one by one, she saved her life—although just
> barely—with her tears.[151]

Given the tendency of both oratory and comedy to refer to contemporary persons and events familiar to the spectators, here stressed by the second-person singular perfect tense, *akekoas*, "you have heard," the fragment is a strong indicator that the trial actually took place. However, it makes no mention of impiety, or any other specific charge, only that Phryne harmed a great many people for which her life seems to have been at stake. Indeed, the terms *blaptein* and *blabe*, if used in a legal sense, imply a private suit, a *dike*, rather than a public *graphe*, involving fraud, breach of contract, or damage to property.[152]

146   Phryne of Thespiae

Notably, the fragment references neither Hyperides nor the hetaera's disrobing. Instead, it depicts the hetaera's legal victory as the result of supplication by weeping and making physical contact with the jurors, "tears and taking the jurors' hands, one by one." The participle *dexioumene* stresses that this was a figurative ritual gesture involving the right hand.[153] For a literary parallel, the goddess Thetis supplicates Zeus on behalf of her son, Achilles, by crouching before him, touching his knee with her left hand, and taking hold of him under the chin with her right.[154] In so doing, she adopts a posture of physical inferiority and self-abasement, much like that of a slave.[155] By the late fourth century, the binding force of supplication had weakened, "becoming more or less emptily metaphorical," in John Gould's words, and yet it continued to be a frequent and often successful tactic for eliciting pity in the courtroom.[156] In Aristophanes' *Wasps*, the elderly juror Philocleon complains about various tactics used by defendants to win acquittal, to wit: the clasping of hands, the same hands that committed the crime (!), supplication, bowing and scraping, wailing, and dragging their weeping children before the jurors.[157] Posidippus' account of the trial, therefore, does not represent Phryne as acting any differently than most defendants in the Athenian legal system.

If the story of Phryne's disrobing did not appear in the original oration or even in the earliest accounts of the trial, how did it enter the later literary tradition? Craig Cooper argues that subsequent retellings resulted from a misreading of Hyperides' original defense speech put into circulation later in the late third or early second century BCE by the biographer Hermippus, who adapted it from Idomeneus of Lampsacus (c. 300 BCE), perhaps as a means of parodying the courtroom displays of Athenian demagogues.[158] Since the accounts of both Athenaeus and Plutarch are embedded in a larger discourse concerning Hyperides' multiple affairs with various hetaeras, they perhaps reflect the interference of Hellenistic biography that may have portrayed a lover's quarrel between Euthias and Hyperides as a motive for the trial.[159] It is possible that these texts first alluded to the orator's disrobing of the hetaera before the jurors. Outside of oratory, Greek poetry from the archaic period onward portrays girls and women, especially mothers, baring their breasts in moments of extreme duress as a gesture of entreaty, exemplified by Hecuba and Clytemnestra. So, too, Iphigeneia in Aeschylus' *Agamemnon* sheds her gown as she begs for her life with her eyes, "Then, as she shed to the ground her saffron robe, she struck each of her sacrificers with a glance from her eyes beseeching pity."[160] Although the text is vague, it nonetheless situates the girl's disrobing as part of a larger attempt to elicit pity in the moments before her death. A closer look at the language of Athenaeus' text further suggests that female nudity in the face of imminent death was associated with vulnerability and supplication rather than eroticism. The verb *perirhegnumi* and its variant, *katarhegnumi*, "to tear apart," recurs in all four Greek passages, not only indicating that the authors must have relied on the same earlier text(s), but also describing an action more often associated with piteous abasement and supplication rather than sexual nudity. The term is regularly followed by a word for clothing, most often *chitonikos*, a shortened version of the full-length, sleeved garment made of linen called a *chiton* worn by women, likely foreign in origins, and probably a general term for a female garment by the first century CE.[161] In the view of Cooper, this description represents an extrapolation of the original peroration, in which Hyperides described bringing Phryne before the jurors in rent garments and striking her breasts, like a tragic character being led to her death.[162] A closer tragic parallel, I would argue, is not Antigone, but rather Xerxes, who tears his garments and laments shrilly at the sight of his defeated army in Aeschylus' *Persians*, actions that portray him as the piteous victim of tragic reversal, just as Iphigeneia above.[163]

The act of stripping women of clothing carries multiple cultural meanings in the Greek literary tradition, none of which are erotic. It can denote enslavement, as evidenced by another Aeschylean passage in which a maiden chorus laments the captive women, both young and old, "dragged by the hair, like horses, with their cloaks torn off them."[164] In a text closer to Hyperides' time, Demosthenes, *On the False Embassy*, relates how a male servant ripped the tunic off the back of a female slave, formerly a modest, free Olynthian woman, and commenced flogging her for refusing to sing at a banquet.[165] The gesture can also signify disgrace, according to the Solonian law on the orderly conduct of women quoted by Aeschines that permitted any man to strip a woman caught in adultery of her mantle, confiscate her jewelry, and beat her, stopping only short of death.[166]

Although the verb *perirhegnumi* occurs in archaic and classical Greek texts, it is much more frequently encountered in later antiquity, again without erotic connotations. It features in scenes of supplication or piteous entreaty, as when a daughter with torn hair and rent garments falls to her knees to beseech her father.[167] As in the Demosthenic passage quoted previously, the violent removal of a woman's clothing may represent a male response to female resistance, as in the case of the brutal

148   Phryne of Thespiae

mercenary, Lucius, who tore the tunic off a young girl and proceeded to whip her naked body when she refused his sexual advances.[168] Or it may denote shame, as when Thamara, after being raped by her brother Ammon, ripped her clothing and bewailed the violence done to her in a portion of Josephus.[169] The laceration of clothing also appears in contexts of deep grief and lamentation, as when Plutarch tells us that Cleopatra rent her garments and beat her breasts in mourning for Antony.[170] Similarly, Dio Chrysostom (c. 40–115 CE) applies the term to his description of the torn clothing worn by supplicating women.[171] The association of the verb *perirhegnumi* with moments of extreme self-abasement, entreaty, or mourning occurs in connection with Phryne in two late, anonymous rhetorical treatises, underscoring that even hundreds of years after the original trial, the disrobing did not necessarily have an erotic meaning. Rather, the gesture served as a rhetorical tactic, much like that enacted upon the body of Manius Aquillius above, aimed at eliciting shock and pity and involving gestures of ritual supplication and lamentation rather than seduction. According to one passage, Phryne "beat her naked breasts once her garment had been torn off."[172] Another does not even mention her nakedness, but rather focuses exclusively on the state of her clothing, again stressing that the speech was meant to win the sympathy of the jurors.[173] Indeed, Sextus Empiricus portrays the hetaera as prostrating herself, *prokulindoumene*, before the judges as she tears open her garment. Whatever the original gesture, by late antiquity, the disrobing had come to signify the vulnerability and self-abasement of the hetaera and a rhetorical stratagem intended to arouse pity rather than pleasure in the jurors.

Athenaeus' account of Phryne's courtroom nudity thus fits with both classical and post-classical discourses on rent clothing as an external marker of distress commonly associated with imminent death, enslavement, extreme grief, or sexual violation. As a rhetorical device, its main purpose was to elicit pity in the viewer, as indicated by the words *oikos* and *eleos*, applied to both the orator and the jurors in Athenaeus' account. To this motif Athenaeus adds a religious spin not found elsewhere: the sight of Phryne causes the jurors "to feel a superstitious fear of this priestess and temple-attendant of Aphrodite."[174] This phrase is the only reference to Phryne as a priestess of Aphrodite, although not as a *hiereia*, the more common term used of the two other fourth-century women charged with impiety, Ninos and Theoris. Instead, the texts identifies her as a *hypophetis* and a *zakoros*, suggesting

The Prosecution of Phryne   149

a late intervention most likely influenced by Phryne's receptions in art.[175] Indeed, the women associated with cults of Aphrodite, whether freeborn women or prostitutes, in the ancient Near East or Attica, do not seem to have been designated by cultic titles during the classical period.[176] The word *hypophetis* means an expounder of the divine, typically used of men, as for example the Selli who declare the oracle of Zeus at Dodona in Homer's *Iliad*.[177] Based on later parallels in Theocritus, where the phrase *Mousaon hypophetai* is a metonym for "poets," we can understand *ten upophetin . . . Aphrodites* to mean something like "embodiment of Aphrodite," or even Aphrodite herself.[178] The word *zakoros*, used of both men and women depending on the definite article, refers to a woman who works in and around the shrine of a deity in a fragment of Menander and seems to be interchangeable with the more common term for cultic personnel, *hiereus/hiereia*.[179] These words expand on the idea of the infinitive, *deisidaimonesai*, literally, "to have fear of the gods," indicating either religious piety or superstitious fear. This language invites the reader to view the disrobing of Phryne as a religious act and her presence in the courtroom as a kind of apotheosis, but since they occur with greater frequency in texts from later antiquity, they likely did not occur in the original speech or excerpts compiled by later authors, but rather indicate the influence of the *Cnidian Aphrodite* and Praxiteles' art more generally on her first-century CE and later receptions.

For parallels to the religious vocabulary in Athenaeus' account, we need look no further than two authors discussed previously in connection with the *Cnidian Aphrodite*, pseudo-Lucian and Alciphron. In [Lucian], *Amores*, the word *zakoros* is used twice of the female temple-attendant at the sanctuary of Aphrodite in Cnidus who recounts the story of the passionate love of the unnamed youth for the statue.[180] It is also used of the personnel who lock the temple doors from the outside at night.[181] Moreover, the unnatural love of the boy for the stone image of the goddess is described as a form of "religious awe," *deisidaimonos*.[182] The use of the same terminology in both Athenaeus and pseudo-Lucian, an unknown author of uncertain date, suggests either that one influenced the other or that both borrowed from the same earlier source.[183] The extended description of the sacred viewing of the Cnidia by the three Greek tourists in *Amores* further resonates with Athenaeus' account of Phryne's disrobing: the image is completely naked, "draped by no garment," and occupies the middle of the temple, where it can be viewed from all sides.[184] These features parallel the judicial viewing of

150   Phryne of Thespiae

the hetaera "in the open," uncovered, and surrounded by male viewers. The idea of a statue inspiring religious awe in the viewer also appears in the letter from Phryne to Praxiteles, in which the marble statue of the hetaera instructs her creator-lover not to fear his own creation:

> Have no fear (*me deises*); for you have made a very beautiful thing, such as no one, in fact, has ever seen before among all things that have been made by hand, having set up your own mistress in the sanctuary. I stand in the middle by Aphrodite and your Eros too. Do not begrudge me this honor.[185]

It is not only the beauty of the statue that gives Praxiteles pause, but the religious power that it emanates by its placement in the sanctuary and proximity to representations of Eros and Aphrodite. The exhortation to "have no fear" (*me deises*) recalls the superstitious effect (*deisidaimonesai*) of Phryne's naked body on her male viewers in the Attic courtroom. Her Thespian image, however, elicits not only fear in the viewer but also desire, inviting the artist to make love to her in the sacred precinct, just as the *Cnidian Aphrodite* beckoned the unnamed youth to satisfy his lust in pseudo-Lucian's tale. Reading back through the linguistic layers of Athenaeus' passage, it is therefore possible to conjecture that Phryne originally appeared at her own trial in torn garments to entreat the jurors with tears and the clasping of hands, conduct commonly associated with defendants in Attic oratory, or that Hyperides engaged in similar behavior on her behalf, like Pericles for Aspasia, displaying the distraught hetaera in mourning dress, like a weeping wife or daughter brought into court by a desperate defendant.[186] Athenaeus retains these elements but adds to it the innovation already well known by the first century CE in which the orator, or hetaera, exposed her breasts in the courtroom. Although the gesture has parallels elsewhere in oratory, as Quintilian relates, it nonetheless suggests a cross-pollination with earlier and subsequent accounts of the *Cnidian Aphrodite* and the danger and power of sacred viewing and the female nude.

Conclusion

The number of interactions of women with the Athenian legal system during the fourth century BCE, the climate of mistrust and social instability that generated their prosecutions (especially for impiety), and the arrival of increasing numbers of immigrants to the city bringing new cults all argue for the historical authenticity of Phryne's trial. These women tended to be foreigners, likely hetaeras, and in most cases associated with enslavement.[187] The ambiguous status of women such as Neaera in forensic oratory posed a potent threat to the social strategies of legitimate marriage, the production of lawful children, and the orderly transmission of property that perpetuated the stability of family and the polis alike. As religious agents, women like Ninos, Theoris, and Phryne not only had the power to corrupt the individual, but also threatened the welfare of the city with their supernatural activities and potential claims to legitimacy. By introducing new private cults, dealing in new forms of ritual action, participating illegitimately in ceremonies of citizen women, and trafficking in potions, these very marginal figures came to loom large in Athenian rhetoric and legal action that defended the piety and purity of the polis, reflecting male anxieties about the potential for female autonomy and power in a democratic society.

Although Phryne's story follows the contours of other impiety prosecutions against women, namely, her marginal status as a metic and hetaera, her introduction of a new cult and participation in disorderly *thiasoi*, the tradition that comes down to us omits these details and focuses instead on her disrobing, an unprecedented rhetorical move not mentioned in connection with either Ninos or Theoris. An analysis of linguistic parallels from classical and later texts, however, indicates that ancient writers viewed Phryne's courtroom nudity as a form of judicial pleading intended to induce pity in the male jurors. As recorded by Posidippus, her conduct at her trial represented a routine act of forensic supplication that conventionally featured tears, physical contact, rent clothing, and the display of family members. By the first century CE, her disrobing had become a rhetorical trope for effectively persuading the juror when all else fails, with parallels in the Roman courts. Athenaeus adds to this earlier tradition the language of sacred viewing, which portrays the hetaera as the apotheosis of Aphrodite, or her sacred handmaid. As this chapter argues, his account reflects the influence of contemporary accounts of Praxiteles' most famous artworks, the statues of Eros and Aphrodite, that first began circulating in Greek epigram around 100 BCE that invented a romance between the artist and hetaera and thereafter gradually merged the story of Phryne's disrobing with the *Cnidian Aphrodite*.

Epilogue

This book has attempted to unsettle contemporary views about the mythology of Phryne—shaped in no small part by nineteenth- and early twentieth-century fine art and popular culture—by demonstrating that key aspects of her ancient biography could have plausibly had some basis in reality, even seemingly implausible scenarios, such as her association with the *Cnidian Aphrodite* and her disrobing at her impiety trial. I began by exploring the challenges posed by the source materials, foremost, that only a handful of fragments from fourth-century texts have survived, such as Hyperides' *In Defense of Phryne* and Posidippus' play *Ephesia*, which offer few insights into the woman. Although Hellenistic prosopographies, geographies, historiographies, and hetaera treatises made frequent reference to Phryne as they developed and embellished her biography, none of these intermediary texts are extant beyond the excerpts quoted or paraphrased by Athenaeus. The primary evidence for her life thus comes down to us from texts composed hundreds of years after her death, all of them written from the perspective of men, whose works reflect the changing tastes and values of Greeks living under Roman rule. For this reason, the book has repeatedly brought to the fore the difficulties, even the impossibilities, of attempting to reconstruct an authentic biography for Phryne, choosing instead to borrow from Saidiya Hartman the idea of critical fabulation in order to imagine or reconstruct a narrative for her life, informed by contemporary scholarship on the ancient world but always written from the perspective of the subjunctive, what "could" or "would" have been, what was "likely," "possible," or "probable."

Phryne of Thespiae. Laura McClure, Oxford University Press. © Oxford University Press 2024.
DOI: 10.1093/9780197580882.003.0007

This approach has necessitated sifting through the vast literary and material debris that constitutes our archive for female prostitution in the ancient world. A review of this evidence—in the form of linguistic terminology, vase iconography, and onomastic practices—demonstrated first the challenges of identifying hetaeras and other types of prostitutes in the historical record. In oratory, the same terms for prostitution could be used of the same woman, depending on the rhetorical aims of the speaker, as exemplified by the prosecution of Neaera. In Attic vase painting, it is often impossible to distinguish hetaeras from other sexual laborers, and even citizen women, apart from the depiction of graphic sexual activities or clear indicia of a sympotic context. And although hetaeras were publicly named, unlike female citizens, their identities are historically occluded by the widespread attribution of aliases, epithets, and homonyms in addition to their given names. The elusiveness of hetaeras in the literary and historical record further attests to their unstable identities, their spatial and social mobility, and the precarity of their lives as women on the margins of fourth-century Athenian society, despite their symbolic centrality.

Chapter 3 situated the narrative of Phryne within the historical realities of prostitution in classical Athens, drawing on contemporary fifth- and fourth-century documentary evidence such as oratory and comedy, historical writing, and archaeological remains. I examined first the connection between prostitution and democratic institutions in the Athenian imaginary, as illustrated by the comic myth of the invention of brothels by the lawgiver Solon and the prosecution of a male citizen on charges of prostitution. Although there seem to have been few state-sanctioned cults beyond that of Aphrodite Pandemos, Greeks of the classical period clearly perceived a close connection between the goddess and female prostitution, whether because she embodied female beauty and sexual allure, or because foreign women brought her worship with them from their native lands. Either way, the identification of female prostitution with Aphrodite ultimately informed the subsequent myth of Phryne as the model for the Cnidia and her mortal embodiment. Commercial sex took place in various civic venues, on the streets for the most vulnerable women, in makeshift brothels and taverns, and at private symposia held by leading men for successful hetaeras, as well as at their own private lodgings maintained for the purpose. Athenian prostitution was legal, taxed and regulated by the state, and even subject to mutually agreed-upon contracts in the case of exclusive liaisons.

154   Phryne of Thespiae

Metic women could own and operate these businesses, gaining financial independence, albeit through the exploitation of younger, more vulnerable women. An analysis of the social and economic conditions of historical hetaeras like Rhodopis, Aspasia, Theodote, and Neaera allowed us to develop a taxonomy of the hetaera that includes foreign and servile origins, spatial and social mobility, physical beauty, geographical migrancy, wealth, notoriety, and public benefactions. Reading Phryne against this model demonstrates the ways in which her story intersects with the historical realities of hetaeras in classical Athens, allowing us to posit a possible biography for her life.

The final chapters explored the two narratives of Phryne most popular among ancient writers and later receptions, her association with various artworks and the disrobing at her impiety trial. Chapter 4 situated the hetaera within a larger, burgeoning discourse on art in antiquity that invented her fictional romance with the sculptor Praxiteles, triangulating it around his Eros, a celebrated subject among Greek epigrammatists, and her role in the creation of the *Cnidian Aphrodite*. A consideration of female portrait statues demonstrated that women in ancient Greece could and did act as dedicators, setting up statues of themselves and family members in prominent sanctuaries, and could in turn be honored by others in the same way. Praxiteles' reputation as a portrait painter, as well as his links to Thespiae, and in particular his Eros, explains the post-classical invention of his passionate love for the hetaera. The international renown of Phryne's portrait statue at Delphi, also attributed to the sculptor, probably also contributed to the evolution of this narrative. Within its historical context, however, the Delphic statue conforms to the pattern of large-scale public dedications by wealthy, independent hetaeras, such as the costly spits set up by Rhodopis, and to fourth-century conventions of portraiture.

Although both the honorific statue and the Thespian Eros point to an economically independent woman who made public benefactions to her community and beyond, the historical basis of these narratives gradually became subsumed by a process of literary invention, embellishment, and romantic fantasy as new genres and interests emerged, especially around the origins of famous artworks. It starts during the early fourth century, as depictions of hetaeras like Theodote serving as models for paintings begin to appear in literature, together with new images of heroic or divine female nudes on Greek vases, prefiguring the development of the monumental female nude in sculpture. The intersection

Epilogue   155

of hetaeras, portraiture, and discrete female nudity during this period provided abundant material for the epigrammatists and later authors interested in erotic subjects to innovate, adapt, and circulate amorous tales of hetaeras and their artist-lovers.

The fabulation of a biography for Phryne culminated with a discussion of the most famous of her ancient narratives, the baring of her breasts at her trial for impiety. It first established the authenticity of the trial by showing that the prosecution of hetaeras in fourth-century Athens were not uncommon, and that several were brought to trial on charges of impiety, including like Aspasia, Ninos, and Theoris. The allegation that such women, all of whom were likely foreigners and metics, promoted new gods and religious practices likely evolved from a climate of fear and suspicion during a tumultuous period of Athenian history. Phryne's prosecution similarly targeted suspicious supernatural activities but differed by the degree of its notoriety and the unprecedented legal strategy of her disrobing. Her conduct, consisting of tears and entreaties, the clasping of the jurors' hands, and even rent clothing, would not have been considered unusual in the Athenian courtroom. Even the baring of her breasts does not have explicit erotic connotations in the later sources, but rather is depicted as a last-ditch effort to elicit the pity of the jurors in the face of death. The religious terminology that informs Athenaeus' account of the disrobing, however, draws on a late tradition that fuses the hetaera with the *Cnidian Aphrodite*, transforming her from mortal woman into the fearful object of sacred viewing.

To return to where we started, Jean-Léon Gérôme's painting, *Phryne before the Aereopagus*, we can see how the painter has combined the latter two strands of Phryne's narrative, her assimilation to the *Cnidian Aphrodite* and her trial for impiety, much as in Athenaeus' original text, but with a view to sexualizing and objectifying the hetaera for nineteenth-century male viewers and the lucrative art market that catered to them. It illustrates how her receptions, from the fourth century BCE to the modern age, continually reinvented Phryne, distorting, mythologizing, and occluding the historical woman, who, despite every effort, still remains beyond our grasp.

Notes

Introduction

1. Posidippus' *Ephesia* (fr. 13 K-A = Ath. 591e), refers to Phryne as "the most renowned by far of the hetaeras" (ἐπιφανεστάτη πολὺ τῶν ἑταιρῶν).

Translations throughout are adapted from the most recent online editions of the Loeb Classical Library, https://www.loebclassics.com.

References to classical authors and works follow the abbreviations in the *Oxford Classical Dictionary*, 4th edition, where possible. Citations of Greek texts not found there use the formats from Liddell and Scott's *Greek-English Lexicon*, 8th edition.

2. The term hetaera first appears in Sappho's poetry, where it is used of the women in her circle, most likely adolescent girls (frr. 120, 126, 142); for a different theory, see Schlesier 2013. Athenaeus argues that the word was used among women to denote a female friend; see Ath. 571d.

As many scholars have observed, there is no modern English equivalent of the Greek word *hetaira*. Although there has been a trend in recent scholarship toward the terms "sexual laborer," "sex worker," "sexual labor," and "sex work" to stress the agency and social legitimacy of such work, I have gravitated toward "prostitute" and "prostitution" as a more accurate reflection of the degree of compulsion and degradation under which these women worked. The phrase "sexual laborers" is occasionally used to distinguish various types of women who earned their living from their bodies from hetaeras. For further discussion, see Glazebrook and Henry 2011: 13 n. 1; McGinn 2014: 89; Cohen 2015: 2 n. 5; Witzke 2015; Glazebrook 2021: 20.

3. House 2008: 266.

4. There are so many visual representations of Phryne from the seventeenth century onward that it is surprising that a unified study has not yet appeared.

5. Von Waldegg 1972: 130.

6. Diog. Laert. 4.2.7; Val. Max. 4.14.3.

7. οὐκ ἀπ᾽ ἀνδρός, ἀλλ᾽ ἀπ᾽ ἀνδριάντος ἀνασταίη, Diog. Laert. 4.2.

8. Pl. *Symp.* 217a–219c.

9. Roworth 1983: 490 and n. 19. The painting is in a collection in Rome.

10. Roworth 2015: 17.

11. On the theme of famous ancient artists in Renaissance painting, see Roworth 1983: 488; on Kauffmann's property inventories, see Roworth 2015.

12. Von Waldegg 1972: 131. The ancient accounts refer to the woman interchangeably as Pancaspe and Pancaste; see Plin. *HN* 35.86-87; Ael. *VH* 12.34. For Kauffmann's *Zeuxis Selecting Models for His Painting of Helen of Troy* (c. 1778), see Annmary Brown

Memorial, Providence, RI. For *Alexander Leaves Campaspe to Apelles* (1783), see Amt der Landeshauptstelle, Kultur, Bregenz.

13. Von Waldegg 1972: 131 n. 57.

14. Roworth 1983: 490.

15. Roworth 1983: 491. For another version, see the drawing of Carl Russ (1811, National Gallery of Art, 2000.71.1).

16. Ath. 591b; for an alternative version of the story, see Paus. 20.1–2. Phryne and Praxiteles' Eros are discussed in greater detail in Chapter 5.

17. Julianus, *Anth. Pal.* 16.204.

18. Roworth 1983.

19. For the painting, see New York, Metropolitan Museum of Art, 61.126.

20. For the painting, see Paris, Louvre INV 23700.

21. For the painting, see Von Waldegg 1972: 132–133 (Abb. 9), who attributes it to Klaus Holma, a pupil of Jacques-Louis David, and locates it in the collection of the Musée Dobrée, Nantes. As of fall 2017, the provenance appears to be Domaine de la Garenne Lemot, Gétigné, France, but I have not been able to locate any further information on the painting.

22. Von Waldegg 1972: 134.

23. Ryan 1993: 1130.

24. For the sketch, see Von Waldegg 1972: 135 Abb. 12 and n. 84.

25. The painting is reproduced and discussed by Von Waldegg 1972: 133, Abb. 10, and the provenance listed as the Musée des Beaux-Arts, Dijon.

26. Von Waldegg 1972: 135.

27. Corpataux 2009: 148.

28. On Gautier's review, see Corpataux 2009: 145 and n. 1.

29. On nudity as an Orientalizing motif in Gérôme's paintings, see Ryan 1993: 1134.

30. For the painting, see the Walters Art Museum, Baltimore, 37.885.

31. House 2008: 272.

32. Ryan 1993: 1135; Von Waldegg 1972: 123.

33. The provenance of the items are as follows: Tuaillon, Berlin, Staatliche Museen, B II 82; Begas, Berlin, Staatliche Museen, Nr. NG 23/60; Maillol, Houston Museum of Fine Art, 28.17; Lepcke, Berlin, Staatliche Museen, B I 286.

34. For the story, see Ath. 590f; the painting is in the collection of the State Russian Museum, St. Petersburg.

35. The painting belongs to the collection of the Museum of Fine Arts, Boston, 1983.683.

36. For the influence of Phryne's receptions in painting on the performing arts, see Von Waldegg 1972: 136–137 and n. 89. For an image of Sanderson in her role as Phryne, see Lucien Augé de Lassus (1914), *Saint-Saëns*, Paris: C. Delgrave, plate between pp. 180 and 181.

37. Toepfer 1997: 23–24.

Chapter 1

1. For a summary of ancient references to Phryne, see Kapparis 2017: 439–41.

2. Diod. Ath. fr. 5 = Ath. 591d–e; διὰ τὴν ὠχρότητα, Plut. *Mor.* 401a.

3. Ath. 590e, 591c, e.

4. Ath. 591c.

5. Ath. 591c–d.

6. Timocles, *Neaera* fr. 25 K-A.= Ath. 567e; Machon fr. 18.385 = Ath. 583b–c. The comic poet Anaxilas compares her to Charybdis for "swallowing" the entire ship of one of her clients, *Neottis* fr. 22 K-A = Ath. 558d. Even as an old woman, she continued to command a high price for her services; see Plut. *Mor.* 125 A.

7. Ath. 591d.

8. *Anth. Plan.* 204 = Ath. 591a–b.

9. Ath. 591b–c.

10. Plut. *Mor.* 401a; Diog. Laert. 6.60.

11. On her rejection of lovers, Timocles, *Neaera* fr. 25 K-A.= Ath. 567e–f, 591d; Machon fr. 450–55 = Ath. 583c. On the provision of a seat at her table to the Athenian Gryllion, see Ath. 591e.

12. Ath. 558a–e, 567e–f, 583c, 588e.

13. Ath. 583c, 584b–d, 585e–f.

14. Gal. *Protr.* 10.43.

15. Ath. 590f–591a; see also Plin. *NH* 35.91, 35.86–87.

16. Ath. 591a; cf. 585f.

17. Ath. 590d–591f = Posidippus, *Ephesia* fr. 13 K-A.

18. Ath. 590d. On Euthias, see Ath. 590e.

19. Ath. 590e.

20. Ath. 591e.

21. For the challenges posed by the ancient evidence, see Treggiari 2007; Skinner 2011; Carney 2013.

22. Plut. *Mor.* 401a–b.

23. For a translation and discussion of the text, see Boehringer 2018. Some ancient writers identify female poets as hetaeras; see McClure 2003a: 84–86. Schlesier 2013 provocatively argues that Sappho, who first uses the word hetaera, depicts not a transitional world of adolescent girls just before marriage but rather mature, autonomous hetaeras.

24. Boehringer 2018; 376. Ancient sources state that the last part of the treatise concerned sexual positions; see Clem. Al. *Protr.* 4.61.2. On Philaenis, see further Kapparis 2017: 53–55.

25. Kennedy 2014 argues that some of the characteristics associated with hetaeras in fourth-century Athens actually belonged to a group of women who were not prostitutes but rather were metic women like Aspasia.

26. See Glazebook 2021 for an excellent analysis of how Attic oratory deploys prostitution as part of a moral discourse that targets women of uncertain status for rhetorical ends.

27. Cohen 2015: 16.

28. For these and other examples, see Cohen 2015: 16–17.

29. Since citing a non-existent law was an offense punishably by death, direct quotation of a law is presumed accurate; see Dem. 26.24.

30. συνθήκας πρὸς αὐτὸν ποιησάμενος, Lysias 3.22.

31. Cohen 2015: 15.

32. Ath. 590e, 591e–f; ps.-Plut. Harpocr. s. v. *Euthias.*

33. Fr. 49 K-A = Ath. 590a; fr. 25 K-A = Ath. 567e, 591c; fr. 2 K-A = Ath. 570b–d; fr. 67 K-A = Ath. 568f; on the interplay of comedy and oratory, see Glazebrook 2021: 13–15 and passim. On fourth-century comedies centered around hetaeras, see Henderson 2000; Glazebrook 2021: 38–40.

34. McClure 2003a: 39 and 210 n. 68; see Henry 1985: 15.

35. Cooper 1995: 314.

36. Fr. 22 K-A = Ath. 558a–e; frr. 25, 27 K-A = Ath. 567e–f; fr. 14 K-A = Ath. 568a, 591d.

37. See Ath. 567a; 586f; 586a; 591c; 587b; 583d. For moral discourse on Phryne, see Dio. Laert. 2.7, 6.2; Plut. *Mor.* 336d; [Lucian] *Dem. Enc.* 12; Tert. *Apol.* 10; for rhetorical treatises, see Ael. *VH* 9.32; for Greek epigram, see *Anth. Pal.* 21.203, 205, 206; *Anth. Plan.* 56; for geography, see Paus. 15.1, 20.1–2, 27.5; for Latin poetry, see Lucil. 7.290; Propert. 2.6.6; for Phryne as the subject of epistolary fictions, see Alc. 4.1, 3–5. It seems noteworthy that she does not feature in Lucian's *Dialogues of the Courtesans*, although he does mention her in a proverbial way at 22. On the genres associated with hetaeras and their influence on Athenaeus, see McClure 2003a: 27–46.

38. Hawley 1993: 75.

39. References to Phryne in *Dining Sophists* are difficult to quantify, but she does seem to get more extensive treatment than the other hetaeras, especially at 583c–585f and 590e–591e; see McClure 2003a: 193–94.

40. Most references to Phryne in Athenaeus are clustered in section 590d–591e; for a list, see McClure 2003a: 192–93 and n. 52, 197.

41. Ath 591c = *FGrH* 405 F 1 (as previously); on Alcetas and this passage, see now Rzepka 2010.

42. Ath. 567a, 591d; see Hawley 1993: 76 and 88 n. 4.

43. Ath. 221f, 335d–e, 457e, 83.

44. Hawley 1993: 76.

45. Plut. *Mor.* 1039b, 125a; Julian 7.226b.; Tert. *Apol* 9; Sext. Emp. *Pyr.* 9.153.

46. Filonik 2013: 33.

47. For recent scholarship on hetaeras in ancient Greece, see Davidson 1997; Ogden 1999; McClure 2003a; Budin 2008; Glazebrook and Henry 2011; Cohen 2015; Glazebrook and Tsakirgis 2016; Kapparis 2017; Silver 2018. The most extensive analyses of Phryne are Raubitschek 1941; Cooper 1995; Eidinow 2010; and Morales 2011, and most recently, a monograph by Melissa Funke, which appeared in print too late in the production process (February 2024) to consult for this project. For comparable monographs on individual hetaeras, see Henry 1995 (Aspasia) and Hamel 2003 (Neaera).

48. Kurke 1997: 107.

49. Gilhuly 2009: 183.

50. Cooper 1995: 303–18; Kowalski 1947: 50–62.

51. Havelock 1995: 3–4.

52. McClure 2003a: 126–36; Morales 2011.

53. Davidson 1997: 202.

54. Morales 2011: 72; see also Davidson 1997: 134.

55. Hawley 1993: 75.

56. McClure 2003a: 167–69; Kapparis 2017: 373.

57. Kapparis 2017: 335, 337.

58. Kapparis 2017: 261; see also Davidson 2006: 30; Hoernes 2012: 61.

59. Kapparis 2017: 441.

60. Eidinow 2010: 14.

61. Keesling 2006: 66–71.

62. Corso 1997: 127–28 and 2004: 239–40.

63. Davidson 2006: 35.

64. Hartman 2008: 11.

65. Morales 2011: 72–73; Cavallini 2010 as cited by Kapparis 2017: 325; Hoernes 2012: 55.

Chapter 2

1. On the inability to distinguish hetaeras from respectable women in terms of dress, see McClure 2015; on the lack of specific names associated with hetaeras, see Taylor 2020.

2. Xen. *Ath. Pol.*1.1.10.

3. Dem. 47.58–59, 61. For the view that slaves are virtually indistinguishable from free persons in art, see Lewis 2002: 140; Rihll 2011: 50; Sommerstein 2013: 136; Cohen 2015: 23.

4. [Dem.] 53.16; Cohen 2015: 24.

5. Ar. *Lys.* 23; Vlassopoulos 2011: 124.

6. Isae. 6.10.

7. Glazebrook 2021: 45.

8. At age seventeen, boys were presented to their father's deme for membership; if approved, his name was entered into the deme rolls, providing incontrovertible proof of citizenship; for the process, see Harrison 1971: 205–7.

9. Kennedy 2014: 98. Kapparis 1999: 34, "It was much easier to question the citizen status of a woman, since women were not included either in the phratry or the deme registers"; for further discussion, see also pp. 192–93. See also Patterson 1994: 208; Davidson 1997: 75; Miner 2003: 25–26; Glazebrook 2021: 5.

10. ποικίλος, Pl. Symp. 182a7–9.

11. Cohen 2015: 72–74 argues that a few citizen women may have operated as independent hetaeras; cf. Lys. fr. 82; Ath. 572a = Antiphanes fr. 210 K-A. See also Hirzel [1918] 1962: 71 n. 1.

12. Harrison 1968: 165; see Kapparis 2021: 33.

13. Jameson 1997: 96.

14. Kapparis 1999: 199–202; on the law, cf. Arist. *Ath.* 26.2; *Pol.* 1275b31, 1278a34; Plut. *Per.* 37.

15. A discussion of terms is central to all contemporary scholarship on prostitution in classical antiquity; see Davidson 1997; McGinn 1998; Kurke 1999: 175–219; Ogden 1999; McClure 2003a: 11–26; Miner 2003; Faraone and McClure 2006: 6–8; Budin 2008; Glazebrook and Henry 2011: 4–8; Corner 2011: 72–75; Kapparis 2011; Goldhill 2015: 185–86; Cohen 2015: ix, 17–18, 31–38.

16. On *porne* and *doule* as a "verbal coupling," see Cohen 2015: 46–47; Glazebrook 2021: 20.

17. πόρνην καὶ δούλην ἄνθρωπον, Lys. 4.19. For the translation of the phrase and discussion of the status of the unnamed woman, see Glazebrook 2021: 26. On sexuality and slavery in this speech, see Marshall 2021.

18. Glazebrook 2021: 3; Kapparis 1999: 409; 2021: 168.

19. Kapparis 1999: 5.

20. Ath. 577c.

21. Ar. *Vesp.* 1353.

22. [Dem.] 59.122.

23. Herter 1960: 83–84; Davidson 1997; Cohen 2015; McClure 2003a; Kapparis 2017.

24. Dem. 23.53; Sommerstein 2013:12.

25. Henry 1995: 14; Kapparis 1999: 9. On the term, see the discussion of Kennedy 2014: 115.

26. Ogden 1996: 80; Kennedy 2014: 97.

27. Kennedy 2014: 115; Goldhill 2015: 186.

28. Henry 1995: 15 and passim believes that Aspasia's true status was a *pallake* rather than hetaera. Cf. Plut. *Per.* 24.2; Pl. *Men.* 235e; Cratinus frr. 258–59 K-A. See further Bicknell 1982; Kennedy 2014: 75–78.

29. Sommerstein 2013: 13–14.

30. Kurke 1999: 180–83, 185–87, 195, 218–19; "highly problematic," according Kapparis 2019: 304 and n. 126; see also McClure 2003a: 9–18; Glazebrook and Henry 2011: 4–8; Glazebrook 2011: 34–35; Corner 2011: 72–78.

31. On the importance of this distinction for the Greeks, see Kurke 1999. On hetaeras and gift exchange, see especially Davidson 1997: 111–12, 120–27; Cohen 2015: 83–86.

32. Kapparis 2019: 304.

33. Ogden 1996: 102 argues for "the absoluteness of the disjunction between the roles of the *hetaera* and the wife"; see also Goldhill 2015: 187.

34. Sommerstein 2013: 15–16; Ogden 1996: 157.

35. Brown 1990: 248–49; Davidson 1997: 99; Miner 2003: 32. Cf. [Andocides] 4.14; Dem. 48.43; [Dem.] 59.22; [Dem.] 49.9.

36. Kennedy 2014: 114.

37. Reinsberg 1993: 87; Davidson 1997: 75.

38. [Dem.] 59.14.17 and passim; Men. *Sam.* 21, 25; see also Reinsberg 1993: 161; Kurke 1999: 181; McClure 2003a: 67; Kennedy 2014: 68–74; Cohen 2015: 10–11.

39. Ῥοδώπιος ἑταίρης γυναικός, Hdt. 2.134.1; κάρτα ἐπαφρόδιτος γενομένη μεγάλα ἐκτήσατο χρήματα, 2.134.2. See also Schlesier 2013: 217, who notes the connection with Sappho.

40. Kapparis 2019: 358 n. 136. On the frequency of the term in Greek literature in the fifth and fourth centuries BCE, see McClure 2003a: 9–11.

41. Kennedy 2014: 86; see also Hirzel [1918] 1962: 71 n. 1; Cohen 2000: 144, "the sale of sexual services by both men and women, including citizens, was a commonplace and lawful aspect of Athenian life"; Cohen 2015: 70–71; Goldhill 2015: 186 and n. 27.

42. πόρνην καὶ δούλην ἄνθρωπον, Lys. 4.9; βασανισθείσης, 4.17; διὰ πόρνην καὶ δούλην ἄνθρωπον, 4.19.

43. ἐλευθέραν, 4.12, 14; αὕτη δὲ ὑπῆρχε κοινή, 4.16.

44. Kapparis 1999: 409; Glazebrook 2021: 32. For her status as a *pallake*, see Todd 2007: 375.

45. ἀπελευθέρα . . . παιδίσκας . . . . ὠνηθεῖσα πολλὰ μὲν ἔτη καθῆστο ἐν οἰκήματι, Isae. 6.19.

46. Isae. 6.20.

47. Glazebrook 2021: 48.

48. οὖσα δούλη, Isae. 6.49–50.

49. On the interchangeability of the terms, see Davidson 1997: 109–36 and 2006: 36–89; MacDowell 2000: 14; Miner 2003: 20, 35; Cohen 2015: 31–36.

50. Ogden 1996: 101.

51. Men. *Sam.* 20–28, 508. On Chrysis' social status, see most recently Sommerstein 2013: 31; see also Patterson 1998: 199–203; Corner 2011: 73.

52. Men. *Sam.* 23, 28.

53. Men. *Sam.* 35–38.

54. γ]αμετὴν ἑταίραν, ὡς ἔοικ᾽, ἐλάνθανον ἔχ]ων, Men. *Sam.* 130.

55. γαμετήν; πῶς; ἀγνοῶ ⟨γὰρ⟩ τὸν λόγον, Men. *Sam.* 131.

56. Ogden 1996: 100.

57. ὅτι ἑταίρα τε ἦν τοῦ βουλομένου, καὶ ὅτι οὐδ᾽ ἐξ ἑνὸς ἄλλου φαίνεται τεκοῦσα, Isae. 3.15; Dem. 48. 52–56.

58. On the date, see Kapparis 1999: 28.

59. ἠσεβηκυῖαν, [Dem.] 59.117. For a discussion of this passage, see Glazebrook 2021: 84–87.

60. For the text and argument, see Kapparis 1999; for an analyses of gender and sexual identity in the oration, see Glazebrook 2021: 63–93.

61. ξένη μὲν γυναικὶ συνοικοῦντα παρὰ τὸν νόμον, [Dem.] 59.13.

62. [Dem.] 59.18.

63. Apollodorus emphasizes her status as a purveyor of venal sex with the repetition of words for labor (ἐργασία) and payment (μισθός); cf. [Dem.] 59.19, 20, 22, 23, 26, 41, and especially 114. See also Glazebrook 2005.

64. ἠργάζετο τῷ σώματι μισθαρνοῦσα τοῖς βουλομένοις αὐτῇ πλησιάζειν, [Dem.] 59.20.

65. ὡς ἂν ἑταίρα οὖσα, [Dem.] 59.24.

66. On Neaera's status as a *doule*, cf. [Dem.] 59.18, 20, 23, 29, 108, 118.

67. αὐτῶν δούλην εἶναι, [Dem.] 59.30; ἑταίραν, 59.31.

68. [Dem.] 59.30.

69. For the transaction, see Glazebrook 2014; Kamen 2013.

70. ὡς ἂν ἑταίρα οὖσα, [Dem.] 59.24, 25, 28, 37, 48, 49.

71. [Dem.] 59.35.

72. προΐσταται, [Dem.] 59.37; γυναῖκα αὐτὴν ἔξω . . . τούς τε παῖδας τοὺς ὄντας αὐτῇ τότε εἰσάξων εἰς τοὺς φράτερας ὡς αὐτοῦ ὄντας καὶ πολίτας ποιήσων, 59.38. On sponsorship and metic women, see Kennedy 2014: 2–3.

73. ἐπὶ προσχήματος ἤδη τινὸς οὖσα καὶ ἀνδρὶ συνοικοῦσα, [Dem.] 59.41.

74. τινα ξένον ἀγνῶτα πλούσιον λάβοι ἐραστὴν αὐτῇ, [Dem.] 59.41.

75. ἄνθρωπον ἐλευθέραν εἶναι καὶ αὐτὴν αὑτῆς κυρίαν, [Dem.] 59.46. Glycera in Men. *Peri.* 497 is similarly described as the guardian of herself (ἑαυτῆς ἐστ᾽ ἐκείνη κυρία).

76. ἐξ ἀρχῆς δούλη ἦν καὶ ἐπράθη δὶς καὶ ἠργάζετο τῷ σώματι ὡς ἑταίρα οὖσα, [Dem.] 59.49.

77. τοιαύτη οὖσα, [Dem.] 59. 73, 81, 85. Kapparis 1999: 37; Miner 2003: 24–26.

78. Patterson 1994: 208; Miner 2003: 27: Glazebrook 2021: 74–75.

79. Miner 2003: 27; McClure 2003a: 76–77; Cohen 2015: 145–53; Glazebrook 2021: 74.

80. [Dem.] 59.50.

81. [Dem.] 59.59–61.

82. πλησιάζουσαν αὐτῷ, [Dem.] 59.67.

83. ὁπόσαι ἂν ἐπ᾽ ἐργαστηρίου καθῶνται ἢ πωλῶνται ἀποπεφασμένως, [Dem.] 59.67.

84. [Dem.] 59.74–78.

85. [Dem.] 59. 107–8.

86. The claims are clearly exaggerated; see Kapparis 1999: 400–1 and Nowak 2010: 189.

87. [Dem.] 59.118.

88. Patterson 1994: 205–7; Glazebrook 2021: 67.

89. Sommerstein 2013: 15 argues that she is a *pallake*, like Chrysis in Menander's *Samia*; on her status, see Ogden 1996: 124; Kennedy 2014: 137–40; Glazebrook 2021: 67.

90. Glazebrook 2021: 67; see also Glazebrook 2005: 162, 182–83. On the ambiguous status of other hetaeras in oratory, see Foxhall 1996: 151; Hunter 1994: 113. *Contra* Hamel 2003 and Kapparis 2019: 243–44, who both assume that she was an active hetaera.

91. τῶν πορνῶν ἐργασία, [Dem.] 59.108; παιδοποιεῖσθαι . . . καὶ τελετῶν καὶ ἱερῶν καὶ τιμῶν μετέχειν τῶν ἐν τῇ πόλει, 59.113.

92. [Dem.] 59.41. On the desirability of passing as wives, see McClure 2003a: 14 and 204 n. 26; Davidson 1997: 125, 132–33; *contra* Ogden 1996: 102.

93. ([Dem.] 59.19.

94. Patterson 1994: 208; Glazebrook 2021: 67. On her uncertain social status, see Cohen 2015: 73 n. 27; Kennedy 2014: 114, who argues that women identified as hetaeras were most frequently metics, and could even be citizens, but they did not necessarily engage in commercial sex.

95. [Dem.].59.122; see Davidson 1997: 73.

96. Assante 2007: 131.

97. Bonfante 1989: 560–61, 567.

98. Reinsberg 1993; see also Peschel 1987; Kurke 1999: 175–219;

99. Neils 2000: 208. On the purse as an attribute of commercial sex, see Keuls 1983: 258–60.

100. Attic red-figure kylix by the Thalia Painter, c. 510 BCE. Berlin, Antikensammlung 3251.

101. For the names Aphrodisia and Obole, see Cohen 2015: 52; Taylor 2020: 71–72, 74-75; for Callisto and Rhodopis, see British Museum E68 and B329, respectively. For hetaera name inscriptions on Attic vases, see Peschel 1987: 74–79, 183–84; Kurke 1999: 201–3. On the status of the female figures depicted on British Museum B329 as citizen women, see Kosso 2009: 95.

102. Attic black figure hydria, British Museum 329. Taylor 2020: 73–74 states that the name Rhodôpis is never attested as a name of real women, although many formed from *rhodos-* are.

103. Rodenwalt 1932.

104. Keuls 1983: 258–60.

105. Davidson 1997: 88; see more recently Ault 2016: 88, 91.

106. See especially Wrenhaven 2009; also Cohen 2015: 49–54, 55–59.

107. Kreilinger 2007.

108. Bonfante 1989: 558–59 and nn. 89, 91; Havelock 1995: 45; cf. *Hom. Hymn Dem.* 198–205; Clem. Al. *Protr.* 2.17; Hom. *Il.* 22.79–81. On supplication as a religious and cultural practice, see Gould 1973: 75.

109. Hom. *Il.* 22.80–83; A. *Cho.* 896–97; but for Menelaus' reaction of Helen's baring of her breasts, cf. Eur. *Andr.* 627–30; Ar. *Lys.* 155–56.

110. On the turn toward male and female nudity in wedding scenes on Attic red-figure vases, see Sutton 1997/98; Sutton 2009a and 200b.

111. Attic red-figure and white-ground amphora by the Andocides Painter, c. 530–520 BCE, Paris, Louvre F 203. Kilmer 1993: 89–90 finds overtones of female homoeroticism ("The fish bear a curious resemblance to olisboi").

112. Lewis 2002: 111; see also Peschel 1987; Kilmer 1993: 159–67; Havelock 1995: 31; Kurke 1997; Sutton 2009a; Kapparis 2019: 349–50.

113. See Lee 2015: 196, 215 (transparent clothing); 164 (footwear); 72, 81 (hairstyles); 167 (mirrors); and 159 (*sakkos*). See also McClure 2015 on Aristophanes' *Lysistrata*.

114. Ferrari 2002: 14–16.

115. Bundrick 2012: 12 and n. 4.

116. Bundrick 2012: 20.

117. Bundrick 2008: 297–301 and Bundrick 2012. See also Kilmer 1993: 164–66.

118. Sutton 2009a: 67.

119. Peschel 1987: 63–65; Kurke 1999: 209–11.

120. Keuls 1983: 176–80, and 167–70.

121. [Dem.] 59.33.

122. Kurke 1999: 2011–13; see also Kilmer 1993: 34–36, 49–50 (R156) and 59–62 (R518).

123. Kapparis 1999: 340.

124. Kapparis 2019: 341.

125. Kapparis 2019: 354.

126. Ar. *Ach.* 1198–1234; *Vesp.* 1326–71; *Av.* 666–74; *Thesm.* 1174–1201.

127. References to the female anatomy, cf. Ar. *Ach.* τῶν τιτθίων, *Ach.* 1299; τὰ τῆς πυγῆς, *Pax* 869; *Lys.* 1158–74; to handling the penis, cf. *Ach.* 1216; *Lys.* 1119–21, *Vesp.* 1342–47; spatial mobility, cf. Ar. *Pax* 874.

128. Most current scholarship rejects Wilamowitz's earlier view that naked hetaeras played the feminine abstractions in these plays; for a summary of this debate, see Henry 1985: 29–30; Henderson 1987: 195–96; Zweig 1992; and Taaffe 1993: 23–47. Stone 1981: 144–46 argues that the term *gumnos* does not always denote actual nudity, but can be figuratively applied to scant clothing.

129. Ath. 569a–c = Xenarchus, *Pentathlete* fr. 4 K-A.

130. On the public display of female bodies in brothels, see Davidson 1997: 130; McClure 2003a: 110–13.

131. Schaps 1977: 323.

132. On the identification of hetaeras by their names, see Wrenhaven 2009: 380–81; Fischer 2013: 248; Kamen 2013: 151–52; Cohen 2015: 58; Ault 2016: 93; Glazebrook 2016: 191–93. On the lack of clear distinction between the names of hetaeras and free women, see McClure 2003a: 64–65, 68; Boehringer 2018.

133. Taylor 2020: 57, 78.

134. Thuc. 2.45.2.

135. Dem. 40.6.

136. Hdt. 2.135.

137. Dem. 30 and passim. See Schaps 1977: 325; Hamel 2003: 28.

138. [Dem.] 59.58.

139. Schaps 1977: 328–29.

140. McClure 2003a 59.

141. See *LGPN* http://clas-lgpn2.classics.ox.ac.uk/cgi-bin/lgpn_search.cgi?status = het.

142. Cohen 2015: 145.

143. Ath. 577d–583d; 585f–587f; 586a, f, 583d, 587b, 591c.

144. ἐκ παιδίου, Ath. 578c.

145. Ath. 578b–c.

146. For a complete list of names associated with hetaeras in Book 13 of Athenaeus, see McClure 2003a: 183–97 (Appendix III).

147. Ath. 576d; Xen. *An.* 1.10.2–3, where she is called a *pallake* rather than hetaera; see further McClure 2003a: 69.

148. Taylor 2020: 57; McClure 2003a: 64–78.

149. Ath. 583e.

150. Schneider 1913.

151. Men. F 96 K-A; Men. *Per.* Cf. Ath. 585c–d, 586b–d, 595d–596b, 605d. See Traill 2012: 33–45; Taylor 2020: 60.

152. Taylor 2020: 66.

153. Taylor 2020: 69–70 nn. 65–66.

154. Taylor 2020: 71–72.

155. [Dem.] 59.19–20; Hyp. 3.3, 5; Hyp. frr. 13–26; Hyp. frr. 171–80. For the theory that persons named in oratory were publicly known and familiar to jurors, see Kapparis 2021: 29–36.

156. On Ninos, cf. Dem. 39.2; Dem. 40.9; [Din.] fr. 33; on Theoris, cf. Dem. 25.79; see also Schaps 1977: 326. The nominative form of Ninos' name is unknown as it only appears in the accusative case in the ancient sources; cf. Dem. 39.2; [Din.] fr. 33.1. Eidinow calls her Ninon in conformance with the entry in *LGPN*; see Eidinow 2015: 17 n. 24; Collins 2001 uses Nino. I follow most scholars in referring to her as Ninos, although the use of a masculine ending -os in a feminine name is unusual; indeed it is at male name in a passage by Phoenix of Colophon quoted by Athenaeus (Ath. 421d). In myth, Ninos was the eponymous Greek founder of Nineveh, the ancient capital of Assyria.

157. Isae. 6.19; Isae. 3.11–14.

158. Neaera is only attested three times in antiquity apart from [Dem.] 59, and not before the second century BCE; see Taylor 2020: 73 n. 83.

159. A possible appearance of Anteia is found in an inscription from Orchomenos dating to the second century BCE, *IG* V (2) 345, 9 (["Ἄν]τεια?: d. Δαμόξενος, m. Δαμόξενος. Even if the correct name is Antheia (Ath. 586e), it only occurs twice in non-Attic context, and very late: *BSA* 61 (1966) p. 199 no. 3, 25("Ἀνθε[ια]) *IG* V (1) 1482.

160. Only found in two very late Athenian inscriptions: possibly *IG* II² 4239, and *IG* II² 3754, 8 (m. Ζήνων III).

161. Unattested outside of literary sources, but occurs three times in oratory: Lys. fr. ep. iii; Hyp. fr. V–vi no. 13; [D.] lix 19–23; cf. Ath. 107e, 584f.

162. Although appearing 150 times in *LGPN*, Phila is never attested at Athens outside of literary sources ([D.] lix 19; *PCG* 7 pp. 326 f. fr. 9); cf. Plut., *Mor.* 849d; *FGrH* 338 F 12, 14.

163. Lys. fr. ep. iii; Hyp. fr. v–vi no. 13; [Dem.] 59.19–23.

164. Ath. 167c, 567c, 586e, 690a.

165. *IG* II² 12672.

166. *IG* II² 12876, *IG* II² 12666, *IG* II² 12877/8 (d. Εὐθυκράτης).

167. BCE *IG* I³ 1328; *IG* II² 12259; *IG* II² 6766; *IG* II² 10774; *IG* II² 10772; *IG* II² 10775; *IG* II² 1534 A.

168. *IG* II² 1533; =Aleshire, *Asklepieion* nv. III, 11.

169. *IG* II² 4627 (? m. Ὀλυμπιόδωρος); *IG* II² 7681 ([Θε]ωρίς?).

170. Taylor 2020: 73 n. 90; Lidov 2002: 227; Boehringer 2018; *pace* Schlesier 2013.

171. Φρύνην ἔχουσαν λήκυθον πρὸς ταῖς γνάθοις, Ar. *Eccl.* 1101; Plut. *Mor.* 401b.

172. My translation is a version of Taillardat. Most agree that Φρύνην here is a proper name, and many texts capitalize it, but the conjecture largely derives from references to Phryne in Athenaeus and Alciphron; for a summary of the arguments, see Ussher 1986: 223–24 and Slater 1989: 47–49.

173. *IG* I³ 700, c. 400–380 BCE; *IG* II² 10233; *IG* II² 10361; =*FRA* 6880; *NScav* 1928, p. 383 no. 2.

174. See *LGPN* http://clas-lgpn2.classics.ox.ac.uk/cgi-bin/lgpn_search.cgi?name = Μνησαρέτη.

175. Thespiae: *IG* VII 1936, *SEG* XIX 353 b ([M]νασαρέτα), *SEG* XIX 355 b; Messene: *SEG* XXXVIII 346 a & XLI 370; cf. *PAE* 1987, pl. 80 α; Phoinike: Cabanes, *L'Épire* pp. 569ff. no. 47, 6; = *SEG* XXVI 720; Larisa: *IG* IX (2) 571; *SEG* XXXV 591, 7 (d. Παντάπονος); Orchomenos: *SEG* XXVIII 455, 13 (or Koroneia); and Koroneia: *SEG* XXXIII 362.

176. Ath. 591c.

177. Ath. 591e.

178. On Phryne's multiple identies, see Cooper 1995: 317 n. 39; Raubitschek 1941; Rzepka 2010.

179. Isae. 6.21; Glazebrook 2011: 51.

180. Cohen 2015: 64; cf. [Dem.] 59.38.

181. βουλομένη ὑπ' ἀμφοτέρων ἐρᾶσθαι, Lys. 4.8.

182. [Dem.] 59.30.

183. [Dem.] 59.33.

184. Lys. fr. 299 Carey = Ath. 586f; see Kapparis 2021: 75–76. For violence and abuse related to hetaeras in oratory more generally, see Kapparis 2019: 209–40.

185. Men. *Sam.* 390–97.

186. Lape 2021: 30.

Chapter 3

1. Ath. 569e.

2. Historical persons regularly appear in Attic old and middle comedy, as well as forensic speeches, and then reappear in philosophical discourse; see Henry 1995: 29. For example, Alce, the freedwoman and brothel manager, is introduced as someone "whom many of you know" (Is. 16.19), suggesting that the jurors had personal knowledge of her or her establishment; see Kapparis 2017: 291.

3. Ath. 569e-f = Philemon, *The Brothers* fr. 3 K-A.

4. Parker 1996: 48 and n. 23. Although some scholars such as Reinsberg 1989: 161–62 and Rosenzweig 2004: 18 treat this anecdote as factual, most scholars find it highly fictionalized; see Rosivach 1995: 2–3; Parker 1996: 40 n. 26; Frost 2002: 34–46; McClure 2003a: 113 and 218 n. 17; Kapparis 2017: 35–46. On prostitution as a democratic institution, see Kurke 1999: 199; Halperin 1990: 100; Cohen 2015: 30.

5. Nowak 2010: 185.

6. ὁπόσαι ἄν ἐπ' ἐγαστηρίου καθῶνται ἢ πωλῶνται ἀποπεφάσμενος, [Dem.] 59.67. For the phrase, see Lys. 10: 19; Plut. *Sol.* 23; Harp. s.v. *polôsi*; Phot. α 2604. For further discussion, see Kapparis 1995: 97–112 and 2019: 37–39, 311–13; *pace* Johnstone 1998: 253.

7. Kapparis 2017: 43–44; Henry 2011: 14–33.

8. Sappho frr. 1–2; see also Burkert 1991: 155; Goff 2004: 236–40.

9. Rosenzweig 2004: 3.

10. παρθενίους τ' ὀάρους μειδήματά τ' ἐξαπάτας τε/τέρψιν τε γλυκερὴν φιλότητά τε μειλιχίην τε, Hes. *Th.* 206–7. A later tradition makes her the daughter of Zeus and Dione, see Pl. *Symp.* 180d; Paus. 1.22.3.

11. Hom. *Il.* 3.383–420; 14.187–223; Sappho fr. 1; E. *Hipp.* 1–57.

12. Rosenzweig 2004: 19, 25–26; see Paus. 1.22.3.

13. Parker 1996: 48–49 and n. 26.

Notes   167

14. Parker 1996: 234 and n. 59; Buxton 1982: 32; Rosenzweig 2004: 19: see Isoc. *Antid.* 249; Paus. 1.22.3.

15. Burkert 1991: 155 and 409 n. 34; Parker 1996: 196 and n. 158; see Pl. *Symp.* 180d–181a; Xen. *Symp.* 8.9; Paus. 1.14.7.

16. Parker 1996: 196.

17. Hdt. 1.199.

18. Budin 2008: 58–92.

19. Ath. 573e = P. fr. 122.7–9.

20. Budin 2008: 119.

21. Neils 2000: 213–14; Dillon 2002: 202–3.

22. Hdt. 1.93; 2.134–35.

23. On the objects found in Building Z3, see Knigge 2005: 68; Glazebrook 2016: 191.

24. Vernant 1969.

25. [Dem.] 59.108.

26. Lape 2021.

27. Hdt. 2.135; Ath. 595a; Paus. 1.37.5.

28. Xen. *Anab.* 1.10.3, 4.3.20; *Cyr.* 4.3.2.

29. Glazebrook 2011: 46.

30. Nowak 2010; Glazebrook 2011: 53; Cohen 2015: 31; Kapparis 2017: 269.

31. Xen. *Mem.* 2.2.4.

32. Aeschin. 1.124. Glazebrook 2011: 36; 2016: 170.

33. Isae. 6.19; Aeschin. 1.74; [Dem.] 59.67. Glazebrook 2011: 35; Cohen 2015: 4–5.

34. Glazebrook 2011: 37.

35. Glazebrook 2011: 41; see Isae. 6.18–21; D. 59.18.

36. Glazebrook 2011; Ault 2016; Kapparis 2017: 285.

37. Ault 2016: 90.

38. Knigge 2005: I. 202, 210; II. Tafel 122, 717, 714/715; Tafel 127, 794.

39. Ault 2016: 92.

40. Glazebrook 2016: 193.

41. Isae. 6.19; [Dem.] 59.41.

42. Davidson 1997: 104–7; Kapparis 2017: 285–86.

43. τὴν οἰκίαν ἀφθόνως κατεσκευασμένην, Xen. Mem. 3.11.4.

44. Ath. 579e–581a = Machon fr. 258–332.

45. Lynch 2007: 243.

46. Murray 1990a: 6.

47. Nevett 1999: 37–39; Lynch 2007: 243.

48. Lynch 2007: 243–44.

49. Lissarague 1990: 7.

50. Murray 1990: 5–6; Lynch 2007: 243–44.

51. Corner 2011: 60.

52. On the difference between the *deipnon* and symposium, see Lissarague 1990: 7.

53. Isae. 3.13; Cic. *Verr.* 2.1.66; Nowak 2010: 191; Kapparis 1999: 220.

54. ἀπὶ τὰ δεῖπνα ἔχων αὐτὴν πανταχοῖ ἐπορεύετο, ὅπου πίνοι, ἐκώμαζέ τ᾽ ἀεὶ μετ᾽ αὐτῆς, συνῆν τ᾽ ἐμφανῶς ὁπότε βουληθείη πανταχοῦ, [Dem.] 59.33.

55. Ar. *Ach.* 1089–93.

56. Isae. 3.13–14.

57. Nowak 2010: 190; see [Dem.] 59.22–23, 24–25, 34, 46, 108; Is. 3.13.

58. [Dem.] 59.24.

59. Davidson 1997: 95.

60. Xen. *Symp.* 2.1–3.

61. Pl. *Symp.* 176e.

62. Pl. *Symp.* 176e, 212c–d.

63. On the witticisms of hetaeras, see Kurke 2002; McClure 2003b.

64. Ath. 583c = Machon 450–55; on the amount, see Loomis 1998: 171, 183, 309.

65. Ath. 585e.

66. Ath. 585e.

67. Ath. 585f.

68. Ath. 585f.

69. Gnom. 577.1.

70. Cohen 2015: 27.

71. Xen. *Oec.* 5.1; Eur. *Or.* 917–22; see Cohen 2015: 25.

72. τὸν τὰ αὑτοῦ πράττοντα τούτον, Pl. *Charm.* 163b6–8, c1–8; see Cohen 2015: 39.

73. Arist. *Rhet.* 1367a33.

74. Cohen 2015: 44.

75. Cohen 2015: 27.

76. Loomis 1998: 166–85; Cohen 2015: 162–70; Kapparis 2017: 306-13.

77. Cohen 2015: 164 and n. 47.

78. Loomis 1998: 184.

79. Loomis 1998: 185, 257; Kapparis 2017: 306–8.

80. Loomis 1998: 185.

81. Men. *Sam.* 390–97; *Col.* 128–30. Cohen 2015: 167 and n. 72.

82. [Dem.] 59.41.

83. Loomis 1998: 184; Glazebrook 2011: 47.

84. [Dem.] 59.29–32 and 46–47; see Kapparis 1999: 227–28; Cohen 2015: 174; Kapparis 2017: 119.

85. Cohen 2015: 164.

86. Men. *Sam.* 13–14; Dem. *Epist.* 3.30; Davidson 1997; Cohen 2015: 176.

87. Aeschin. 1.119; Fisher 2001: 258–59; Glazebrook 2011: 46–49; Cohen 2015: 13, 30, 116–18, 176–78; Kapparis 2017: 273.

88. καὶ τοὺς πριαμένους τὸ τέλος οὐκ εἰκάζειν, ἀλλ᾽ ἀκριβῶς εἰδέναι τοὺς ταύτῃ χρωμένους τῇ ἐργασίᾳ, Aeschin. 1.119.

89. Nowak 2010: 186.

90. Dem. 22.56–57.

91. Cohen 2015: 177 and n. 21.

92. Kapparis 2017: 273.

93. ἐλευθέραν εἶναι καὶ αὐτὴν αὑτῆς κυρίαν, [Dem.] 59.64.

94. Kapparis 1999: 235.

95. φοβουμένη δὲ τὸν Φρυνίωνα διὰ τὸ ἠδικηκέναι μὲν αὐτή, [Dem.] 59.37.

96. [Dem.] 59.46.

97. [Dem.] 59.29–32, 36–37. On binding contracts for sex between prostitutes and clients, see Lys. 3.22; Aeschin. 1.160, 165; Poll. 8.140; Plaut. *Asin.* 746–809. See also Davidson 1997: 100; Cohen 2015: 97–114; Kapparis 2017: 155.

98. ἔχεις τὰ σαυτῆς πάντα. προστίθημί σοι/ἐγὼ θεραπαίνας, Χρυσί, Men. *Sam.* 381–2. If Χρυσί is understood as χρυσί, then the implication is that she also can also take her gold jewelry with her. See also the discussion of Cohen 2015: 100–1.

99. κατὰ γραμματεῖον ἤδη τινὲς ἡταίρησαν, Aeschin. 1.165; Cohen 2015: 29, 97–98.

100. Cohen 2015: 103–6.

101. Lape 2021: 38.

102. Glazebrook 2011: 50; Cohen 2015: 138–43.

103. Glazebrook 2011: 51; Cohen 2015: 175.

104. Cohen 2015: 138.

105. [Dem.] 59.18–20.

106. Hyp. *Ath.* 2–3; Glazebrook 2021: 68.

107. Hyp. *Ath.* 2.

108. Xen. *Mem.* 3.11.4–5; Glazebrook 2011: 51–52; Cohen 2015: 139.

109. Isae. 6.21, 6.18.

110. τὴν Στεφάνου οἰκίαν, καὶ τὴν ἐργασίαν ταύτην εἶναι, [Dem.] 59.67.

111. Ogden 1996: 94–95; McClure 2003a: 76–77; Cohen 2015: 145–46.

112. For Callistion, see *IG* II².11793; Ath. 583a, quoting Machon, identifies Corone as the nickname of the mother of Callistion.

113. *IG* II².12026; *CIA* App. 102 b, 18.

114. *IG* II².10892.

115. On mother-daughter hetaeras, see McClure 2003a: 76–77; Cohen 2015: 149–50.

116. Ath. 583c = Machon fr. 18.385; =Ath. 567e = Timocles, *Neaera* fr. 25 K-A.

117. Plut. *Mor.* 125.

118. Ath. 591d = Callistratus, *On Hetaeras* = *FGrH* 348 F 1.

119. Ath. 591a–b *Anth. Pal.* 204 = *FGE* 910–13.

120. Plut. *Mor.* 400f–401; Ath. 596c; Dio. Sic. 1.14; Plin. *NH* 36.83. Another tradition, that an eagle swooped down and carried off one of her shoes while she was bathing and dropped it into the lap of the Egyptian pharaoh, Psammetichus, who promptly married her, is not recorded in any archaic or classical Greek text; see Strabo 17.1.33; Ael. 13.33.

121. Hdt. 2.134.

122. Hdt. 2.135.

123. Sappho fr. 7; see Strab. 17.1.33, Ath. 596b–c; see further Mueller 2016.

124. κάρτα ἐπαφρόδιτος γενομένη μεγάλα ἐκτήσατο χρήματα, Hdt. 2.135.2.

125. Hdt. 2.134–35.

126. Hdt. 2.135.

127. *GerKeram* 635; *SEG* 13.634; Keesling 2006: 61; Kapparis 2017: 317 and n. 7. There is also a vase inscription of the same name, although probably unrelated; see *BM Vases* II B 329; = *ABV* p. 334 no. 1.

128. Ehlers 1966: 90–93 argues that Aspasia was a hetaera, and the post-classical tradition often treats her as such, but most recent scholars assume she was free woman metic; see Bicknell 1982: 245; Henry 1995; Kennedy 2014: 74, 86.

129. Ath. 533d.

130. Ath. 219c; 569f; 589d. Other references include Ath. 220b–c, 533d, 599b, 569f–570a, 589e. On Aspasia as a wise woman, see Henry 1995: 66–67. On hetaeras and philosophers, see Kapparis 2017: 125–38.

131. Cratin. fr. 259 K-A; Eupol. fr. 110 K-A; Plut. *Per.* 24.6.

132. Plut. *Per.* 24, 32. For a comprehensive list of sources, see *RE* 2.2 (1896/ 1958): columns 1716–21.

133. *IG* II² 7394; see Bicknell 1982; Henry 1995: 10–11; see Plut. *Per.* 24.2.

134. Bicknell 1982: 244.

135. Henry 1995: 12.

136. Bicknell 1982: 243; Kennedy 2014: 75; see Plut. *Per.* 37; Arist. *Ath. Pol.* 26.3.

137. Bicknell 1982: 244; on this marriage, see Plut. *Per.* 24, 2–6; Schol. Pl. *Menex.* 235e, Harp. s.v. *Aspasia*; Suda. s.v. A.

138. Alternatively, Duris, *FGrH* 76 F 65 makes Aspasia responsible for the Samian War.

139. Ar. *Ach.* 524–34.

140. The allegation of Aspasia as a *pornoboskousa* is also recorded by Plut. *Per.* 32.1, while the women are called *auletrides* at Ath. 220f.

141. A contemporary comic fragment identifies Aspasia with Helen, Eupol. fr. 267 K-A, and another with Hera, the wife of Pericles-Zeus, Cratin. fr. 259 K-A; see Plut. *Per.* 24. 9; schol. Pl. *Menex.* 235e.

142. Plut. *Per.* 24.1.

143. Plut. *Per.* 32.1. Henry 1995: 14 believes Hermippus conjured up the impiety trial as a "dramatic fantasy."

144. Henry 1995: 32–33.

145. Xen. *Mem.* 2.6.36; Xen. *Oec.* 14.

146. Pl. *Men.* 234b4–7.

147. Pl. *Men.* 236d4–249c8.

148. Thuc. 2.45.2.

149. Xen. *Mem.* 3.11–16; see *SEMA* 1936, *SEMA* 1937 (d. Ἀγρέανος); *IG* II² 7869 (d. Νικόστρατος); *SEG* XXVI 267; *IG* II² 11103; see *SEG* XXVI 346 (?m. Δημήτριος). For Theodote in Athenaeus, see 220f, 535c, 574f, 588d–e.

150. Ath. 220f, 588d; *Anth. Pal.* 7.565; as travel companion of Alcibiades, Ath. 535c, 574e.

151. Γυναικὸς δέ ποτε οὔσης ἐν τῇ πόλει καλῆς, ἧ ὄνομα ἦν Θεοδότη, οἵας συνεῖναι τῷ πείθοντι, Xen. *Mem.* 3.11.1), while the men who patronize her are coyly called "friends" (φίλος, Xen. *Mem.* 3.11.4).

152. Xen. *Mem.* 3.11.4. On the dialogue and the culture of viewing in Athens, see Goldhill 1998.

153. οἷς ἐκείνην ἐπιδεικνύειν ἑαυτῆς ὅσα καλῶς ἔχοι, Xen. *Mem.* 3.11.1; τοὺς μαστοὺς καὶ τὰ στέρνα, Ath. 588d–e.

154. Xen. *Mem.* 3.11.3.

155. Xen. *Mem.* 3.11.4. On expensive clothing, jewelry, and attendants as the personal property of hetaeras, see Dem. 48.55; [Dem.] 59.35.

156. Socrates' queries assume that she might be a citizen (*politis*). For the vignette, see Goldhill 1998; Cartledge 2001: 159–60; Cohen 2015: 61.

157. τοὺς φιλοκάλους καὶ πλουσίους εὑρήσει, *Mem.* 3.11.9.

158. Xen. *Mem.* 3.11.10.

159. Xen. *Mem.* 3.11.14.

160. Cohen 2015: 62.

161. συνθηρατὴς τῶν φίλων, Xen. *Mem.* 3.11.15.

162. This discussion largely follows Corso 1997: 128–29; see also Corso 2004: 239–40; Eidinow 2010: 14 and 2015: 17–23; Kapparis 2017: 439–41.

163. On her status as a citizen of Thespiae, see Kapparis 2017: 440. As a parallel, the name appears on the stele of a young woman (c. 380 BCE), "Mnesarete, daughter of Socrates"; see Munich, Glyptothek 491 n. 1. Corso 2004: 239 asserts, without evidence, that she was descended from a noble family of Thespiae.

164. Ἀσπασίας τῆς Μιλησίας, Pl. *Men.* 249d.

165. Tuplin 1986.

166. I am grateful to my colleague at the University of Wisconsin, Claire Taylor, for this observation.

167. Fossey 1988: I.134–64; Corso 2004: 240.

168. Choricius, *Declamations* 8.

Chapter 4

1. Ath. 590f–591b.

2. Athenaeus is the only extant ancient account that makes Phryne the model for the Cnidian Aphrodite, although he does not name his source; see Ath. 591a; cf. 585f. The extant fragments of the comic poet Posidippus, who knew of her trial (Ath. 591e), do not link her to the statue, although Duris of Samos (c. 240–260 BCE), one of Pliny's sources for Greek artists, may have initiated the stories of the Cnidia, Phryne, and Praxiteles; for the view, see Havelock 1995: 55 and n. 1. Clement identifies the model as another of Praxiteles' mistresses, Cratina, and attributes this information to the historical treatise of Posidippus, *On Cnidus* (*FGrH* iv. p. 482); Clem. Al. *Protr.* 4.47; see also McClure 2003a: 130 and 221 n. 67. Choricius states that Phryne served as Praxiteles' model for an Aphrodite commissioned by the Spartans; see Choricius *Declamations* 8; Kapparis 2017: 324 and n. 29. Of the numerous epigrams in the Greek anthology that mention the Cnidian Aphrodite, not one of them involves Phryne; see *Anth. Pal.* 16.159–70.

3. On Praxiteles' Eros, Phryne, and the Thespian triad, see *Anth. Pal.* 6.260; 16.203, 204, 205, 206; Ath. 591a–b = Simon. *Anth. Plan.* 204, *FGE* 910–13; Paus. 9.27.3; 1.20.1–2; Suda th. 278. On Phryne's statue at Delphi, see Paus. 10.15.1; Ael. *VH* 9.32; Plut. *Mor.* 336d, 401a–b; Ath. 591b–c = Alcetas, *On the Dedications at Delphi FGrH* 405 F 1; [Dio. Chrys.] 37.28; as a statue of Aphrodite dedicated by Phryne, see Diog. Laert. 6.60. See further Corso 1997, 2004: 256–62.

4. On the Happy Hetaera, see Plin. *HN* 34.70–71; Tatianus *Ad Gr.* 33.3.55; see further Corso 2004: 308–11.

5. Ath. 591d = Callistratus, *On Courtesans, FrGH* 348 F1; Hor. Ep.

6. Havelock 1995: 134; Keesling 2006; Kapparis 2017: 337.

7. *Anth. Pal.* 16.159, 160, 161, 162, 163, 165, 166, 167, 168, 169, 170.

8. On Phryne and Praxiteles, see *Anth. Pal.* 6.260; 16.203, 204, 205, 206; *Anth. Plan.* 204. See Havelock 1995: 134–35.

9. Havelock 1995: 3; see also Dillon 2002: 195; Morales 2011.

10. Dillon 2010: 11 and 182 n. 26.

11. Athens National Museum Inv. 1, see Dillon 2010: 22.

12. Translation by Gisela Richter (1968: 26); see Dillon 2010: 185 n. 66.

13. Keesling 2006: 67.

14. Dillon 2010: 12.

15. Ajootian 2007: 30; Dillon 2010: 38.

16. Dillon 2010: 6.

17. Dillon 2010: 99.

18. Dillon 2010: 26.

19. Dillon 2010: 48–49.

20. Keesling 2006: 66.

21. Ma 2007: 207; Dillon 2010: 207.

22. Agora I 4568l; see Ajootian 2007: 19–20; Dillon 2010: 47 and 169.

23. Trans. Mabel Lang from Connelly 2007: 139; see also Keesling 2006: 76 n. 39; Dillon 2010: 9, 108–81 n. 14.

172   Notes

24. Ajootian 2007: 20 and 32 n. 67; Dillon 2010: 41.

25. *IG* II² 3454; see Dillon 2010: 40 and n. 146 and 169.

26. Paus. 1.27.4; *IG* II² 3464. See Dillon 2010: 40, 169.

27. Paus. 9.30.1; Corso 1997: 128.

28. Athens, National Archaeological Museum, no. 1463; Corso 2004: 143, 175–85.

29. Plin. *HN* 34.58; Havelock 1995: 41–42; Corso 2004: 111 n. 97; Ajootian 2007: 13.

30. Ajootian 2007; see also Dillon 2010: 40, 42.

31. *Ad veritatem*, Quint. 12.10.9.

32. Ajootian 2007: 28.

33. *IG* VII 1831; Ajootian 2007: 16–17.

34. Ajootian 2007: 30.

35. Paus. 9.27.5; [Dio. Chrys.] 37.28; Alciphr. 4.1 fr. 3; see also Pirenne-Delforge 1994: 289–93; Corso 2004: 257–81; Kapparis 2017: 322–24.

36. Paus. 9.21.7.

37. Pirenne-Delforge 1994: 292–93 argues that although Eros was the object of great veneration at Thespiae, evidence for his worship is relatively late; most of the ancient testimonia suggests that the cult of Aphrodite in Thespiae dates to the fifth century. On the Erotideia, see Paus. 9.31.3; Ath. 561e; Corso 2004: 278; Gutzwiller 2004: 386 and n. 2.

38. Plut. *Mor.* 753f; Alciphr. 4.1. fr. 3; Pirenne-Delforge 1994: 290.

39. Keesling 2006: 69, 76 n. 42. On Phryne as dedicator of the Eros only, see Ath. 591b; Strabo 9.2.25 (Glycera); Paus. 9.27.3–5 (implicit). On Praxiteles as dedicator, Alciphr. 4.1. Plutarch states that she shares a temple and worship with Eros (ἡ δὲ σύνναος μὲν ἐνταυθοῖ καὶ συνίερος τοῦ Ἔρωτος, Plut. *Mor.* 753f). According to Keesling, "the placement of her portrait next to a divine image in a temple would have implied deification in the late Hellenistic and Roman periods, not yet in the fourth century."

40. Pirenne-Delforge 1994: 290; Corso 2004: 261–62, fig. 105; Gutzwiller 2004: 87–88.

41. Corso 1997.

42. Corso 2004: 262–65.

43. Καλλιφάν Πεδαγένης Ἀφροδίτῃ εὐακόοι, *SEG* XXXI, 515; see Pirenne-Delforge 1994: 291–92, who also cites a bronze dedicatory hydria addressed to Aphrodite Thespiae.

44. Pirenne-Delforge 1994: 290–92, basing his argument on literary sources, incorrectly states that Aphrodite was the only female deity worshipped at Thespiae. For inscriptional evidence on the worship of Athena in the area of Thespiae, see Ajootian 2007: 16 and 31 n. 37.

45. Cic. *Ver.* 2.4.4, 2.60.135; see [Lucian] *Amores* 11; see Corso 2004: 277.

46. [Lucian] *Am.* 15–17.

47. Strabo 9.2.25; Plin. 36.22; Paus. 1.20.1–2 and 9.27.3–5; see Corso 2004: 278.

48. Corso 2004: 310.

49. Οὗτος Ἔρως ἐδίδαξε πόθους. Αὐτὴ φάτο Κύπρις| ποῦ σ' ἄρα δὴ σὺν ἐμοὶ δέρξατο Πραξιτέλη[ς]; Thebes inv. 310; see Plassart 1926: 404–6, no. 20; Corso 2004: 278. For an analysis of the inscription, see Gutzwiller 2004.

50. Ποῦ γυμνὴν εἶδέ με Πραξιτέλης. Plato, *Anth. Pal.* 16.160, 162; see Antipater of Sidon, *Anth. Pal.* 16.168.

51. Gutzwiller 2004: 406.

52. Ath. 590f–91a; Raubitschek 1941: 899; Rosenmeyer 2001: 254 n. 37. Two other epigrams mention Praxiteles' Eros, but not Phryne, see *Anth. Pal.* 12.56–57.

53. Ath. 591a = Simonides, *Anth. Pal.* 16.204.

Notes   173

54. Ἀντί μ' ἔρωτος Ἔρωτα, Geminus, *Anth. Pal.* 16.205; γέρας φιλίης, Julian, *Anth. Pal.* 16.203; λύτρον ἔδωκε πόθων, Leonidas, *Anth. Pal.* 16.206.

55. Geminus, *Anth. Pal.* 6.260.

56. Alciphr. 4.1 fr. 3.

57. Ov. *Met.* 10.243–97. See Havelock 1995: 130–31; Rosenmeyer 2001.

58. Anonymous, *Anth. Pal.* 16.162.

59. Corso 2004: 276.

60. Keesling 2006; Dillon 2010: 25–26.

61. Plin. *HN* 34.70–71.

62. Ath. 591a–b.

63. Corso 2004: 310 n. 510.

64. Tatianus *Ad Gr.* 33.3; for a full discussion of the Happy Hetaera, see Corso 2004: 308–17.

65. Strabo 9.2.25; Tatianus, *Ad Gr.* 34.4; see Corso 2004: 311.

66. *IG* 14.1146.6; see Corso 2004: 311 n. 515.

67. Choricius, *Declamationes* 8.57.

68. Ath. 591b–c.

69. Keesling 2006: 67.

70. Corso 1997: 123; see Ath. 591b = Alcestas *FGrHist* 405 F 1; [Dio. Chrys.] 37.28; Plut. *Mor.* 336d, 401a–b, 753f; Paus. 10.15.1; Ael. *VH* 9.32; Diog. Laert. 6.2.60; Lib. *Decl.* 25.40.

71. Corso 1997: 124.

72. Corso 1997 132 dates the statue to 335 or 334 BCE, after the neighboring monuments of Archidamus III and Philip II had been installed, probably around 338 and 336 respectively.

73. As *agalma*, see Ael. *VH* 9.32; as *andrias* or human subject, see Ath. 591b; as an *eikon* or portrait, see Paus. 10.15.1; Plut. *Mor.* 336d.

74. Diog. Laert. 37.28.

75. Corso 1997: 126.

76. Corso 1997: 132–34.

77. Keesling 2006: 66.

78. οἱ περικτίονες, Ath. 591b–c. As a dedication from the citizens of Delphi, see Keesling 2006: 47; Dillon 2010: 48. For an anti-Theban message on behalf of the Thespians, see Corso 1997: 132–33.

79. Keesling 2006: 66.

80. Paus. 10.15.1; Plut. *Mor.* 336d, 401b; Diog. Laert. 6.60 states that Phryne dedicated an image of Aphrodite.

81. Ath. 574c–d.

82. Corso 1997: 129; Keesling 2006: 61–63.

83. Hdt. 2.135; see Ath. 596c, who calls her Doricha, and the spits *obeliskoi*, "little spits." See Keesling 2006: 59–63.

84. *SEG* XIII.364; see Keesling 2006: 72 n. 6.

85. ἀνέθηκε Ῥοδῶπις; Mastrokostas as paraphrased by Keesling 2006: 61 and 72 n. 7.

86. Solid gold: Ath. 591b; Plut. *Mor.* 336d, 401a; Ael. *VH* 9.32; [Dio. Chrys.] 37.28–29; Lib. *Decl.* 25.40; gilded bronze: Paus. 10.15.1. See Corso 1997: 130; Keesling 2006: 68; Ajootian 2007: 14.

87. Hdt. 8.121.2; Paus. 10.18.7. Corso 1997: 130 believes the portrait statues of Archidamus III and Philip II were also of gilded bronze.

88. Dillon 2010: 25, 186 n. 93; Keesling 2006: 68–69.

89. Plut. *Mor.* 401a.

174   Notes

90. Keesling 2006; Ajootian 2007: 14; Dillon 2010: 48. Pausanias (10.15.1) locates it near two statues of Apollo.

91. Keesling 2006: 67.

92. Corso 1997: 123–50; Keesling 2006; Dillon 2010: 48.

93. *Pace* Keesling 2006: 68, who argues that the words stress "the anomaly of Phryne's portrait in the midst of the sanctuary in which most honorific portraits on display represented men, and a few women, of aristocratic status."

94. Keesling 2006: 66.

95. Ath. 594e–595b; Keesling 2006: 59.

96. Ath. 594e.

97. Plut. *Mor.* 401a.

98. Plut. *Mor.* 753f; Plut. *Mor.* 336d and 401a; see Diog. Laert. 6.60; Ael. *HV* 9.32; [Dio Chrys.] 37.28; Ath. 591b–c.

99. Ath. 577c = Polemen fr. 14 Preller.

100. Ath. 591c = Callistratus *FGrH* F 1.

101. Hom. *Od.* 6.79–96; Hes. *Op.* 519–24.

102. Hom. *Il.* 14.170–72.

103. Hes. *Theog.* 188–99; *Hom. h. Ven.* 5.62–64; Hom. *Od.* 8.362–66.

104. Glazebrook 2016: 181, 191.

105. Hom. *h. Ven.* 5.83–91.

106. Hom. *Il.* 3.397; Hom. *h. Ven.* 6.10–11.

107. Eur. *An.* 627–30; parodied at *Lys.* 155–56.

108. Sutton 2009a: 74–77.

109. Sutton 2009a.

110. Tallboy lekythos attributed to the Shuvalov Painter (private collection), see Sutton 2009b: 272–73 and Pl. 21C.

111. Only 10 percent of kneeling bathers are found on drinking cups, for which see Sutton 2009a: 83–84, fig. 8; Sutton 2009b: 274.

112. Sutton 2009b: 273.

113. Xen. *Mem.* 3.11.1.

114. γραφῇ, Xen. *Oec.* 10.19.1.

115. Sutton 2009:b 274.

116. Sutton 2009b: 274 and nn. 26–27.

117. Cic. *Inv. rhet.* 2.1–3; Plin. *NH* 35.64, 66; Dion. Hal. *De imit.* 6.31; see also Corso 2007: 16; Sutton 2009a–b; Dillon 2010: 1, 6–7, 167.

118. Cic. *Inv. rhet.* 2.1.

119. Sutton 2009b: 275.

120. Hom. *Il.* 3.157–58; Val. Max. 3.7.3; Arist. *Or.* 49.386.

121. Sutton 2009b: 275.

122. Sutton 2009b: 276.

123. Ael. *VH* 4.12; Sutton 2009b: 275.

124. Plin. *NH* 35.125.

125. Plin. *NH* 35.100.

126. Plin. *NH* 35.86; Ath. 588d.

127. Ath. 590f.

128. Ath. 588e.

129. ἤνθει, Clem. Al. *Protr.* 4.

130. Although the two women visiting the temple of Asclepius at Cos in Herod. 4 remark on the marvelous statues housed within and even paintings by Apelles, they do not mention an Aphrodite; see Havelock 1995: 86.

131. Plin. *HN* 35.79–90.

132. Plin. *HN* 35.91. On Pancaspe as model, see NH 35.87

133. Havelock 1995: 86–87, 130 and n. 47; see Ov. *Met.* 10.243–97.

134. Antipater of Sidon, *Anth. Pal.* 16.178.

135. Plin. *HN* 35.91.

136. Corso 2004: 239–40.

137. On Zeuxis' *Helen* as a prototype for the *Cnidian Aphrodite*, see Corso 2004: 16; on the influence of the kneeling bather, see Sutton 2009a–b.

138. Ath. 591a; Ath. 585f. Corso 2007: 11; on Cratina as the model, see references in n. 1 above.

139. On the date, see Corso 2007: 9; *NH* 36.20–21.

140. Plin. *HN* 36.20–21.

141. Havelock 1995: 60–63.

142. Plin. *HN* 36.21–22.

143. [Lucian] *Am.* 17.

144. As a votive dedication, see Havelock 1995: 31, 134; Corso 2004: 31.

145. Bonfante 1989: 546.

146. Havelock 1995: 1–2.

147. Havelock 1995: 9; Osborne 1998: 230–35; Pasquier 2007. The original was destroyed in a fire in Constantinople in 476 CE.

148. Havelock 1995: 14.

149. Plin. *HN* 35.130–33.

150. Havelock 1995: 55; Corso 2007: 39 cites Alexis' (c. 375–275 BCE) *Cnidia* ("Girl from Cnidos"; Ath. 165e) as evidence of the fame of the statue in Athens during the fourth century, although the surviving fragments do not contain any explicit reference to it. A later comic poet, Sopater (second cent. BCE), is also said to have produced play entitled *Cnidia* (Ath. 109f). It is likely that both plays simply followed comic convention in featuring as female protagonists foreign hetaeras, on the model of Menander's *Samia*.

151. Cic. *Verr.* 2.6.135.

152. Havelock 1995: 4–5.

153. Havelock 1995: 135. For the statue in literary sources, see Plin. *HN* 36.29; [Lucian] *Am.* 13–14; Ath. 590a–b; epigrams: Anonymous *Anth. Pal.* 16.159, 162, 168, 169; Plato *Anth. Pal.* 16.160, 161; Lucian *Anth. Pal.* 16.163; Evenus *Anth. Pal.* 16.165, 166; Antipater of Sidon *Anth. Pal.* 16.167; Hermodorus *Anth. Pal.* 16.170.

154. Antipater of Sidon *Anth. Pal.* 16.167.

155. Plato *Anth. Pal.* 16.160; cf. Anonymous *Anth. Pal.* 16.159, 162, 168.

156. ἃ μὴ θέμις, Plato *Anth. Pal.* 16.160.

157. Plin. *HN* 36.20021; [Lucian] *Am.* 13–14.

158. [Lucian] *Am.* 13.

159. μειδιαίσαισα, Sappho fr. 1.

Chapter 5

1. Ath. 590d–e.

2. Ath. 590f–591a.

3. Ancient sources: Ath. 590d–e; [Plut.] *Mor.* 849c–e; Sext. Emp. *Math.* 2.2; Quint. *Orat.* 10.5.3; Poll. 5.93, 2.124; Syrian. Ad. Herm. 4, p. 20; Harp. s.v. Euthias,

Isodaites; Corvinus F 21–22; [Longinus] *De subl.* 34.2–3; Alciphr. 4.4. Modern scholarship: Semenov 1935; Raubitschek 1941: 893–907; Kowalski 1947; Cooper 1995; Cavallini 2004 and 2014; Pernot 2004; Eidinow 2010, 2015: 23–30; Morales 2011; O'Connell 2013; Kapparis 2017: 257–61 and 2021: 76–82.

4. Macdowell 1978: 27–28.

5. For a brief overview of the Athenian legal system, see Carey 1997: 1–25; Glazebrook 2021: 9–12. On the qualifications of jurors, see Harris 1971: 46–48; Filonik 15–16 n. 19.

6. Loomis 1998: 104–8; Glazebrook 2021: 9.

7. Macdowell 1978: 36–40.

8. Macdowell 1978: 24–27.

9. For a detailed account of the Athenian legal process, from initiating a case to the final outcome between 410 and 340 BCE, see Boegehold 1995: 30–36. On public trials, see Macdowell 1978: 61–62.

10. Macdowell 1978: 62–66.

11. Arist. *Pol.* 1268b9; Harrison 1971: 164.

12. Eidinow 2016: 49 n. 41; cf. [Arist.] *Ath. Pol.* 57.2–3, Dem. 35.48.

13. Boegehold 1995: 30–31; Glazebrook 2021: 10; cf. Dem. 21.103, 45.8.

14. On Athenian women and the legal system, see Foxhall 1996: 140–49; Gagarin 1998; Johnstone 1998; Kamen 2013: 91; Kapparis 2020 and 2021; and Glazebrook 2021.

15. Foxhall 1996 first challenged the prevailing orthodoxy that women played no role in the Athenian legal system; see now Kapparis 2021.

16. In Dem. 57, the speaker defends his mother's legitimate citizen status, not only to defend his own citizen status, but also for the sake of her honor. In Aeschin. 2.172–73, the citizen status of Demosthenes' mother is called into question, implying that his own citizenship is doubtful; see Foxhall 1996: 140.

17. Dem. 27–30; see Foxhall 1996: 144–47.

18. Kapparis 2021: 2–3.

19. Lys. 32.11–18; Dem. 39.3–4; Dem. 40.10–11; see Foxhall 1996: 143–44.

20. Glazebrook 2021: 11.

21. Kapparis: 2021: 23–101.

22. On citizenship and immigration violations, see Kapparis 2021: 131–35; economic disputes, 143–46; violent crime, 147–48. On religious offenses, see Eidinow 2010: 9–35, 2016; Dillon 2002: 183–208; Filonik 2013: 11–96; 2016: 125–45; Kapparis 2021: 136–42.

23. Fragmentary testimonia for other trials involving *epikleroi* include Lysias, *On the Daughter of Antiphon*, probably an *epidokasia*, a processes to determine who was the closest male relative of a deceased man named Antiphon and eligible to marry his only daughter (Kapparis 2021: 26–29); several by Dinarchus, including *The Daughters Are Aristophon Are Not Heiresses, or Diamartyria, the Daughter of Aristophon Is Not an Heiress, Synegoria to Hegelochos, for the* Epikleros, and *For an Epikleros, Daughter of Iophon* (Kapparis 2021: 36–39, 52, 66–67); Lysias, *On the Daughter of Onomakles*, a historically attested man whose daughter may have been an *epikleros* and quite possibly had property inherited under the thirty (Kaparis 2021: 73); and Isaeus, *To Satyros, for the Epikleros* (Kapparis 2021: 83–84). On the women in Lys. 32; see Foxhall 1996: 147–49.

24. For the fragments, see [Dinarchus] frr. 35.1–3 Conomis; Lycurg. frr. 6.1–20 Conomis; see Kapparis 2021: 56–57, 60–66.

25. Lys. frr. 20a–d, 22, 23 Carey; see Kapparis 2021: 23–26.

26. Kapparis 2021: 84.

27. Kapparis 2017: 241–63 and 2021: 23–101.

28. Harrison 1971: 15, 23-24, 82, 86, 193 n. 1, 195, 204; Kapparis 2021: 33, 34, 92, 151, 167, 179, 222.

29. Macdowell 1978: 74-75.

30. Ath. 590d; [Plut.] *Mor.* 849; Hyp. frr. 13-16 Jensen; see Kapparis 2021: 29-36.

31. Ath. 587d.

32. Ath. 586b.

33. Kapparis 2021: 35.

34. [Dem.] 59.19; Lys. fr. 208 Carey. On allusions to hetaeras to establish a male bond, see Kapparis 2021: 35, 53-56.

35. Hyp. fr. 93 Jensen; see Kapparis 2021: 46-47; Din. frr. 55.1, 2 Conomis; see Kapparis 2021: 52-53.

36. Lys. Fr. 208 Carey; see Kapparis 2021: 53-54. Hyp. frr. 125 and 164-65 Jensen; Kapparis 2021: 67-68, 88-90; Lys. fr. 257 Carey; Kaparis 2021: 68-69.

37. Lys. fr. 299 Carey; cf. Ar. *Plu.* 179; Harp. s.v. Nais; Ath. 592c-d; see Kapparis 2017: 210-17 and 2021: 75-76.

38. Ath. 592c-d.

39. ἐρᾷ δὲ Ναῖς οὐ διὰ σὲ Φιλωνίδου;, Ar. *Plu.* 179.

40. On the ancient sources, see Kapparis 2017: 211 nn. 174-180.

41. Breitenbach 1908: 29; Kapparis 2017: 21, cf. Dem. 29.49; 27.57.

42. Kapparis 2017: 211-12.

43. On the *graphe asebeias*, see Harris 1971: 62-63, 82, 104 n. 3, 175 n. 4.

44. Filonik 2013: 4; Eidinow 2016: 49.

45. Arist. *Virt. Vit.* 1251a30; Dem. 20.22; see Eidinow 2016: 50.

46. Dem. 19.293; Antiph. 2.1.6; Lys. 7.

47. Eidinow 2016: 61; cf. Ar. *Eccl.* 214-40; *Lys.* 638-47.

48. Parker 1996: 217; Eidinow 2016: 62.

49. Thuc. 6.27-29, 53, 60-61.

50. Murray 1990b: 155-56; Wallace 1992: 328 n. 2; Filonik 2013: 40 n. 103. Timandra (Ath. 535c, 574e) has been variously identified by ancient authors as Damasandra (Plut. *Alc.* 39) and Epimandra (schol. Ar. *Plut.* 179); see McClure 2003a: 63.

51. Thuc. 6.27, 53, 60; Xen. *Hell.* 1.4.14-23; Filonik 2013: 40-46.

52. Thuc. 6.27-28, 60; And. 1.11-17, 34-25; Filonik 2013: 41.

53. And. 1.32-35; Thuc. 6.27.2, 60.3; Filonik 2013: 42-43.

54. And. 1.10, 29-32, 58, 71; Thuc. 6.53.1. On the decree prohibiting individuals who had admitted to acts of impiety from entering temples, see Filonik 2013: 42 n. 119; Eidinow 2016: 51-52.

55. Eidinow 2016: 52 n. 53.

56. Eidinow 2016: 266.

57. Thuc. 7.87.6; see Eidinow 2016: 269.

58. Isoc. 8.88; Thuc. 7.27.4-5; see Eidinow 2016: 269-70.

59. Ar. *Eccl.* 415-21; *Plut.* 535-47; And. 3.36; Eidinow 2016: 272-74.

60. Isoc. 14.48-49; Eidinow 2016: 289.

61. Isoc. 19.19, 25; Eidinow 2016: 290.

62. Xen. *Mem.* 2.7.2. Eidinow 2016: 292

63. [Dem.] 59.50 and 72, 57.25; Isae. 12.2; see Ogden 1996: 124; Eidinow 2016: 304.

64. [Dem.] 59.111-14; see Isae. 3.17.18; Antiphanes fr. 210 K-A.

65. On the prosecution as a *graphe asebeias*, see Pl. *Euthphr.* 5c, schol. Pl. *Ap.* 18b.

66. τούς τε νέους διαφθείροντα καὶ θεοὺς οὓς ἡ πόλις νομίζει οὐ νομίζοντα, ἕτερα δὲ δαιμόνια καινά, Pl. *Ap.* 24b-c. On the charges, see Favorinus *ap.* Diog. Laert. 2.40;

Xen. *Mem.* 1.1.1; Pl. *Ap.* 24b–c; *Euthphr.* 3b, 5c; see Filonik 2013: 52–57; Phillips 2013: 410–11; Eidinow 2016: 52 n. 54.

67. Filonik 2013: 29; see Plut. *Per.* 32.1.

68. Eidinow 2016: 59.

69. Versnel 1990: 102–23, 128; Parker 1996: 152, 2002; Filonik 2013: 19; Eidinow 2016: 52–54.

70. Strabo 10.3.18. Parker 1996: 152.

71. Eidinow 2016: 53 n. 57.

72. Eidinow 2016: 53 n. 58; Parker 1996: 199.

73. Jameson 1997: 102; Eidinow 2016: 3.

74. On these trials, see Parker 1996: 162–63 and n. 34; Kapparis 2021: 137–42 (quote from p. 142); Eidinow 2016 offers a detailed and sophisticated analysis of the suits involving Ninos, Theoris, and Phryne that has been invaluable to this study.

75. On the sexual status of all three women, see Trampedach 2001: 148; Eidinow 2016: 63.

76. Jameson 1997: 103.

77. Eidinow 2016: 167–264. See also Filonik 2013: 51–60; Kapparis 2021: 143.

78. Kapparis 2021: 88.

79. Ar. *Lys.* 1–3.

80. Ar. *Lys.* 376; Men. *Sam.* 41; see Parker 1996: 162.

81. Henderson 1987: 118.

82. Ar. *Vesp.* 9–10.

83. Ar. *Lys.* 388–90.

84. Dem. 18.259–60.

85. Dem. 18.131, 284. The *tympanon* was a kettle drum or tambourine used especially in Dionysiac celebrations; see E. *Ba.* 124, DFA pl. 22. On Glaucothea as a hetaera, see Cooper 1995: 304.

86. Eidinow 2016: 9.

87. Plut. *Per.* 32.1–6; Ath. 589e; Hermippus fr. 5 K-A. See Henry 1985: 19–28; Cooper 1995: 315; Filonik 2013: 28–33; Eidinow 2016: 322–23; Kapparis 2021: 39–43

88. Plut. *Per.* 32.1–2.

89. Ar. *Ach.* 524–29; Ath. 570a.

90. Phillips 2013: 120–22, see Aeschin. 1.14, 184.

91. πάνυ παρὰ τὴν δίκην, ὡς Αἰσχίνης φησίν, ἀφεὶς ὑπὲρ αὐτῆς δάκρυα καὶ δεηθεὶς τῶν δικαστῶν, Plut. *Per.* 32.4. Bers 2009: 46 argues that the description Pericles' entreaties illustrates his devotion to Aspasia and his skill with democratic audiences.

92. ἱκέτευσε τοὺς δικαστὰς μετὰ πολλῶν δακρύων, Pl. *Ap.* 34b7–35b8. Cooper 1995: 312–13 n. 24; on supplication, see Gould 1973: 77. On the use of the topos in oratory, see Bers 2009: 121–53.

93. Henry 1985: 24; Filonik 2013: 33.

94. Lefkowitz 1976: 110–11; 2012: 93–95, 104–12.

95. Kapparis 2021: 41.

96. Eidinow 2016: 66, 192.

97. Eidinow 2016: 20 n. 38. For a discussion of this trial, see Filonik 2013: 67–68; Eidinow 2016: 17–23; Kapparis 2021: 69–72.

98. Dem. 39.2, 40.9.

99. Din. fr. 33.1.

100. Dem. 19.281.

101. Schol. Dem. 19.281: 495A.

102. Eidinow 2016: 56 believes that the unnamed priestess is Ninos; *pace* Kapparis 2021: 72.

103. Schol. Dem. 19.281: 495B.

104. Kapparis 2021: 72.

105. ξένους ἐμύει θεούς, Joseph. *Ap.* 2.267–68.

106. Eidinow 2016: 57–58.

107. Eidinow 2016: 60.

108. On the trial of Theoris, see Collins 2001; Eidinow 2016: 11–17, 57–64; Kapparis 2021: 85–88.

109. *LGPN IG* II² 4627 (? m. Ὀλυμπιόδορος); *IG* II² 7681 ([Θε]ωρίς?). On Theoris the hetaera, see Ath. 592a–b.

110. Dem. 25.79–80.

111. Eidinow 2016: 12 argues that Theoris could have been a citizen since Lemnos fell under Athenian control after the Peloponnesian War.

112. Kapparis 2021: 87.

113. Plut. *Dem.* 14.6.2.

114. Harp. s.v. Theoris.

115. Kapparis 2021: 67, 82–83.

116. Dem. 57.8.

117. Kapparis 2021: 67.

118. Harp. s.v. *Arkteusai, dekateuin.*

119. On the trial, see Cooper 1995; Filonik 2013: 63–66; Eidinow 2016: 23–30; Kapparis 2021: 76–82.

120. Quint. *Inst.* 10.5.2; [Longinus] *Subl.* 34.2–4; Messala frr. 21–22.

121. Eidinow 2016: 23 n. 47.

122. Cooper 1995; Havelock 1995: 3–4, 42–47; Morales 2011: 100.

123. Scholars arguing for the historicity of the trial all agree that the romantic elements, such as the affair between Phryne and Hyperides, the sexual rivalry between the two orators, and the disrobing, were literary inventions that had become firmly fixed in the hetaera's reception by the time of the Second Sophistic period; see Cooper 1995; Havelock 1995: 46; Filonik 2013: 66; Eidinow 2016: 23–30; Kapparis 2021: 261.

124. On the fragments, see Hyp. frr. 171–80 Jensen; Marzi 1977 retains Jensen's numbering but supplies only eight fragments; O'Connell (2013) proposes a further fragment (Poll. 8.123–24).

125. Ath. 591e.

126. For the translation and discussion, see Eidinow 2016: 27.

127. Anonymous Seguerianus 215 = Euthias fr. 2 Baiter-Saupe.

128. Eidinow 2016: 28.

129. Harp. s.v. *Isodaites.*

130. Plut. *Mor.* 398a, Hyp. Fr. 177; Hsch. s.v. Isodaites; see Eidinow 2016: 29 n. 72.

131. Eidnow 2016: 30.

132. ἀνεπόπτευτος, Hyp. fr. 174; ἐπωπτευκότων, fr. 175. Foucart 1902: 216–18 and Marzi 1977: 306–7; Raubitschek 1941: 905 argus that the terms refer specifically to the ritual bathing of the participants. But see O'Connell 2013: 111, who argues that Hyperides provided an extensive description of legal procedures for cases involving Eleusinian Mysteries; he suggests Poll. 8.123–24, which also includes these rare terms for participants, comprises a missing fragment from that speech; see Eidinow 2016: 30 n. 75.

133. Ath. 590d–e = Baiter-Saupe ii.319–20; Hermippus fr. 68a I Wehrli.

134. δημιόπρατα, Lys. fr. xlviii, Baiter-Saupe. On the term δημιόπρατα, see Ar. *Vesp.* 659, Ath. 476e, Pollux 10.96. On public debtors, see Harrison 1971: 172–76.

135. Harp. s.v. Euthias.

136. Fr. 172 Jensen = Syrian. *ad Herm.* 4 p. 120 Walz = 2.31 Rabe.

137. Bacchis to Hyperides, Alciphr. 4.1.

138. Ath. 591e = Diodorus *FGrH* 372 F 36 and 72 T 17a.

139. Ath. 590d = *FGrH* 338 F 14.

140. Ath. 590d = Hyp. fr. 171 Jensen (ἐρᾶν); see [Plut.] *Mor.* 849e (ὁμιληκώς); Poll. 5.93 (διελέχθην), 2.1.24 (διειλεγμενος ἐπί ἀφροδισίων).

141. [Plut.] *Mor.* 849E.

142. Ath. 591e = Aristogeiton IV, Baiter-Sauppe ii.310; see Eidinow 2016: 26. For references in oratory, see Dem. 25.41–42, 64, and 94; 26.17; *Ep.* 3.16; Din. 2.12–13.

143. Quint. *Inst.* 2.15.6–9: Nam et Manium Aquilium defendens Antonius, cum scissa veste cicatrices quas is pro patria pectore adverso suscepisset ostendit, non orationis habuit fiduciam, sed oculis populi Romani vim attulit: quem illo ipso aspectu maxime motum in hoc, ut absolveret reum, creditum est. Servium quidem Galbam miseratione sola, qua non suos modo liberos parvolos in contione produxerat, sed Galli etiam Sulpici filium suis ipse manibus circumtulerat, elapsum esse cum aliorum monumentis, tum Catonis oratione testatum est. Et Phrynen non Hyperidis actione quamquam admirabili, sed conspectu corporis, quod illa speciosissimum alioqui diducta nudaverat tunica, putant periculo liberatam.

144. Plut. *Mor.* 849e: ὡμιληκὼς δέ, ὡς εἰκός δή, καὶ Φρύνη τῇ ἑταίρᾳ ἀσεβεῖν κρινομένῃ συνεστάθη. αὐτὸς γὰρ τοῦτο ἐν ἀρχῇ τοῦ λόγου δηλοῖ· μελλούσης δ᾽ αὐτῆς ἁλίσκεσθαι, παραγαγὼν εἰς μέσον καὶ περιρρήξας τὴν ἐσθῆτα ἐπέδειξε τὰ στέρνα τῆς γυναικός· καὶ τῶν δικαστῶν εἰς τὸ κάλλος ἀπιδόντων, ἀφείθη.

145. Sext. Emp. *Math.* 2.3–4: οἱ γοῦν παρὰ τῷ ποιητῇ δημογέροντες, καίπερ ἐκπεπολεμωμένοι καὶ τελέως ἀπηλλοτριωμένοι πρὸς τὴν Ἑλένην ὡς κακῶν αἰτίαν γενομένην αὐτοῖς, ὅμως ὑπὸ τοῦ περὶ αὐτὴν κάλλους πείθονται, καὶ προσιούσης τοιαῦτά τινα πρὸς ἀλλήλους διεξίασιν, "οὐ νέμεσις Τρῶας καὶ ἐυκνήμιδας Ἀχαιοὺς τοιῆδ᾽ ἀμφὶ γυναικὶ πολὺν χρόνον ἄλγεα πάσχειν."Φρύνη τε, ὡς φασίν, ἐπεὶ συνηγοροῦντος αὐτῇ Ὑπερίδου ἔμελλε καταδικάζεσθαι, καταρρηξαμένη τοὺς χιτωνίσκους καὶ γυμνοῖς στήθεσι προκυλινδουμένη τῶν δικαστῶν πλεῖον ἴσχυσε διὰ τὸ κάλλος τοὺς δικαστὰς πεῖσαι τῆς τοῦ συνηγοροῦντος ῥητορείας.

146. Ath. 590d–e: ὁ δὲ Ὑπερείδης συναγορεύων τῇ Φρύνῃ, ὡς οὐδὲν ἤνυε λέγων ἐπίδοξοί τε ἦσαν οἱ δικασταὶ καταψηφιούμενοι, παραγαγὼν αὐτὴν εἰς τοὐμφανὲς καὶ περιρήξας τοὺς χιτωνίσκους γυμνά τε τὰ στέρνα ποιήσας τοὺς ἐπιλογικοὺς οἴκτους ἐκ τῆς ὄψεως αὐτῆς ἐπερρητόρευσεν δεισιδαιμονῆσαί τε ἐποίησεν τοὺς δικαστὰς τὴν ὑποφῆτιν καὶ ζάκορον Ἀφροδίτης ἐλέῳ χαρισαμένους μὴ ἀποκτεῖναι. καὶ ἀφεθείσης ἐγράφη μετὰ ταῦτα ψήφισμα, μηδένα οἰκτίζεσθαι τῶν λεγόντων ὑπέρ τινος μηδὲ βλεπόμενον τὸν κατηγορούμενον ἢ τὴν κατηγορουμένην κρίνεσθαι.

147. Alciphr. 4.4: τὴν γὰρ δίκην σοι καὶ πρὸς εὐτυχίαν³γεγονέναι νομίζω . . . . μὴ δὴ καταδιαιτήσης ἡμῶν, ὦ φιλτάτη, τῶν ἑταιρῶν, μηδ᾽ Ὑπερείδην κακῶς δόξαι βεβουλεῦσθαι ποιήσῃς τὰς Εὐθίου ἱκεσίας προσιεμένη, μηδὲ τοῖς λέγουσί σοι ὅτι, εἰ μὴ τὸν χιτωνίσκον περιρρηξαμένη τὰ μαστάρια τοῖς δικασταῖς ἐπέδειξας, οὐδὲν ὁ ῥήτωρ ὠφέλει, πείθου. καὶ γὰρ αὐτὸ τοῦτο ἵνα ἐν καιρῷ γένηταί σοι ἡ ἐκείνου παρέσχε συνηγορία.

148. On this device in connection with Marcus Antonius and Manius Aquilius, see Cic. *Verr.* 2.5.3; *de orat.* 2.124, 194; Sall. *Iug.* 85.30; Macrob. *Sat.* 2.4.27; Dio Chrys. *Or.* 55.4.2.

149. ὡς ἐσεῖδες μαστόν, ἐκβαλὼν ξίφος φίλημ' ἐδέξω, E. *Andr.* 627–30; parodied at Ar. *Lys.* 155–56.

150. Previous scholars largely accepted that the disrobing actually took place; see Cantarelli 1885: 465–82; Foucart 1902; Semenov 1935: 271–79; Raubitschek 1941: 893–99; Kowalski 1947: 50–62. Most recent scholarship follows Cooper 1995 in treating the event as the invention of later writers; see further Bollansée 1999: 336 n. 22; Filonik 2013: 64; Eidinow 2016: 26 n. 56.

151. Ath. 591e–f = fr. 13 K-A:

Φρύνη πρό <γ'> ἡμῶν γέγονεν ἐπιφανεστάτη
πολὺ τῶν ἑταιρῶν· καὶ γὰρ εἰ νεωτέρα
τῶν τότε χρόνων εἶ, τόν γ' ἀγῶν' ἀκήκοας.
βλάπτειν δοκοῦσα τοὺς βίους μείζους βλάβας
τὴν ἡλιαίαν εἶλε περὶ τοῦ σώματος
καὶ τῶν δικαστῶν καθ' ἕνα δεξιουμένη
μετὰ δακρύων διέσωσε τὴν ψυχὴν μόλις.

152. Harrison 1971: 115–18, 141–44.

153. For a taxonomy of the ritual and its various forms in Greek literature, see Gould 1973.

154. Hom. *Il.* 1.500–2; see Gould 1973: 75–76.

155. Gould 1973: 94.

156. Gould 1973: 101; Johnstone 1999: 116 n. 44, 121; Bers 2009: 137.

157. ἐμβάλλει μοι τὴν χεῖρ' ἀπαλήν; ἱκετεύουσίν; ὑποκύπτοντες; οἰκτροχοοῦντες, Ar. *Vesp.* 548–75.

158. Cooper 1995: 304–5 n. 7, 315.

159. Cooper 1995: 309; Eidinow 2016: 27 n. 57.

160. κρόκου βαφὰς δ' ἐς πέδον χέουσα/ ἔβαλλ' ἕκαστον θυτήρ/ων ἀπ' ὄμματος βέλει/ φιλοίκτῳ, A. *Ag.* 206, 239.

161. On the *chiton* and *chitoniskos*, see Lee 2015: 106–10.

162. Kowalski 1947: 53; Cooper 1995: 312; for tragic parallels, see E. *An.* 502; S. *Ant.* 891–928.

163. A. *Pers.* 468, 199.

164. A. *Sept.* 329.

165. περιρρήξας τὸν χιτωνίσκον, Dem. 14.197–98.

166. καταρρηγνύναι τὰ ἵματα, Aesch. 1.183.6.

167. Xen. Ephes. 2.5.6.

168. ὁ χιτώνιον περιρρήξας ἐμαστίγου γυμνήν, Plut. *De mul. vir.* 242e–263c.

169. περιρρήξασα τὸν χιτωνίσκον . . . ὀδυρομένη τὴν βίαν, Joseph. *AJ* 7.171.

170. περιερρήξατο τε τοὺς πέπλους ἐπ' αὐτῷ, καὶ τὰ στέρνα τυπτομένη, Plut. *Ant.* 77.3; cf. Arr. *Anab.* 7.24.3.

171. περιερρηγμένας καὶ ἱκετευούσας ὑμᾶς, Dio Chrys. *Or.* 46. 12; cf. 35. 9.

172. παιομένην τὰ στήθη γυμνά, καὶ χιτῶνα περιρρήξασαν, 7.335 Walz; Cooper 1995: 313.

173. (ἐλεεινολογίας τε πλήθει καὶ τῇ περιρρήξει τῆς ἐσθῆτος, 4.414 Walz; Cooper 1995: 313.

174. δεισιδαιμονῆσαί τε ἐποίησεν τοὺς δικαστὰς τὴν ὑποφῆτιν καὶ ζάκορον Ἀφροδίτης, Ath. 590e.

175. On religious awe in this passage, see Naiden 2006: 102; Eidinow 2016: 24–25.

176. For further discussion, see Budin 2008 and Chapter 3 in this volume.

177. Hom. *Il.* 16.235; cf. Ap. Rhod. 1.1311. Pindar uses the term to refer to "purveyors of slander"; see Pind. *Pyth.* 2.76.

178. On the term in Hellenistic poetry, see Theoc. *Id.* 16.29, 17.1115, 22.16.

179. Men. frr. 126 (male), 311 (female); ἱερεῖς καὶ ζάκοροι θεῶν, Plut. *Cam.* 30.2.

180. [Luc.] *Am.* 15.13, 17.1.

181. [Luc.] *Am.* 16.23.

182. δεισιδαίμονος ἁγιστείας, [Luc.] *Am.* 15.19.

183. But note the absence of such terms in another version of the youth and the Cnidia at Lucian *Im.* 4.

184. [Lucian] *Am.* 13.

185. Alciphr. 4.1 fr. 3.

186. On the presence of women and children in the Athenian courtroom, see Lys. 20.34; Dem. 19.283, 25.84, 48.57; Isoc. 18.52-54; Aeschin. 2.152; Pl. *Ap.* 34b7–35b8. See also Gagarin 1998. Many thanks to Allison Glazebrook for bringing these examples to my attention.

187. Jameson 1997: 102; Eidinow 2016: 312.

Works Cited

Ajootian, A. 2007. "Praxiteles and Fourth-Century Athenian Portraiture." In P. Schultz and R. von den Hoff, eds., *Early Hellenistic Portraiture: Image, Style, Context*. Cambridge: Cambridge University Press, 13–33.

Assante, J. 2007. "What Makes a 'Prostitute' a Prostitute? Modern Definitions and Ancient Meanings." *Historiae* 4: 117–32.

Ault, B. A. 2016. "Building Z in the Athenian Kerameikos: House, Tavern, Inn, Brothel?" In A. Glazebrook and B. Tsakirgis, eds., *Houses of Ill-Repute: the Archaeology of Brothels, Houses, and Taverns in the Greek World*. Philadelphia: University of Pennsylvania Press, 75–102.

Baiter, J., and H. Sauppe. 1850. *Oratories attici, ii*. Zurich: Hoehr.

Bers, V. 2009. *Genos Dikanikon: Amateur and Professional Speech in the Courtrooms of Classical Athens*. Center for Hellenic Studies. Cambridge, MA: Harvard University Press.

Bicknell, P. 1982. "Axiochos Alkibiadou, Aspasia and Aspasios." *L'antiquité classique* 51: 240–50.

Boegehold, A. 1995. *The Lawcourts at Athens: Sites, Buildings, Equipment, Procedure, and Testimonia*. The Athenian Agora 28. Princeton, NJ: American School of Classical Studies at Athens.

Boehringer, S. 2018. "What Is Named by the Name 'Philaenis'? Gender, Function, and Authority of an Antonomastic Figure." In M. Masterson, N. S. Rabinowitz, and J. Robson, eds., *Sex in Antiquity: Exploring Gender and Sexuality in the Ancient World*. London: Routledge, 374–92.

Bollansée, J. 1999. *Hermippos of Smyrna and his Biographical Writings: A Reappraisal*. Leuven: Peeters.

Bonfante, L. 1989. "Nudity as Costume in Classical Art." *American Journal of Archaeology* 93: 543–70.

Breitenbach, H. 1908. *De genere quodam titulorum comoediae atticae*. Basel: Werner-Riehm.

Brown, P. G. 1990. "Plots and Prostitutes in Greek New Comedy." *Papers of the Leeds International Seminar* 6: 241–66.

Budin, S. 2008. *The Myth of Sacred Prostitution in Antiquity*. Cambridge: Cambridge University Press.

Bundrick, S. 2008. "The Fabric of the City: Imaging Textile Production in Classical Athens." *Hesperia* 77: 283–334.

Bundrick, S. 2012. "Housewives, Hetairai, and the Ambiguity of Genre in Attic Vase Painting." *Phoenix* 66: 11–35.

Burkert, W. 1991. *Greek Religion*. Trans. J. Raffan. Cambridge, MA: Harvard University Press.

Buxton, R. 1982. *Persuasion in Greek Tragedy: A Study of Peitho*. Cambridge.

Cantarelli, L. 1885. "Osservazione sul processo di Frine." *RIFC* 13: 465–82.

Carey, C. 1997. *Trials from Classical Athens*. London and New York: Routledge.

Carney, E. 2013. *Arsinoe of Egypt and Macedon: A Royal Life*. Oxford: Oxford University Press.

Cartledge, P. 2001. "The Political Economy of Greek Slavery." In P. Cartledge, E. Cohen, and L. Foxhall, eds., *Money, Labour and Land: Approaches to the Economies of Ancient Greece*. London and New York: Routledge, 156–66.

Cavallini, E. 2004. "Il processo contro Frine: l'accusa e la difesa." *Labeo* 50: 231–38.

Cavallini, E. 2014. "Esibizionismo o propaganda politica?: Frine tra storia e aneddotica." In U. Bultrighini and E. Dimauro, eds., *Donne che contano nella storia greca*. Lanciano: Carabba, 127–51.

Cohen, E. 2000. "'Whoring Under Contract': The Legal Context of Prostitution in Fourth-Century Athens." In V. Hunter and J. Edmondson, eds., *Law and Social Status in Classical Athens*. Oxford: Oxford University Press, 113–47.

Cohen, E. 2015. *Athenian Prostitution: the Business of Sex*. Oxford: Oxford University Press.

Collins, D. 2001. "Theoris of Lemnos and the Criminalization of Magic in Fourth-century Athens." *Classical Quarterly* n.s. 51: 477–93.

Connelly. J. 2007. *Portrait of a Priestess: Women and Ritual in Ancient Greece*. Princeton, NJ: Princeton University Press.

Connolly, B., and M. Fuentes. 2016. "Introduction: From Archives of Slavery to Liberated Futures?" *History of the Present: A Journal of Critical History* 6.2: 105–16.

Cooper, C. 1995. "Hyperides and the Trial of Phryne." *Phoenix* 49: 303–18.

Corner, S. 2011. "Bringing the Outside In: The *Andron* as Brothel and the Symposium's Civic Sexuality." In A. Glazebrook and M. Henry, eds. *Greek Prostitutes in the Ancient Mediterranean, 800 BCE–200 CE*. Madison: University of Wisconsin Press, 60–85.

Corpataux, J.-F. 2009. "Phryné, Vénus et Galatée dans l'atelier de Jean-Léon Gérôme." *Artibus et Historiae* 30: 145–58.

Corso, A. 1997. "The Monument of Phryne at Delphi." *Numismatica e Antichità Classiche* 26: 123–50.

Corso, A. 1997. "Love as Suffering: the Eros of Thespiae of Praxiteles." *BICS* 42: 63–91.

Corso, A. 2004. *The Art of Praxiteles: The Development of Praxiteles' Workshop and Its Cultural Tradition until the Sculptor's Acme (364–1 BC)*. Studia Archaologica 153. Rome: L'ERMA di Bretschneider.

Corso, A. 2007. *The Art of Praxiteles II: The Mature Years*. Studia Archaologica 153. Rome: L'ERMA di Bretschneider.

Davidson, J. 1997. *Courtesans and Fishcakes: The Consuming Passions of Classical Athens*. Chicago: University of Chicago Press.

Davidson, J. 2006. "Making a Spectacle of Her(self): the Greek Courtesan and the Art of the Present." In M. Feldman and B. Gordon, eds., *The Courtesan's Arts: Cross-cultural Perspectives*. Oxford: Oxford University Press, 29–51.

Dillon, M. 2002. *Girls and Women in Classical Greek Religion*. London and New York: Routledge.

Dillon, S. 2010. *The Female Portrait Statue in the Greek World*. Cambridge: Cambridge University Press.

Ehlers, B. 1966. *Eine vorplatonische Deutung des sokratischen Eros: Der Dialog Aspasia des Sokratikers Aischines*. München: C. H. Beck.

Eidinow, E. 2010. "Patterns of Persecution: 'Witchcraft' trials in Classical Athens." *Past and Present* 208: 9–35.

Eidinow, E. 2016. *Envy, Poison, and Death: Women on Trial in Classical Athens*. Oxford: Oxford University Press.

Faraone, C., and L. McClure, eds. 2006. *Prostitutes and Courtesans in the Ancient World*. Madison: University of Wisconsin Press.

Ferrari, G. 2002. *Figures of Speech: Men and Maidens in Ancient Greece*. Chicago: University of Chicago Press.

Filonik, J. 2013. "Impiety Trials: A Reappraisal." *Dike* 16: 11–96.

Fischer, M. 2013. "Ancient Greek Prostitutes and the Textile Industry in Attic Vase-Paintings ca. 550–450 BCE." *Classical World* 106: 219–56.

Fisher, N. 2001. *Aeschines Against Timarchus*. Oxford: Clarendon Press.

Fossey, J. 1988. *Topography and Population of Ancient Boiotia*. 2 vols. Chicago: Ares.

Foucart, P. 1902. "L'Accusation de Phryne." *Revue de philologie, de littérature et d'histoire anciennes* 26: 216–18.

Foxhall, L. 1996. "The Law and the Lady: Women and Legal Proceedings in Classical Athens." In L. Foxhall and A. Lewis, eds., *Greek Law in Its Political Settings: Justifications not Justice*. Oxford: Oxford University Press, 133–52.

Frost, F. 2002. "Solon *Pornoboskos* and Aphrodite Pandemos." *Syllecta Classica* 13: 34–46.

Gagarin, M. 1998. "Women in Athenian Courts." *Dike* 1: 39–51.

Gilhuly, K. 2009. *The Feminine Matrix of Sex and Gender in Classical Athens*. Cambridge: Cambridge University Press.

Glazebrook, A. 2005. "The Making of a Prostitute: Apollodoros's Portrait of Neaira." *Arethusa* 38: 161–87.

Glazebrook, A. 2011. "*Porneion*: Prostitution in Athenian Civic Space." Glazebrook and Henry 2011: 34–59.

Works Cited   187

Glazebrook, A. 2016. "Is There an Archaeology of Prostitution?" In A. Glazebrook and B. Tsakirgis, eds., *Houses of Ill-Repute: the Archaeology of Brothels, Houses, and Taverns in the Greek World*. Pennsylvania: University of Pennsylvania Press, 169–96.

Glazebrook, A. 2021. *Sexual Labor in the Athenian Courts*. Austin: University of Texas Press.

Glazebrook, A., and M. Henry, eds. 2011. *Greek Prostitutes in the Ancient Mediterranean, 800 BCE–200 CE*. Madison: University of Wisconsin Press.

Glazebrook, A., and B. Tsakirgis, eds. 2016. *Houses of Ill-Repute: the Archaeology of Brothels, Houses, and Taverns in the Greek World*. Pennsylvania: University of Pennsylvania Press.

Goff, B. 2004. *Citizen Bacchae: Women's Ritual Practice in Ancient Greece*. Berkeley: University of California Press.

Goldhill, S. 1998. "The Seductions of the Gaze: Socrates and His Girlfriends." In P. Cartledge, P. Millet, and S. von Reden, eds., *Kosmos: Essays in Order, Conflict and Community in Classical Athens*. Cambridge: Cambridge University Press, 105–24.

Goldhill, S. 2015. "Is There a History of Prostitution?" In M. Masterson, N. S. Rabinowitz, and J. Robson, eds., *Sex in Antiquity: Exploring Gender and Sexuality in the Ancient World*. London: Routledge, 179–97.

Gould, J. 1973. "Hiketeia." *Journal of Hellenic Studies* 93: 73–193.

Gutzwiller, K. 2004. "Gender and the Inscribed Epigram: Herennia Procula and the Thespian Eros." *Transactions of the American Philological Society* 134: 383–418.

Halperin, D. 1990. *One Hundred Years of Homosexuality and Other Essays on Greek Love*. New York and London: Routledge.

Hamel, D. 2003. *Trying Neaera: The True Story of a Courtesan's Scandalous Life in Ancient Greece*. New Haven, CT: Yale University Press.

Harrison, A. R. W. 1968. *The Law of Athens*. Vol. 1. Oxford: Clarendon Press.

Harrison, A. R. W. 1971. *The Law of Athens*. Vol. 2. Oxford: Clarendon Press.

Hartman, S. 2008. "Venus in Two Acts." *Small Axe* 12.2: 1–14.

Havelock, C. 1995. *The Aphrodite of Cnidos and Her Successors*. Ann Arbor: University of Michigan Press.

Hawley, R. 1993. " 'Pretty, Witty and Wise': Courtesans in Athenaeus' *Deipnosophistae* Book 13." *International Journal of Moral and Social Studies* 8.1: 73–89.

Henderson, J. 1987. *Aristophanes' Lysistrata*. Newburyport: Focus Publishing.

Henderson, J. 2000. "Pherekrates and the Women of Old Comedy." In F. Harvey and J. Wilkins, eds., *The Rivals of Aristophanes: Studies in Athenian Old Comedy*. London: Duckworth, 135–50.

Henry, M. 1985. *Menander's Courtesans and the Greek Comic Tradition*. Frankfurt am Main, Bern, New York: Peter Lang.

Henry, M. 1995. *Prisoner of History: Aspasia of Miletus and Her Biographical Tradition*. New York and Oxford: Oxford University Press.

Henry, M. 2011. "The Traffic in Women: From Homer to Hipponax." In A. Glazebrook and M. Henry, eds., *Greek Prostitutes in the Ancient Mediterranean, 800 BCE–200 CE.* Madison: University of Wisconsin Press, 14–33.

Herter, H. 1960 [2003]. "The Sociology of Prostitution in Ancient Greece." In M. Golden and P. Toohey (eds.), *Sex and Difference in Ancient Greece and Rome.* Edinburgh: University of Edinburgh Press, 57–113.

Hirzel, R. [1918] 1962. *Der Name. Ein Beitrag zu seiner Geschichte im Altertum und besonders bei den Griechen.* Amsterdam: A.M. Hakkert.

Hoernes, M. 2012. "Bilder und Konstruktionen einer Hetäre: 'Und Phryne soll nicht durch die Gerichtsrede des Hypereides, sondern durch den Anblick ihres Körpers gerettet worden sein.'" In F. Müller, V. Sossau, and F. El-Nagashi, eds., *Gefährtinnen: vom Umgang mit Prostitution in der griechischen Antike und Heute.* Innsbruch: Spectanda, 5–70.

House, J. 2008. "History without Values? Gérôme's History Paintings." *Journal of the Warburg Institute* 71: 261–76.

Hunter, V. 1994. *Policing Athens: Social Control in the Attic Lawsuits, 420–320 B.C.* Princeton, NJ: Princeton University Press.

Jameson, M. 1997. "Women and Democracy in Fourth Century Athens." In P. Brulé and J. Oulhen, eds., *Esclavage, guerre, économie en Grèce ancienne: hommages à` Yvon Garlan.* Rennes, France: Presses universitaires de Rennes, 96–107.

Jensen, C. 1917. *Hyperidis Orationes Sex cum Ceterarum Fragmentis.* Leipzig: Teubner.

Johnstone, S. 1998. "Cracking the Code of Silence: Athenian Legal Oratory and the Histories of Slaves and Women." In S. Murnaghan and S. R. Joshel, eds., *Women and Slaves in Greco-Roman Culture.* London and New York: Routledge, 221–35.

Johnstone, S. 1999. *Disputes and Democracy: The Consequences of Litigation in Ancient Athens.* Austin: University of Texas Press.

Kamen, D. 2013. *Status in Classical Athens.* Princeton, NJ: Princeton University Press.

Kapparis, K. 1995. "Critical Notes on D.59 *Against Neaira.*" *Hermes* 123: 19–27.

Kapparis, K. 1999. *Apollodoros Against Neara [D 59].* Berlin and New York: De Gruyter.

Kapparis, K. 2011. "The Terminology of Prostitution in the Ancient Greek World." In A. Glazebrook and M. Henry, eds., *Greek Prostitutes in the Ancient Mediterranean, 800 BCE–200 CE.* Madison: University of Wisconsin Press, 222–55.

Kapparis, K. 2017 *Prostitution in the Ancient Greek World.* Berlin and New York: De Gruyter.

Kapparis, K. 2020. "Constructing Gender Identity: Women in Athenian Trials." In J. Filonik, B. Griffith-Williams, and J. Kucharski, eds., *The Making of Identities in Athenian Oratory.* London and New York: Routledge, 63–80.

Kapparis, K. 2021. *Women in the Law Courts of Classical Athens.* Edinburgh: Edinburgh University Press.

Keesling, C. 2006. "Heavenly Bodies: Monuments to Prostitutes in Greek Sanctuaries." In C. Faraone and L. McClure, eds., *Prostitutes and Courtesans in the Ancient World.* Madison: University of Wisconsin Press, 59–76.

Works Cited 189

Kennedy, R. 2014. *Immigrant Women in Athens: Gender, Ethnicity, and Citizenship in the Classical City.* London and New York: Routledge.

Keuls, E. 1983. "'The Hetaira and the Housewife': the Splitting of the Female Psyche in Greek Art." *Mededelingen van het Nederlands Historisch Instituut te Rome* 44–45: 23–40.

Kilmer, M. 1993. *Greek Erotica on Attic Red-Figure Vases.* London: Duckworth.

Knigge, U. 2005. *Der Bau Z. Kerameikos, Ergebnisse der Ausgrabungen.* Vol. 17.1–2. Munich: Hirmer Verlag.

Kosso, C. 2009. "Women at the Fountain and the Well: Imagining Experience." In C. Kosso and A. Scott, eds., *The Nature and Function of Water, Baths, Bathing and Hygiene from Antiquity through the Renaissance.* Leiden: Brill, 87–108.

Kowalski, G. 1947. "De Phrynes pectore nudato." *Eos* 42: 50–62.

Kreilinger, U. 2007. *Anständige Nackheit: Körperpflege, Reinigungsriten und das Phänomen weiblicher Nackheit im achaisch-klassichen Athen.* Rahden/Westfalen: Marie Leidorf.

Kurke, L. 1997. "Inventing the *Hetaira*: Sex, Politics, and Discursive Conflict in Archaic Greece." *CA* 16: 106–50.

Kurke, L. 1999. *Coins, Bodies, Games, and Gold: The Politics of Meaning in Archaic Greece.* Princeton, NJ: Princeton University Press.

Kurke, L. 2002. "Gender, Politics, and Subversion in the *Chreiai* of Machon." *Proceedings of the Cambridge Philological Society* 48: 20–65.

Lape, S. 2021. "Mobility and Sexual Laborers in Menander's *Dis Exapaton* and Plautus' *Bacchides.*" *Ramus* 50: 25–42.

Lee, M. 2015. *Body, Dress and Identity in Ancient Greece.* Cambridge: Cambridge University Press.

Lefkowitz, M. 1976. "Fictions in Literary Biography: the New Poem and the Archilochus Legend." *Arethusa* 9: 181–89.

Lefkowitz, M. 1981. *Lives of the Greek Poets.* London.

Lewis, Sian. 2002. *The Athenian Woman: An Iconographic Handbook.* London: Routledge.

Lidov, J. 2002. "Sappho, Herodotus, and the 'Hetaira.'" *CP* 97: 203–37.

Lissarrague, F. 1990. *The Aesthetics of the Greek Banquet.* Princeton, NJ: Princeton University Press.

Lloyd, A. B. 1988. *Herodotus Book II.* Vol. 3. Leiden: Brill.

Loomis, W. 1998. *Wages, Welfare Costs, and Inflation in Classical Athens.* Ann Arbor: University of Michigan Press.

Lynch, K. 2007. "More Thoughts on the Space of the Symposium." In R. Westgate, N. R. E. Fisher, and J. Whitley, eds., *Building Communities: House, Settlement and Society in the Aegean and Beyond: Proceedings of a Conference Held at Cardiff University, 17–21 April 2001.* London: British School at Athens, 243–49.

Ma, J. 2007. "Hellenistic Honorific Statues and Their Inscriptions." In Z. Newby and R. Leader-Newby, eds., *Art and Inscriptions in the Ancient World.* Cambridge: Cambridge University Press, 203–20.

Macdowell, D. 1978. *The Law in Classical Athens.* Ithaca, NY: Cornell University Press.

Macdowell, D. 2000. "Athenian Laws about Homosexuality." *Revue internationale des droits de l'antiquité* 3rd ser. 47: 14–27.

Marshall, C. W. 2021. "Love-Sick in a Different Way: Sex and Desire in Lysias 4." In D. Kamen and C. W. Marshall, eds., *Slavery and Sexuality in Classical Antiquity.* Madison: University of Wisconsin Press, 124–41.

Marzi, M. 1977. "Iperide." In M. Marzi, P. Leone, and E. Malcovati, eds., *Oratori Attici minori*, Vol. 1. Turin: Utet, 9–328.

McClure, L. 2003a. *Courtesans at Table: Gender and Greek Literary Culture in Athenaeus.* London: Routledge.

McClure, L. 2003b. "Subversive Laughter: The Sayings of Courtesans in Book 13 of Athenaeus' *Deipnosophistae.*" *American Journal of Philology* 124.2: 259–94.

McClure, L. 2015. "Courtesans Reconsidered: Women in Aristophanes' *Lysistrata.*" *EuGeStA* 5: 54–84.

McGinn, T. 1998. *Prostitution, Sexuality and the Law in Ancient Rome.* Oxford.

McGinn, T. 2014. "Introduction: Problems of Evidence." In T. Hubbard, ed., *A Companion to Greek and Roman Sexualities.* Chichester, England and Malden, MA: Wiley-Blackwell, 87–105.

Miner, J. 2003. "Courtesan, Concubine, Whore: Apollodorus's Deliberate Use of Terms for Prostitutes." *AJP* 124: 19–38.

Morales, H. 2011. "Fantasising Phryne: The Psychology and Ethics of 'Ecphrasis.'" *Cambridge Classical Journal* 57: 71–104.

Mueller, M. 2016. "Re-centering Epic Nostos: Gender and Genre in Sappho's Brother's Poem." *Arethusa* 49: 25–46.

Murray, O., ed. 1990a. *Sympotica: A Symposium on the Symposion.* Oxford: Oxford University Press.

Murray, O. 1990b. "The Affair of the Mysteries: Democracy and the Drinking Group." In O. Murray, ed., *Sympotica: A Symposium on the Symposion.* Oxford: Oxford University Press, 149–61.

Naiden, F. 2006. *Ancient Supplication.* Oxford: Oxford University Press.

Neils, J. 2000. "Others within the Other: An Intimate Look at Hetairai and Maenads." In B. Cohen, ed., *Not the Classical Ideal: Athens and the Construction of the Other in Greek Art.* Leiden: Brill, 203–26.

Nevett, L. 1999. *House and Society in the Ancient Greek World.* Cambridge: Cambridge University Press.

Nowak, M. 2010. "Defining Prostitution in Athenian Legal Rhetorics." *Tijdschrift voor Rechtsgeschiedenis / The Legal History Review* 78: 183–97.

O'Connell, P. 2013. "Hyperides and 'epopteia': A New Fragment of the 'Defense of Phryne.'" *Greek, Roman and Byzantine Studies* 53: 90–116.

Ogden, D. 1996. *Greek Bastardy in the Classical and Hellenistic Periods.* Oxford: Clarendon Press.

Ogden, D. 1999. *Polygamy, Prostitutes and Death: the Hellenistic Dynasties.* London: Duckworth with the Classical Press of Wales.

Osborne, R. 1998. *Archaic and Classical Greek Art.* Oxford: Oxford University Press.

Parker, R. 1996. *Athenian Religion: A History.* Oxford: Clarendon Press.

Parker, R. 2002. "The Trial of Socrates: And a Religious Crisis?" In Th. C. Brickhouse and N. D. Smith, eds., *The Trial and Execution of Socrates. Sources and Controversies.* Oxford and New York: Oxford University Press, 145–61.

Pasquier, A. 2007. "Les Aphrodites de Praxitèle." In A. Pasquier and J.-L. Martinez, eds., *Praxitèle, un maître de la sculpture antique.* Paris: Somogy éditions d'art, 130–201.

Patterson, C. 1994. "The Case against Neaera and the Public Ideology of the Athenian Family." In A. Boegehold and A. Scafuro, eds., *Athenian Identity and Civic Ideology.* Baltimore: Johns Hopkins University Press, 199–216.

Patterson, C. 1998. *The Family in Greek History.* Cambridge, MA: Harvard University Press.

Pernot, L. 2004. "Femmes devant l'assemblée en Grèce et à Rome." *Logo* 7: 201–11.

Peschel, I. 1987. *Die Hetäre bei Symposium und Komos in der attisch-rotfigurigen Vasenmalerei eds 6-4 Jahr. v. Chr.* Frankfurt am Main and New York: P. Lang.

Phillips, D. 2013. *The Law of Ancient Athens.* Ann Arbor: University of Michigan Press.

Pirenne-Delforge, V. 1994. *L'Aphrodite grecque. Contribution à l'étude de ses cultes et de sa personnalité dans le panthéon archaïque et classique. Kernos* supplement 4. Athens and Liege: Centre international de l'Étude de la Religion antique.

Plassart, A. 1926. "Fouilles de Thespies et de l'hiéron des muses de l'Helicon. Inscriptions 6. Dédicaces de caractère religieux ou honorifique: Bornes de domaines sacrés." *Bulletin de correspondance hellénique* 50: 383–462.

Raubitschek, A. E. 1941. "Phryne." *RE* 20.1: 893–907.

Reinsberg, C. 1993. *Ehe, Hetärentum und Knabenlieb im antiken Griechenland.* Munich: Beck.

Richter, G. 1968. *Korai: Archaic Greek Maidens: a Study of the Development of the Kore Type in Greek Sculpture.* London: Phaidon.

Rihll, E. 2011. "Classical Athens." In K. Bradley and P. Cartledge, eds., *The Cambridge World History of Slavery*: Vol. 1, *The Ancient Mediterranean World.* Cambridge: Cambridge University Press, 48–73.

Rodenwalt, G. 1932. "Spinnende Hetären." *Archäologischer Anzeiger* 47: 7–22.

Rosenmeyer, P. 2001. "(In-)versions of Pygmalion: The Statue Talks Back." In A. Lardinois and L. McClure, eds., *Making Silence Speak: Women's Voices in Greek Literature and Society.* Madison: Wisconsin University Press, 240–60.

Rosenzweig, R. 2004. *Worshipping Aphrodite: Art and Cult in Classical Athens.* Michigan: University of Michigan Press.

Rosivach, V. 1995. "Solon Brothels." *Liverpool Classical Monthly* 20.1–2: 2–3.

Roworth, W. 1983. "The Gentle Art of Persuasion: Angelica Kauffman's Praxiteles and Phryne." *The Art Bulletin* 65.3: 488–92.

Roworth, W. 2015. "The Angelica Kauffmann Inventories: An Artist's Property and Legacy in Early- Nineteenth-Century Rome." *Getty Research Journal* 7: 17–68.

Ryan, J. 1993. "More Seductive than Phryne: Baudelaire, Gérôme, Rilke, and the Problem of Autonomous Art." *Proceedings of the Modern Language Association* 108: 1128–41.

Rzepka, J. 2010. "Alketas." In I. Worthington, *Jacoby Online: Brill's New Jacoby.* Leiden: Brill. http://referenceworks.brillonline.com/cluster/Jacoby%20Online.

Schaps, David. 1977. "The Woman Least Mentioned: Etiquette and Women's Names." *Classical Quarterly* 27: 323–30.

Schlesier, R. 2013. "Atthis, Gyrinno, and other *HETAIRAI*: Female Personal Names in Sappho's Poetry." *Philologus* 157: 199–222.

Schneider, K. 1913. "*Hetairai.*" In Pauly-Wissowa, *Real-encyclopädie der classichen Altertumwissenschaft.* Stuttgart: Metzler, 8–2, col. 1331–72.

Semenov, A. 1935. "Hypereides und Phryne." *Klio* 28: 271–79.

Sidwell, K. 2000. "Athenaeus, Lucian, and Fifth-Century Comedy." In D. Braund and J. Wilkins, eds., *Athenaeus and His World: Reading Greek Culture in the Roman Empire.* Exeter: University of Exeter Press, 136–52.

Silver, M. 2018. *Slave-wives, Single Women and "Bastards" in the Ancient Greek World: Law and Economics Perspectives.* Oxford: Oxbow Books.

Skinner, M. 2011. *Clodia Metelli: The Tribune's Sister.* Oxford and New York: Oxford University Press.

Slater, N. 1989. "Lekythoi in Aristophanes' *Ecclesiazusae.*" *Lexis* 3: 43–51.

Sommerstein, A. 2013. *Menander and the Pallake.* London and New York: Routledge.

Stone, L. 1981. *Costume in Aristophanic Comedy.* New York: Cambridge University Press.

Sutton, R. 1997/8. "Nuptial Eros: The Visual Discourse of Marriage in Classical Athens." *Journal of the Walters Art Gallery* 55/56: 27–48.

Sutton, R. 2009a. "Female Bathers and the Emergence of the Female Nude in Greek Art." In C. Kosso and A. Scott, eds., *The Nature and Function of Water, Baths, Bathing and Hygiene from Antiquity through the Renaissance.* Leiden: Brill, 61–86.

Sutton, R. 2009b. "The Invention of the Female Nude: Zeuxis, Vase-Painting, and the Kneeling Bather." In J. Boardman and O. Palagia, eds., *Athenian Potters and Painters.* Vol. 2. Oxford and Oakville: Oxbow Books, 270–79.

Taaffe, L. 1993. *Aristophanes and Women.* London and New York: Routledge.

Taylor, C. 2020. "Onomastic Patterns of So-Called *Hetaira* Names in the Greek World." *Métis* n. s. 18: 55–82.

Todd, S. C. 2007. *A Commentary on Lysias: Speeches 1–11.* New York: Oxford University Press.

Toepfer, K. 1997. *Empire of Ecstasy: Nudity and Movement in German Body Culture.* Berkeley and Los Angeles: University of California Press. E-Books Collection: https://publishing.cdlib.org/ucpressebooks/view?docId = ft167nb0sp;brand = ucpress.

Trampedach, K. 2001. "Gefärliche Frauen. Zu athenischen Asebie-Prozessen im 4. Jh. v. Chr." In R. von den Hoff and S. Schmidt, eds., *Konstruktionen von Wirklichkeit: Bilder im Griechenland des 5. und 4. Jahrhunderts v. Chr.* Stuttgart, 137–55.

Treggiari, S. 2007. *Terentia, Tullia and Publilia: the Women of Cicero's Family.* London/ New York: Routledge.

Tuplin, C. 1986. "The Fate of Thespiae during the Theban Hegemony." *Athenaeum* 64: 321–41.

Ussher, R. 1986. *Aristophanes Ecclesiazusae.* New Rochelle: Caratzas.

Vernant, J.-P. 1969. "Hestia-Hermes: The Religious Expression of Space and Movement among the Greeks." *Social Science Information* 8: 131–68.

Versnel, H. S. 1990. *Inconsistencies in Greek and Roman Religion, I, Ter Unus. Isis, Dionysos, Hermes. Three Studies in Henotheism.* Leiden: Brill.

Vlassopoulos, K. 2011. "Greek Slavery: From Domination to Property and Back Again." *Journal of Hellenic Studies* 131: 115–30.

Von Waldegg, J. 1972. "Jean-Léon Gérome's *Phryne vor den Richtern.*" *Jahrbuch der Hamburger Kunstsammlungen* 17: 122-42.

Wallace, R. 1992. "Charmides, Agariste and Damon: Andokides 1.16." *Classical Quarterly* 42.2: 328–35.

Witzke, S. 2015. "Harlots, Tarts and Hussies? A Problem of Terminology for Sex Labor in Roman Comedy." *Helios* 42: 7–27.

Wrenhaven, K. 2009. "The Identity of the 'Wool-Workers' in Attic Manumissions." *Hesperia* 78: 367–86.

Zweig, B. 1992. "The Mute Nude Female Characters in Aristophanes' Plays." In A. Richlin, ed., *Pornography and Representation in Greece and Rome.* Oxford: Oxford University Press, 73–89.

Index

For the benefit of digital users, indexed terms that span two pages (e.g., 52–53) may, on occasion, appear on only one of those pages.

Figures are indicated by an italic *f* following the page number.

adultery, 37, 38–39, 40–41, 52–53, 67, 148

Aeschines, 21–22, 73–74, 128
  Against Timarchus, 128
  involvement in ecstatic rites, 134–37

Aeschylus
  Agamemnon, 147–48
  Persians, 147–48

Ajootian, A., 98

Alce, 34, 40–41, 57–59, 60–62, 74, 75, 82

Alcetas, 23–24, 105

Alciphron, 23–24, 59, 102–3, 120, 123–24, 142, 143–44, 145, 150–51

Alexander the Great, 3–4, 18–19, 20, 59, 83–84, 112–13

Andocides, 130–31, 133

Antiphon, *Against the Stepmother for Poisoning*, 127–28

Apelles' Anadyomene (*Aphrodite Rising from the Sea*). *See* Aphrodite

Aphrodite
  Apelles' Anadyomene (*Aphrodite Rising from the Sea*), 3–4, 19, 90–91, 92, 99–101, 113–14, 115–16, 115*f*, 121–22, 123–24
  Arles type, 99, 100*f*, 104–5, 115–16
  and bathing, 108–10, 111*f*, 111*f*
  and hetaeras, 69, 70–71, 82, 84–85, 88–89, 110–13, 114, 144, 145–46, 151, 154–55
  in the *Homeric Hymn to Aphrodite*, 109

and the Ludovisi Throne, 69–72
  and nudity, 116–19, 118*f*, 119*f*, 120, 121
  Ourania, 67–68
  Pandemos, 65, 66–68, 69–70, 154–55
  and Peitho, 67–68
  and portrait statues of women, 94–95
  and sacred prostitution, 69–70
  and sacred viewing, 102–3, 116–17, 150–52, 156
  worship of, 69–71
  See also Cnidian Aphrodite

Apollodorus, 35–41, 55, 82, 128–29, 132–33

Archidamus III, 104, 106–7

Archippe, 96

Aristaeneta, 95–96

Aristagora
  in Attic oratory, 128–29, 143
  name, 57–59

Aristophanes, 50–52, 76, 129–30
  Acharnians, 50–52, 86–87, 136
  Ecclesiazusae, 59–60, 67
  Lysistrata, 134–35
  Wasps, 30–31, 50–52, 134–35, 147
  See also Comedy, Greek; nudity, female

asebeia. *See* impiety trials

Aspasia, 85–88
  as brothel-keeper, 86–88
  engagement with Athenian politics, 87–88
  foreign origins, 31–32, 85–86

Aspasia (*cont.*)
hetaera, 85
name, 56, 82–83
and the Peloponnesian War, 86–87
and Pericles 31–32, 85–86, 136–37
in Plato's *Menexenus*, 87–88
prosecution for impiety, 87, 134, 136–37, 156
and Socrates, 87–88
Athenaeus, 23–24
and the *Cnidian Aphrodite*, 92–93, 113–14, 122
on hetaera names, 55–57
and Phryne's impiety trial, 123–24, 129, 143, 147–51, 153–56
and Phryne's name, 18–19, 59–60
and Phryne's portrait statue at Delphi, 18–19, 23–24, 104–8
Athenian legal system
asebeia (*see* impiety trials)
dike, 125, 146
graphe, 125, 128–29
graphe asebeias, 130–32, 136
hetaera trials, 128–30, 137–39
male jurors, 39–40
familiarity with famous hetaeras, 57–59, 65–66, 128–29
at Phryne's trial, 1–3, 6–8, 102–3, 123–24, 145–50
susceptibility to emotional displays of defendants, 136–37
See also Phryne; Socrates
Athens
and ambiguous social identity, 28–29, 34, 35, 39–41, 60–62
deme, 28–29, 35–36
labor, free and unfree, 78–79
oligarchy, 132
phratry, 28–29, 34, 35–36
and prostitution, 65–67
See also Peloponnesian War
auletris, 30–31, 63–64, 69–70, 71*f*, 107–8
defined, 30–31
and the symposium, 49–50, 51*f*, 51*f*, 75–77
in vase painting, 47–50, 51*f*, 51*f*, 53
See also Lamia

Bicknell, P., 85–86

Bonfante, L., 41–42, 116–17
Botticelli, 19, 114
Boulanger, G., 8–9, 9*f*
brothels, 46–47, 52, 62, 65–67, 70–75
absence of purpose-built brothels in Athens, 73–74
Building Z, 42–44, 70–71
and enslaved women, 30–31, 34, 36, 47–49
established by Solon, 65, 66–67, 154–55
Kerameikos, 42–44*porneion* 74
as a safe alternative to adultery, 52
woman-owned, 81, 82
and wool working, 42–44, 44*f*, 53, 74–75
Budin, S., 69
Bundrick, S., 46–47

Campaspe, 3–4, 112–13, 114
See also Pancaspe
Clytemnestra, 44–46, 147–48
Cnidian Aphrodite by Praxiteles, 3–4, 17, 19, 26, 44–46, 70–71, 90–91, 92–93, 102–3, 118*f*, 119*f*
in (Lucian), *Amores,* 99–101, 150–51
on Cnidian coinage, 117–19, 119*f*
influence on accounts of Phryne's disrobing, 123–24, 146, 149–50, 151–52
as inspiration for epigram, 114, 119–21
kneeling bather as prototype, 108–10, 111*f*, 111*f*
popularity during the first century BCE, 18–19, 93, 115–21, 122
and sacred viewing, 103, 116–17, 123–24, 150–52, 156
Thespian Aphrodite as prototype, 104–5
See also Phryne
comedy, Greek, 21–23, 50–52, 84–85, 87, 103–4, 146
Cooper, C., 25–26, 147–48
Corso, A., 26, 90–91, 99, 102–4, 115–16
Crates, 18–19, 104, 107–8
critical fabulation. *See* Hartman, S.

d'Antigny, B., 14–17
David, J. -L., 6–8, 8*f*
Davidson, J., 25, 26–27, 32–33

Demosthenes, pseudo-Demosthenes, 35–
    36, 126, 129–30, 140–41
  Against Aristogeiton I, 138–39
  Against Boeotus I, 54, 137
  Against Boeotus II, 54, 126–27, 137
  Against Euboulides, 139–40
  Against Neaera, 21–22, 35–41, 55
  Against Onetor, 55
  On the Crown, 134–36
  On the False Embassy, 137, 148
Diogenes Laertius, 3–4, 23–24, 104–5

Eidinow, E., 26, 90, 133–35, 136–37
entertainers, female, 30–31, 49–52, 50*f*, 51*f*,
    51*f*, 69–70, 71*f*, 105, 135–36
  See also auletris
epigram, Greek, 4–6, 23–24, 93, 99–102,
    114–15, 119–20, 122, 151–52
Eros by Praxiteles, 4–5, 5*f*, 13–14, 15*f*, 18–
    19, 83–84, 90–91, 92–93, 99–103,
    115–16, 121–22, 123–24, 151, 155
Euctemon, 28–29, 34, 57–58, 60–61, 74
Euthias, 19, 22–23, 123–24, 141, 142–
    43, 147–48

Ferrari, G., 46–47

Gérôme, J. -L., 1–4, 2*f*, 6–17, 123–24, 156
Gilhuly, K., 25
Gillam, B., 12–13, 13*f*
Gillray, J., 6, 7*f*
Glaucothea, 134–36, 137, 142
Gnathaena, 18–19, 75
Grottger, A., 13–14, 15*f*

Hartman, S., 26–27, 153
Havelock, C., 25–26, 93, 116–17, 119–20
Hecuba, 44–46, 147–48
Helen of Troy, 67–68, 87, 109
  and Zeuxis' painting, 4, 110–12, 115–16,
    144, 145–46
Herennia Procula, 99–101, 102–3
Hermippus, 87, 136, 142, 147–48
Herodotus, 33–34, 65–66, 68–70, 84–85,
    87, 103–4, 105–6
hetaeras
  as brothel owners, 36, 82–83
    Nicarete, 36–37, 40–41, 42–44, 57–58,
    61–62, 82

Theodote, 88–89
  and citizen wives, 29, 31–32, 35–36, 44–
    46, 60–61, 62–64
  and contracts, 31–32, 33, 81–82, 90–
    91, 154–55
  cost, 52, 66, 79–80, 81
  defined, 32–33
  naming practices, 54–60, 63–
    64, 126–27
  public benefactions, 18–19, 84–85, 102,
    107–8, 154–55
  social mobility, 28–29, 34, 62, 85, 90–
    91, 154–55
  spatial mobility, 39–40, 50–52, 54, 65–
    66, 72–73, 85, 154–55
  taxation, 79–68, 154–55
  treatises about, 23–24, 56, 153
  witticisms, 75, 77–78, 83–84, 85, 90–91
  wool-working, 42–44, 43*f*, 44*f*,
    53, 74–75
  See also Athenian legal system;
    prostitution
Hyperides 1
  Aspasia, 87, 134, 136–37
  In Defense of Phryne, 1–3, 9–10, 19,
    22–24, 91, 123–24, 128–29, 136–37,
    140–41, 151
  as lover of Phryne, 90–91, 123–
    24, 128–29

impiety trials
  Ninos, 57–58, 134, 137–38, 139–40, 142,
    149–50, 151–52, 156
  Socrates, 133–34
  Theoris, 57–58, 134, 138–40, 149–50,
    151–52, 156
  See also Phryne
Isaeus, 21–22, 28–29, 34–35, 60–61, 76,
    82, 126–27
Isocrates, 105, 132–33

Kapparis, K., 26, 32–34, 90, 126–27, 128,
    134, 136–37, 138, 139
Kauffmann, A., 4–5, 5*f*, 6–8, 110–12
Keesling, C., 26
Kennedy, R., 28–29, 32–33
komos, 33, 37, 49–52, 54,
    75–77, 141
kore, 94

Index   197

kouros, 94
Kreilinger, U., 44–46
Kurke, L., 25, 32–33, 49

Lais, 3–4, 18–19, 22–24, 112–13, 114, 128–29
Lamia, 30–31, 107–8
  See also auletris
Lape, S., 62, 81–82
liturgy, 79–80, 97–98
Loomis, W., 79–80
Lucian, pseudo-Lucian, 59, 119–20
  Amores, 99–101, 116–17, 120–21, 123–24, 150–51
  Dialogues of the Courtesans, 23–24, 82–83
Ludovisi Throne, 69–70, 70*f*, 113–14
Lynceus, 77–78
Lysias, 21–22, 30, 33–34, 47–49, 60–62, 126–30, 139–40, 142
Lysimache, 97

Machon, 55–56, 77–78, 82–83
Mania, 55–56, 82–83
Menander, 21–22, 149–50
  Samia, 21–22, 35, 62, 79–80, 81, 143
metics, 21, 30, 56–58, 97–98, 125, 126, 130–31
  and foreign cults, 134–35, 138, 139
  hetaeras as, 21, 30, 32–34, 35, 37, 63–64, 65–66, 85–86
  and illegal marriage, 31–32, 35–36, 128
  and immigration violations, 128–29
  involvement in commercial activities, 78–79
  Neaera as, 35–36, 38–39
  Phryne as, 90–91, 151–52
  prostates, 30, 33–34, 126
  taxation, 30, 79–80
  unstable identities, 32–33, 60–61, 62
Morales, H., 25–26
mother-daughter pairs, 40–41, 42–44, 75, 82–84, 88–89
mutilation of the Herms, 130–31

Nadar (Gaspard-Félix Tournachon), 10–12, 11*f*
Nais, 61–62, 129–30
Neaera, 22–23, 31–32
  (Demosthenes), *Against Neaera*, 35–41

Nicarete, 36–37, 40–41, 42–44, 57–58, 61–62, 72–73, 82, 128–29
Phano, 35–36, 38–41, 55, 58–59, 82–83, 132–33
Phrastor, 38, 55, 132–33
Phrynion, 37, 47–49, 60–62, 72–73, 76, 81
spatial mobility, 37, 39–40, 72–73, 77, 154–55
Stephanus, 35–36, 37–40, 62, 72–73, 75, 79–80, 81, 82, 132–33, 136–37
Theogenes, 38–39, 132–33
uncertain social status, 38, 39–41, 61–62
  See also Apollodorus
Nicander, 66, 68
Ninos, 57–59, 134, 137–38, 139–40, 142, 149–50, 151–52, 156
nudity, female, 41–42, 44–46, 47–50, 48*f*, 51*f*, 66–67
  ambiguity of, 46–47, 53
  brothel slaves, 52–53, 66–67
  Cassandra at the altar, 44–46, 45*f*
  in the context of bathing, 44–46, 93, 108–10, 111*f*, 114–15
  display of breasts, 1–3, 6–8, 14, 19, 44–46, 52, 70*f*, 88–89, 109, 117–19, 123, 144–46, 151, 156
    in supplication, 147–49
  in Greek comedy, 50–53, 66–67
  and prostitution, 41–42
  'respectable' or idealized, 44–46, 53, 63–64, 88–89, 108–10, 111–93, 111–93, 114–15
  at the symposium, 47–50, 48*f*, 51*f*
  and torn garments, 148–49, 151
  See also Aphrodite; Cnidian Aphrodite; Phryne

Ogden, D., 32–33, 35
Olympias, 20, 59

pallake, 30–33, 34–35, 39–40, 61–62
  Aspasia as, 32–33, 56, 85
  defined, 31–32
  interchangeability with hetaera, 31–33, 35, 40–41, 62
  Neaera as, 39–40, 62–63
Panathenaea, 33, 37, 67–68, 77, 113–14
Pancaspe (or Pancaste), 113, 114

198   Index

See also Campaspe

Pausanias, 23–24, 97, 99–101, 119–20

Peloponnesian War, 30, 86, 132, 136

  effect on women, 132–33

Pericles

  and Aspasia, 31–32, 85–88, 136–37, 151

  funeral oration, 54, 87–88

  marriage law, 30, 85–86

  and the Peloponnesian War, 86–87

  portrait statue, 94–95

  and Socrates' trial, 133, 136

Phano. *See* Neaera

Philaenis, 20, 23–24

Phile, 40–41, 57–59

Philemon, 22–23, 66, 79–80

Philip II, 18–19, 104–7

Phryne

  beauty of, 19, 144–46

  dedications

    portrait statue at Delphi, 18–19,
      23–24, 26, 72–73, 91, 92–94, 95–96,
      99, 104–8, 115–16, 121–22, 155

  disrobing

    at the Eleusinia, 19, 92, 113–14, 116–
      17, 123–24

    at her impiety trial, 2*f*, 6–12, 8*f*, 13–17,
      19, 25–26, 70–71, 123–24, 125–26,
      140–41, 143–51

    at the Posidonia, 14, 19, 92, 113–14,
      116–17, 123–24

  as model for images of Aphrodite,
    113–14

    for Apelles' Anadyomene, 3–4, 19,
      92–93, 113–14, 115–16, 121–22

    for Praxiteles' *Cnidian Aphrodite*,
      3–4, 19, 26, 90–91, 92–93, 115–
      16, 154–55

    for statue of Aphrodite at Sparta,
      90–91, 103–4, 115–16, 121–22

  names and nicknames, 18–19, 20, 22–
    23, 59–60

  rebuilding walls of Thebes 83–84,
    91, 107–8

  romance with Praxiteles, 3–6, 5*f*, 18–
    19, 25–26, 90–91, 92–93, 101–3,
    113, 114, 122, 151–52, 155

  witticisms, 3–4, 77–78, 83–84

  See also Hyperides; Praxiteles

Pindar, 69

Plato, 3–4, 21

  Menexenus, 87–88

  Symposium, 3–4, 75–77

Pliny the Elder, 97–98, 99–101, 103–4,
    112–13, 114–15, 116–20

Plutarch, 20, 23–24, 59–60, 85–
    86, 148–49

  on Phryne's disrobing, 136–37, 143,
    144, 147–48

porne, 62

  Aspasia as, 85, 87–88

  defined, 30–31

  interchangeability with hetaera
    and *pallake*, 30–31, 32–33,
    34, 62–63

  Neaera as, 36, 39–40, 62–63

  opposite of hetaera, 32–33

portrait statues of women, 94–97

  Archippe, 96

  Aristaeneta, 95–96

  Lysimache, 97

  Nicandre, 94

  Simo, 96–97

  Syeris, 97

Posidippus, *Ephesia* (*Woman from
    Ephesus*), 19, 22–23, 57–58, 140–41,
    146–47, 151–52, 153

Praxiteles, 3–6, 5*f*, 18–19, 90–91, 97–98

  Aphrodite at Sparta, 90–91, 103–4, 115–
    16, 121–22

  Aphrodite statue at Thespiae, 99, 102–
    3, 104–5

  Happy Hetaera, 92–93, 103–4

  Portrait statues, 98

  Thespian triad, 99–103, 107–8, 115–16

  wealth, 97–98

  See also Cnidian Aphrodite; Eros; Phryne

profanation of the Eleusinian Mysteries,
    130–32, 139

prostitution

  and Athens, 66–67

  as a business, 78–83

  cost, 52, 66, 79–80, 81

  male, 98, 128

  and oratory, 21–23, 28, 33–34 (*see also*
    Demosthenes)

  sacred, 69–70

  scholarship on, 25, 30–32

  terms for, 30–33

Index   199

prostitution (*cont.*)
   tax, 80
   topography, 72–75
   See also Hetaeras; Solon
Pygmalion, 10–12, 102–3
Pythionice, 72–73, 107–8

Quintilian, 98, 140–41
   on Phryne's disrobing, 143–44, 145–46, 151

religion, Greek
   dedications, 3–4, 18–19, 26, 56–57, 84–68, 93, 94–97, 98, 105–95, 121–22, 155
   Eleusinian Mysteries, 33, 130–31, 137, 142
   foreign cults, 123–24, 134–35, 139
      Isodaites, 141–42
      Sabazius, 134–36, 141
   priestesses, 69–70, 72f
      and foreign cults, 135–36, 137–38, 139
      Phryne as, 19, 149–50
      and religious prosecution, 127–28, 138–39
      and votive statues, 94, 96–97, 102–3, 137–38
   supplication, 44–46, 45f, 53, 136–37, 147–48, 151–52
   Thesmophoria, 34, 60–61
   thiasoi, 123–24, 134–23, 137, 141, 142, 151–52
   See also mutilation of the Herms; Panathenaea; profanation of the Eleusinian Mysteries
Rhodopis, 69–70, 84–85
   beauty, 33–34, 84–85
   dedication at Delphi, 84–85, 91, 105–7, 121–22, 154–55
   earliest attested hetaera in Greek literature, 33–34
   and Egypt, 69–70, 84–85
   name, 42, 59
   notoriety, 55
   and Sappho, 84–85
   servile origins 33, 84–85
   spatial mobility, 72–73
   wealth, 33–34, 85

Rodenwalt, G., 42–44
Roux, M., 9–10

Saint-Saëns, C., 14–17
sakkos, 46–47, 47f, 53, 69–70, 71f
Sanderson, S., 14–17
Sappho, 67–68, 84–85, 121
Schaps, D., 54, 57–58
Sextus Empiricus, 143–44, 145–46, 148–49
Siemiradzki, H., 14, 113
Socrates, 3–4, 75–77
   and Aspasia, 85, 87–88, 136
   impiety trial, 123–24, 132, 133–35, 136–37
   and Theodote, 88–89, 110–12
Solon, 65–68, 148, 154–55
Stephanus. *See* Neaera
supplication. *See* religion, Greek
Sutton, R., 109–93
symposium, Greek, 25, 30–31, 69, 75–76, 130–31
   and Athenaeus' *Dining Sophists*, 23–24
   and domestic space, 75–76
   entertainment, 30–31, 33, 41–42, 47–50, 50f, 51f, 51f, 75–77
   exclusion of wives, 76
   and hetaeras and prostitutes, 25, 41–42, 47–49, 53, 63–64, 75–78
   and sexual activity, 47–49, 48f, 109–10
   sympotic scenes in vase painting, 47–50, 48f, 50f, 51f, 51f, 53, 63–64, 154
   and sympotic verse, 20
   witticisms, 3–4, 75, 77–78, 90–91
   See also auletris; Plato, *Symposium*

Thebes, 83–84, 90, 91, 99, 107–8
Theodote, 130–31, 154–55
   beauty, 88–89
   as madame, 75, 82
   as model for painters, 88–89, 110–12
   and 'respectable' nudity, 89, 90–91, 99, 109
   and Socrates, 88–89
   wealth, 75
   See also Xenophon

Theoris, 57–59, 134, 138–40, 149–50, 151–52, 156
Thespiae, 18–19, 30, 72–73, 83–84, 90–91, 98, 99–102, 114–15, 116–17, 155
  See also Phryne; Praxiteles
Thucydides, 65–66, 130–31

vase painting
  bathing scenes, 44–46, 53, 108–10, 111*f*, 111*f*
  epinetron, 47–49, 110–12
  kylikes, 41–44, 44*f*, 47–50, 48*f*, 50*f*, 51*f*, 53, 63–64, 109–10
  lekythos, 109–10
  money bag, 41–44, 43*f*, 46–47, 47*f*
  pyxis, 109–10, 111*f*, 111*f*
  wool-working, 42–44, 43*f*, 44*f*, 53
  *See also auletris;*nudity, female; symposium

Villany, A., 14–17, 16*f*

women, citizen
  avoidance of public naming, 54–55, 59, 126–27
  contrasted with prostitutes, 31–32, 35, 52–53, 72–73
  epikleros, 126–27
  guardianship, 46–47, 126–27, 132–33
  and lawful marriage, 20, 21–22, 28–29, 30, 31, 35–30, 37, 40–41, 54–55, 60–61, 77, 85–86, 151–52
  and legitimate children, 20, 28–29, 31, 35, 40–41, 85–86, 151–52
  See also Athenian legal system

Xenophon, 21, 65–66, 73–74, 77, 88–89, 109, 112–13, 130–31

Zeuxis, 4, 110–12, 115–16, 145–46

The manufacturer's authorised representative in the EU for product safety is Oxford
University Press España S.A. of El Parque Empresarial San Fernando de Henares,
Avenida de Castilla, 2 – 28830 Madrid (www.oup.es/en or product.safety@oup.com).
OUP España S.A. also acts as importer into Spain of products made by the manufacturer.

Printed in the USA/Agawam, MA
May 16, 2025

887590.006